TIME

and

the Erotic

in Horace's

Odes

TIME

and

the Erotic

in Horace's

Odes

Ronnie Ancona

Duke University Press   Durham and London

1994

© 1994 Duke University Press

All rights reserved

Printed in the United States of America

on acid-free paper ∞

Designed by Cherie Holma Westmoreland

Typeset in Palatino with Optima Display

by Keystone Typesetting, Inc.

Library of Congress Cataloging-in-Publication

Data appear on the last printed page of

this book.

CONTENTS

PREFACE

This study of time and the erotic in Horace's *Odes* is an attempt to explore how temporality functions as a defining feature of Horace's love poems. My purpose is not to address all aspects of Horace's erotic lyric or all of the love odes, but rather to focus on what I think is perhaps their most significant feature—temporality—in order to show how Horace can be seen as both a more interesting and a more troubling love poet than previous critics have thought.

My approach, while somewhat unorthodox in terms of Horatian scholarship, is best seen as part of a broader project in recent classical studies, a project that aims not only to enlarge the scope of the field of classics to include discussion of features of classical literature, such as sexuality and gender, previously considered less worthy of critical attention,[1] but also to read classical literature, as one classicist has put it, with more suspicion than celebration.[2] Drawing on contemporary theory, including recent work in feminist criticism, I hope to address aspects of Horace as a love poet—most especially the dynamics of gender relations—that critics have tended to ignore and to articulate Horace's version of love not as something to be championed (or condemned), but rather to be seen as challengingly problematic.

Although this book is intended primarily for classical scholars—particularly those interested in Horace, love poetry, or, specifically, Horace as love poet—I hope it may also be of value to others in the humanities with specializations in gender, sexuality, or contempo- rary theory. To make the book accessible to that wider audience, I have included translations of all the Latin. My sole aim in these translations has been to produce literal renditions so that readers with little or no Latin can follow my arguments with the least diffi- culty. (All translations are mine unless otherwise noted.) I regret that my translations—or any English translations—cannot reflect Hor- ace's amazingly flexible handling of word order, one of his greatest talents as a poet.[3]

In all but a few places the text of Horace I have followed is that of the Teubner edition by Shackleton Bailey (Stuttgart, 1985).[4] The bibliography on Horace is vast. Although I hope to have included most references relevant to my discussions, I do not claim to have been exhaustive.

ACKNOWLEDGMENTS

The completion of this book was aided by support from several sources. From Hunter College I received a Junior Faculty Development Award, a Eugene Lang Junior Faculty Award, and grants from the Professional Staff Congress-City University of New York Research Awards program. While at Carleton College, I was given a Faculty Development Endowment Grant. I am very grateful for all of this support.

Versions of my discussions of *Odes* 1.23 and *Odes* 1.25 have appeared previously in *Helios* and *Collection Latomus: Studies in Latin Literature and Roman History*, respectively. I would like to thank the editors of these journals for permission to use this material.

Participation in several seminars helped me to develop my feminist critical perspective. These include Carleton College's Faculty Development Seminar on Feminism and Literary Criticism; Hunter College's Women's Studies Theory Group; Carol Gilligan's seminar "On the Psychology of Love," held at Douglass College; and the Penn Mid-Atlantic Seminar on the Study of Women in Society.

I would like to acknowledge my debt to many who offered responses to versions of this work in progress. These include audiences at the College of St. Benedict, Franklin and Marshall College, the Hunter College Women's Studies Theory Group, the Brooklyn Polytechnic Preparatory Country Day School, the 1992 Cincinnati Symposium on Feminism and Classics, as well as at meetings of the American Philological Association, the American Comparative Literature Association, the Classical Association of the Atlantic States, and the Classical Association of the Middle West and South.

Charles Babcock gave me encouragement from the book's beginnings as a seminar paper, and then, as a dissertation under his direction at the Ohio State University. He was the first person to listen to my thoughts on several of the poems I discuss here. I am very grateful for his continued interest, including the reading of this manuscript. In addition, my students and colleagues over the years have given me opportunities to test out many of my ideas. To them I express my thanks.

Rachel Toor's immediate and sustained enthusiasm for this project made the prospect of publishing with Duke University Press a pleasure. Pam Morrison's advice and patience eased the last stages of publication. I would like to thank Sheila Dickison for her positive and encouraging response to the manuscript. To Michael Putnam and Judith Hallett, who generously offered extensive comments and criticisms that certainly helped me to make this a better book, I am extremely grateful. The final product benefited from the careful copyediting of Katherine Malin. Of course, I alone am responsible for the faults that remain.

Finally, the help and support of Steven Cole has meant more to me than I can say. To him and to our young son, David Ancona-Cole, who continually and delightfully reminded me of the world outside of work, I dedicate this book.

Philadelphia, Pennsylvania
September 1993

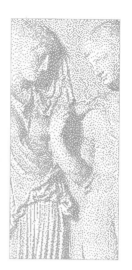

INTRODUCTION

Literary critics concerned with the nature of love in the *Odes* have for the most part focused their discussions on the attitudes of the poet/lover, which thus become the source of the claim that love in the *Odes* cannot last. Such a focus, however, while addressing a significant issue for our understanding of the erotic in the *Odes*, remains blind to how thoroughly what we might call the defeat of love in the *Odes*—its inability either to endure into the future or to be reciprocated passionately in the present—is itself shaped by the poet/lover's desire to dominate the temporality of the beloved. Rather than exploring how the poet/lover's desire itself produces the belief that temporality poses a threat to love, critics have instead sought to find in Horace's lyrics either a view of love that can be championed or one that must be rejected.

Broadly, most such efforts have taken one of two positions: the claim that Horace fails as a love poet because of the unromantic or antiromantic nature of the love poems, or the claim that Horace succeeds as a love poet because of his rational and realistic approach to love. Each of these characterizations assumes that temporality in the erotic odes must be seen as necessarily opposed to love: in the first, Horace fails as a love poet because he employs strategies that undermine the romantic ideal that love conquers time, while in the second, Horace succeeds as a love poet for not having unrealistic illusions about love's ability to endure, that is, for recognizing that time conquers love. The aim of this book is to challenge the assumption that temporality must inevitably pose a threat to the erotic by examining how temporality functions within the construction of love in the *Odes*.

Traditional criticism of Horace's poetry has begun by privileging the perspective of the male poet/lover and has derived its understanding of temporality from what that perspective has to say. What I want to do is offer an approach that breaks free of the gender assumptions that have so frequently guided such criticism. My own approach will seek rather to discover how the poet/lover's perspective is itself a consequence of the role that temporality plays in shaping his desire.

It seems plausible to argue that the fact that Horatian scholarship has for the most part been a male bastion has greatly affected the degree to which the perspective the male poet adopts as lover or commentator on love has itself been seen as the proper locus for understanding the relation of temporality to love. This in turn suggests a need for rethinking not merely Horace's lyrics but also the assumptions that guide our discussions of them. My hope is that the feminist approach I take, in refusing to accept as authoritative the perspective of the poet/lover, will allow us to see both that the construction of the beloved is the locus of the problematic status of temporality in Horace's version of love and, furthermore, that the lover is the fashioner of his own erotic difficulties and thus is implicated in his own unsuccessful strategies of desire.

My method has been to combine close readings of fourteen of the love odes with analysis that helps to articulate the consequences in each poem of the particular configurations of time and the erotic. I begin in the first chapter by critiquing the predominant modes of recent Horatian scholarship on the love odes, offering as an alternative a view that takes into account the male gender of the lover and its effect upon the relationship between time and the erotic in the poems' structures of desire. In the second, third, and fourth chapters I show the extent to which the issue of temporality pervades the love odes. Through a discussion of the poet's use of various temporal devices—the temporal adverb (*Odes* 1.25, 2.5, 3.7), seasonal imagery (*Odes* 1.4, 4.7, 1.9, 1.23), and the lover or beloved's own temporality, that is, their age or experience (*Odes* 2.8, 4.1, 4.13)—I show both how Horace makes time dominate erotic contexts and, further, how the prevailing version of love that emerges is characterized by the lover's desire to control the beloved. The fifth chapter

(*Odes* 2.9, 1.22, 1.13, 3.9) focuses on the ways in which the romantic ideal of a timeless love, which Horace seems to reject, in fact under-lies his version of love. I conclude that temporality, understood as the contingency the male poet/lover wants to but cannot control, explains why love "fails" in the *Odes*.

Throughout my analysis I use the term "erotic" in its broadest sense, to include any and all aspects of love, desire, and sexuality. The poems I discuss I call "love odes" or "erotic odes" without distinction. I use the term "temporality" to mean the condition or state of being temporal, or related to time. The terms "lover" and "beloved," although problematic, remain useful. That they inher-ently split a relationship or structure into subject and object presents a difficulty when dealing with potentially equal and reciprocal rela-tionships; however in the *Odes*—and, I should add, in much love poetry—there is usually a clear subject/lover and object/beloved.[1] By using these terms I do not mean to suggest that I endorse this kind of polarity with respect to love; rather the terms (perhaps unfortunately) fit well the structures of desire I shall be discussing. The term "love object" I use interchangeably with "beloved." When I use the term "poet/lover" for the persona of the poet as lover (as, e.g., in my discussions of *Odes* 1.25 and 4.1), I do not mean to suggest an identity with the historical poet Horace. When speaking generally, I refer to the beloved as female, for the male beloved—by sharing in the object status of the female—in a sense becomes femi-nized himself.[2]

ONE

Time, Gender, and

the Erotic: Critical Orthodoxy

and the Prospects for a

Feminist Critique

The vast majority of recent commentary on Horace as a love poet falls into one of two categories: criticism informed by the privileging of a romantic version of love, or criticism informed by what might be called a notion of the poet as universal spokesman.[1] In the first kind of criticism, what occurs is a deprecation of Horace's love poems for not according with the model of a Catullus, many of whose love poems seem to be a direct outpouring of emotion toward an idealized beloved with whom he wants a lasting relationship. In the second kind of criticism, Horace is hailed as a sober and wise man, with whom we should all identify, who "correctly observes" that love does not last. Thus in the first kind of criticism Horace is condemned for having the wrong approach to love—at least the wrong approach to be chosen for expression in love poetry—and in the second, he is endorsed for bringing a necessary realism to the area of love.

While these approaches at first glance appear to be radically different, they in fact share a common assumption, namely, that the proper focus of criticism is the reproduction of the poet's own conceptions of love. In the first case the result is a devaluation of Horace as a love poet for not producing a version of love characterized by the romantic ideal of timelessness. In the second, the result is a lauding of Horace for "correctly" perceiving romantic love as an impossibility. The problem with both positions, however, is that their effort to provide an accurate reproduction of Horace's view of love precludes any genuine critique of that view. The critics who devalue Horace because of his failure to accord with a romantic version of love assume that Horace's own views are self-evident, and thus do little to set the internal dynamics of the poems they discuss in relation to the romantic model of love that they privilege. While the critics who seek to defend Horace's view of love offer a needed corrective to such devaluation and also provide insightful explications of many of the love poems, their approach is limited, in turn, by an unconscious identification with the poet/lover, which produces a blindness to the problems that his male desire produces both for the beloved and for himself.

The critical approach to Horace as a love poet that privileges a romantic version of love is perhaps best exemplified by the statement of R. G. M. Nisbet: "None of Horace's love-poems (if that is the right name for them) reaches the first rank."[2] Implicit in this remark is a judgment about Horace's love poetry that is based on an unstated assumption of what a love poem should be, yet Nisbet offers no clear and consistent notion of what would constitute a love poem, or more specifically, a good love poem. Nevertheless, the faults that he attributes to Horace as a love poet (lack of seriousness and involvement, artificiality, and unbelievability), and the poets with whom he compares Horace unfavorably (Catullus and Propertius), would suggest that the model that Horace fails to live up to is that of the romantic love poet. What Nisbet finds disturbing about Horace's love poetry is its remoteness from a romanticism that exhibits desire with the kind of directness and immediacy of, for example, a Propertius, whose poems (according to Nisbet) "are written with an earnestness and intensity that seem to be derived at least partly from real life."[3] Thus, because Horace deals with desire in less overt ways than do romantic poets, he is unable to meet Nisbet's standards for good love poetry.[4]

While somewhat less negative, the perspective of R. G. M. Nisbet and Margaret Hubbard on the love poems, as expressed in the introduction to their commentary on Book 1 of the *Odes*, retains the general sense of Nisbet's earlier criticisms. Their perspective is worth discussing at some length, both for the notions it contains, and for the influence that those notions have by appearing in the current standard commentary in English on the *Odes*. For them, the problem with Horace as a love poet seems to be his failure to produce the kind of love poetry with which they can be comfortable, that is, love poetry in the Catullan tradition. They assume that other present-day readers will have a similar response: "[t]he modern reader is apt to draw unfavorable comparisons with Catullus and Propertius, but they were intending something very different." What that "something . . . different" is remains unstated, but one imagines that it has something to do with how Horace is perceived to handle the emotions of love: "Horace is not concerned with his own emotions; exceptions are embarrassing, however explicable in the context."[5]

As far as the first part of this remark is concerned, what Nisbet and Hubbard do not seem to recognize is that "concern with one's emotions" need not be directly expressed. By the 1920s, literary critics outside of classics had already seen the problem with this reductive notion of what it means to deal with emotion, and it is worth recalling how fully New Criticism succeeded in exposing the inadequacy of reducing poetry to what is assumed to be the emotional life of the author. Thus, T. S. Eliot, in his essay "Tradition and the Individual Talent" (1919), written in response to Romantic assumptions about poetry—most notably expressed in Wordsworth's description of poetry as "emotion recollected in tranquility"—attacks the notion that a poet in any straightforward fashion expresses his personality or his emotions through his poetry.[6] Eliot argues that the poet works not in isolation but in relation to a literary tradition and that poetry is, in fact, in some sense "an escape from emotion" and "an escape from personality" although "only those who have personality and emotions know what it means to want to escape from these things."[7]

Still further, I. A. Richards, in *Practical Criticism* (1929), had eloquently challenged the notion that emotion mediated by reflection is somehow "insincere." Thus irony, "where the feeling really present is often the exact contrary to that overtly professed," should not be viewed "as insincere as simple readers often suppose it must be."[8] The classicist Archibald Allen, writing more than three decades later, addresses some of these same issues in "Sunt qui Propertium malint," published, interestingly enough, in the same book of essays on elegy and lyric in which Nisbet's negative comment upon Horace's love odes appears.[9] Allen persuasively argues that the seemingly spontaneous expression of emotion commonly identified with Propertius, for example, and not with Ovid, is in fact not always present in Propertius. More importantly, he discusses the fact that an ancient audience would have identified sincerity as a function of style, not of personality, and that as a consequence, sincerity has more to do with the persuasiveness of the poet's style than with the relationship between the poet's style and his personality. Although Eliot, Richards, and even Allen are themselves now dated, their critique helps us to see how Nisbet and Hubbard, in claiming that "Horace is not concerned with his own emotions," rely upon discredited assumptions that a transparent relationship can be found between a poet and the emotions his poems express.

The real difficulty in relying upon such assumptions can be seen in considering the second part of Nisbet and Hubbard's remark, where we might ask for whom Horace's "exceptions" to concerns with his emotions are supposed to be embarrassing. Presumably they would be embarrassing either to the poet himself, to the poet/lover, to Nisbet and Hubbard, or to other readers, but the notion that embarrassment has such a univocal content seems dubious. Presumably, for Nisbet and Hubbard these exceptions do not fit comfortably with their notion (or their notion of others' notions) of Horace or the poet/lover as somehow "beyond desire." The poet/lover of *Odes* 4.1 (to whom they refer) is embarrassed by his continuing susceptibility to love, and the conclusion seems to be either that readers who have judged Horatian love as somehow transcending desire share the poet/lover's own embarrassment here, or that readers are embarrassed by the poet/lover's expression of his embarrassment.

But implicit in each of these kinds of embarrassment is the assumption that the poem itself reflects some Horatian "view," which exists independently of the poem, and we have noted how dubious such an assumption is. Still further, the belief that readers either can share an embarrassment that they find in the poem (regardless of whether the poem is itself a reflection of the author) or that they are embarrassed by their distance from what the poem expresses, assumes that readers themselves seek to identify with what they read. Such an assumption ignores both the complexity of how embarrassment might be constructed within a poem (with which of the elements contributing to embarrassment is the reader to identify?) and the heterogeneity of responses that the embarrassment might produce. The emotional expression that Nisbet and Hubbard presumably find embarrassing is the expression of a *male* lover for whom emotion poses a threat to autonomy. Insofar as autonomy is a feature of the dynamic of male eroticism, it seems fair to argue that embar-

rassment is itself gendered: a reader will identify with the embar-
rassment (will *feel* embarrassment) produced by Horace's emotional
expression only if she is willing to identify as well with the perspec-
tive of the male lover.

In both the criticism of Horace's poetry for its separation from the
presumed emotional life of the poet and the description of the "em-
barrassment" that some of the poetry is supposed to produce, we
can see how Nisbet and Hubbard develop a critical strategy that
seeks to circumscribe those aspects of Horace's poetry that are most
distant from the Catullan model of romantic love. Their assumption
seems to be that the romantic model comes closest to capturing the
actual dynamics of erotic love, and thus that those moments in
Horace's poetry that challenge this model are separated from such
presumed actuality. Thus, the expression of erotic emotion is de-
tached from what they presume would have been Horace's real
feelings, or it is seen to produce an embarrassment whose source is
finally the impossibility of imagining how such feelings might really
occur.

This attempt to separate what is disturbing in Horace's poetry
from the actualities of erotic love is perhaps clearest in their claim
that Horace owes more to the conventions of erotic writing than to
the realities of Roman life in the first century B.C.E. By positing an
artificial separation between "art" and "life," they can dismiss as
"merely literary" aspects of the love poems with which they are
uncomfortable.[10] For example, although offering evidence for the
widespread practice of homosexuality in Horace's time,[11] they de-
clare that references to homosexual love "should not be over-literally
interpreted," and, specifically in regard to *Odes* 1.4, that "the homo-
sexual implication has no bearing on Sestius' actual behaviour, but is
a conventional motif derived from Greek poetry." In addition, they
cite *Odes* 4.13 and *Odes* 1.25 as examples of "Horace imitat[ing] the
more pungent side of Hellenistic literature," and then proceed to
what seems to be their underlying characterization of Horace as a
love poet: "Really *serious* [emphasis mine] notes, as opposed to this
factitious realism, are rather rare."[12]

The idea here seems to be that "serious" romantic poetry would
somehow replace "factitious realism" with the emotional intensity
that is presumed to mark actual erotic experience, and perhaps it is
because such poetry is "rare" for Horace that Nisbet and Hubbard
are led to the following (surprisingly sympathetic) summary of Hor-

ace as a love poet: "More normally he assumes a detached, ironic pose, which as far as love-poetry is concerned seems very original."[13] What is worthy of note here is how the opposition between seriousness and detached irony leaves in place the assumption that the erotic feelings of the lover are the primary object of concern for the critic. If "detachment" and "seriousness" characterize not just the *attitudes* of the lover within a love poem, but also the emotional significance of the poem itself, then it is no wonder that Nisbet and Hubbard see the "detachment" of erotic feeling in Horace's odes as precluding the judgment that Horace was himself a serious love poet. The distanced, ironic stance, despite its acknowledged originality, is seen as automatically diminishing the odes' possibilities as love poems.

However, the error in such an argument is the assumption that the purpose of criticism is to reproduce whatever in the poem is taken to be the expression of the poets' own views. Nisbet and Hubbard assume that because the *lover* in many of Horace's love poems is detached, such detachment must also be taken as an expression of Horace's views, and they assume further that the only possible response to such detachment is to judge it as inadequate love poetry. Rather than working to discover *why* erotic feeling is expressed in an ironic, detached manner, Nisbet and Hubbard assume that Horace must himself have failed to understand the reality of erotic intensity that can be seen in a poet such as Catullus. But what such privileging of a romantic view of love precludes is seeing the relation between the ironic, detached pose of the lover and the world that he seeks to control. As we shall see, the lover's distance does not indicate an absence of erotic feeling, but rather indicates how fully the lover has responded to the beloved's threat to his own autonomy. In focusing so completely on the lover, criticism that accepts a romantic model of love must necessarily fail to understand the relational dynamics of lover and beloved, which Horace's "detachment" displays so fully.

While the critical responses that have challenged the type of criticism exemplified by Nisbet and Hubbard have taken many forms, they share, for the most part, a rejection of the notion of Horace as unconcerned with the emotions and instead propose what amounts to a Horace who can stand as a universal authority on love. Rather than judging the detached Horatian poet/lover as unsuitable for real love poems, they champion his posture with regard to love as sensible and realistic. In other words, they reject the romantic position that Horace knew nothing about love and substitute the universalist assumption that he knew all about love. But as we shall see, such an inversion of judgment leaves in place the centrality of the lover's perspective, which we have seen in the romantic view of love. In each case, the critic's job is to judge the adequacy of Horace's love poetry by examining whether or not the lover's expression of emotion is itself acceptable. The mutuality of erotic love is thus reduced to the perspective of a single desiring self, and that self is itself praised or blamed on the basis of its response to what it desires. Although it seeks to counter the tradition that privileges a romantic view of love by trying to show that detachment is as worthy of attention as passionate involvement, recent criticism that praises Horace as a love poet leaves unquestioned the assumption that the beloved's independent existence has meaning for the lover only as a difficulty that must somehow be surmounted.

We can see such a privileging of the lover's perspective in A. J. Boyle's essay on Horace's love odes, which argues that the "Romantic prejudice and myopic *Philologie*" and "*Quellenforschungen*" of previous criticism must be replaced by examining the "poems themselves" and "the poetic construct itself."[14] Boyle's goal is "to further the critical understanding of the nature and quality of Horace's achievement as a love-poet," and he does profitably discuss such features of the love odes as Horace's "astute use of commonplaces, verbal wit, liveliness of language, metrical control, firmness of organization and structure, and . . . gently ironic tone."[15] However, he remains unaware that he does not simply look at the poems themselves—the very possibility of which most contemporary literary theorists would question[16]—but rather, through an unacknowledged identification with the male poet's desire, takes the poet's themes and the way they are presented as human or universal.

In his discussion of *Odes* 1.25 (a poem I discuss in Chapter 2), for example, he rejects the approaches both of Collinge and of Nisbet and Hubbard as failing to account for what he characterizes as Horace's realism: "To regard it either as a crude and nasty piece of verse [Collinge] or as a conventional literary exercise [Nisbet and Hubbard] is to fail to perceive the poet's forceful and *realistic* presentation of the terrible consequences of time's passing upon a specific, and especially vulnerable, *human individual*" [emphasis mine].[17]

But while Boyle succeeds here in taking this poem seriously, he fails in not acknowledging the extent to which the poem's so-called "realism" is in fact a construct of a male poet/lover's imagination, an imagination that then creates this particular image of the woman growing increasingly less desirable to him and to others. It is the poet/lover who determines the "terrible consequences of time's passing," the poet/lover who makes those consequences seem natural and universal: "the explicit nature symbolism of the final stanza [Lydia turned to dry leaves] . . . places the personal devastation to be suffered by Lydia within the context of a universal law of nature."[18] What Boyle is unable to recognize is that the association of Lydia's decline with that of nature is not realistic, but rather represents a strategy on the part of the poet/lover that supports his discrediting of Lydia. Generalizing Lydia's situation into an example of universal erotic decline over time shows a blindness to the significance of Lydia's gender.

Part of Boyle's recuperation of Horace's amatory odes is based on seeing in them universal concerns:

> . . . some of Horace's main intent in the amatory odes is thematic, that is to say, is directed towards the analysis or exploration of important human concerns. . . . Certainly the themes which pervade the amatory odes . . . are bound up with basic, recurring constituents of human behaviour, with integral, indeed nucleic features of man's [sic] experience. Consider, for example, the following select list of matters surveyed by the poet: . . . the emotional vulnerability of the female sex; female unresponsiveness or obstinacy. . . . Nobody can deny that the topics around which Horace builds his amatory odes are constructs of, and have direct reference to, major elements of human experience, elements which are situated not at the periphery of man's [sic] existence, but at its emotional, intellectual and moral centre.[19]

But the difficulty of generalizing from the specificity of female gender becomes apparent when we see that *Odes* 1.25 is taken to be a "universal" story, yet, at the same time, Lydia's particularized experience becomes tied up with such "nucleic features of man's [sic] experience" as "the emotional vulnerability of the female sex." Boyle tries to have it both ways: he wants to universalize Lydia's situation yet keep Lydia for an example of things female, such as "the emotional vulnerability of the female sex." What Boyle is evading is the gender specificity of both the portrayal of the beloved and of the writing poet/lover. Femaleness is not incidental to Lydia's erotic decline over time. Rather than rejecting Horace's portrait of Lydia as offensive, as other critics have done, Boyle embraces it as universal, but this is impossible, for Lydia's being a woman is central to how Horace has time shape her sexuality. Boyle's essay has the virtue of taking the love poems seriously and of elucidating many of the techniques that make them work. It falls short, though, in its blindness to the extent to which gender, as we shall see in the following chapters, frames both the male poet/lover's strategies and the consequent image of the beloved in the odes.[20]

The degree to which a concentration on the erotic strategies of the poet/lover occludes a recognition of the significance of gender can be seen even in Michael Putnam's excellent contribution to criticism of Horace as a love poet.[21] In his recent book, *Artifices of Eternity: Horace's Fourth Book of Odes*, Putnam shows how the move from what he calls "personal trials . . . to public, historical occasions" (298) can be understood only by recognizing that the public itself functions as "a sublimation of the individual's amatory cravings" (298). Putnam's great advance on earlier criticism of Horace as a love poet lies in the subtlety of his analysis of the *motives* that lie behind the transformations of the erotic in the *Odes*, for he reads eroticism in Horace not as a failure to accord with a romantic ideal, nor as a "thematic" concern with "nucleic features of man's experience," but rather as an integral aspect of Horace's struggle to find "a continuity in art which nature's linear inexorability patently denies" (298). By connecting eroticism, art, and temporality, Putnam is able to show that both eroticism and the creation of art are driven by the hope that the self might be freed from the ravages of time, and he thus succeeds in establishing that any account of Horace's view of love must recognize how thoroughly eroticism is connected to the lover's anxious uncertainty about the relationship of his identity to the world in which he lives.

But while Putnam's argument hints at times of a *critique* of this conception of the erotic, his analysis largely remains anchored in the assumption that criticism must aim at a sympathetic reproduction of the ideas that he discusses. Consider, for example, his analysis of what he calls the change from "erotic to spiritual" (70) love in *Odes* 4.3. He argues that where eroticism produces a lover who is little more than "a mesmerized pursuer of the passing and the vanishing," here instead the speaker, by becoming the "producer of enchanting, enduring *melos*," is able to become "one with the permanence of his lovely song, an example of the highest form of eros, with art constantly renewing itself" (70). However, the claim here that this transformation from the erotic to the spiritual produces a speaker who "instead of being centrifugal is himself the center" (70) raises suspicions about the cost of such a transformation. Where Plato's conception of the beautiful or the good demanded that the self be recognized as at best illusory, here the "permanence of his lovely song" suggests instead a narcissistic aggrandizement of the self. What has been lost, in the move from the erotic to the spiritual, seems to be the troubling relatedness of the self demanded by erotic desire, and the self as the center of its experiences which remains would seem to have no way of explaining why the art with which it is now merged is anything other than a mesmerizing fantasy of escape.

At one point, Putnam does suggest that the "message . . . that art . . . can abstract its creator and audience from time" is "delusive" as well as "comforting" (305), but he seems unwilling to explore how the recognition that the "message" of escape is "delusive" might allow a rethinking of the initial conception of the self as motivated by its hope to be abstracted out of time. In describing Horace's increasing turn to political and historical themes, Putnam speaks of "a sublimation of the individual's amatory cravings, ever a victim of time's flow, into the larger, more constant love of Rome and the common rituals of song which betoken her eternity" (298), and this sense of the individual lover as victimized by time is, of course, central not just to the turn to the "constant love of Rome," but more generally to the lover's desperate refusal to situate his own identity in any real relation to the uncontrollable temporality of the beloved. Putnam's use of the term "sublimation" suggests a recognition of the compensatory function that "constant love" is supposed to play for the lover, but what goes unexplored is how the constancy of Rome is meant to compensate for the human beloved, whose temporality defies any static constancy.

By sublimating, Horace attempts to find satisfaction for his desire in precisely the manner we would expect at this point in our discussion: through an evasion of the temporality of the other. The substitution of "yearning for Augustus and devotion to poetry" (324) for desire for the human beloved is not seriously questioned by Putnam, but I would argue that this erotic move on Horace's part should be seen as a kind of failure. For what is suggested by this "sublimation of the individual's amatory cravings" is a belief that the only solution to the unsettling role that temporality plays in the erotic lies in the elimination of the human beloved, for her humanity of necessity entails an acceptance of the very contingency of time that so threatens the lover. In the substitution of "yearning for Augustus and devotion to poetry" for an actual erotic relationship, Horace eliminates the difficulty of a self whose desires bring it in relation to what it cannot control. In the externalization of his own poetic powers the poet has found his ideal beloved: she is self in the guise of other. Finally, Horace's sublimation of desire should be seen not as a genuine conquering of time, but rather as the ultimate, unsuccessful, stage in the attempt to control the temporality of the beloved.

Horatian critics such as Boyle and Putnam, who do not privilege a romantic view of love, force us to take Horace as a love poet more seriously. In addition, they contribute to a fuller explication of Horace's version of love. However they fail to address the consequences of Horace's version of desire, largely because they unconsciously and perhaps of necessity identify themselves with Horace as poet/ lover and thus universalize his position. By assuming identity with the male poet/lover, these critics preclude both any identification with the beloved, which might help to shape a full examination of her, and a sufficiently distanced critique of the poet/lover. Without necessarily intending to, they have allowed their identification with the poet/lover to shape their view of his version of the erotic, and they have thus failed to see the extent to which gender interacts with temporality in the construction of love, and, further, how Horace's distanced, ironic stance functions as a male strategy of desire designed to control temporality. Part of the reason for this failure undoubtedly lies in assumptions about male autonomy or identity, which naturalize or keep unobserved the extent to which the issue of temporality in the love situation is an issue of power and control. If the critic or the dominant culture from which the critic writes sees the poet/lover's attempts to control the temporality of the beloved only from the point of view of the poet/lover, what is lost is the self of the beloved and thus the possibility of offering a critique of the lover.

To combat this problematic identification with the poet/lover and to provide a larger theoretical framework, I turn now to some recent work in the theory of gender relations and erotic identity, which can allow a reconceptualizing of both the erotic dynamics of lyric poetry and the reader's relationship to those dynamics. I look first at Judith Fetterley's notion of the "resisting reader" and examine how her arguments provide a way of responding to texts that employ universalizing strategies that privilege the male. I then look at Jan Montefiore's work on love poetry to see how such a "resisting" strategy can be useful specifically in approaching love poetry.[22] Finally, I present some recent psychoanalytic work on human development that has illuminated such issues as male identity and the creation of a self, and which will thus help us to understand the erotic dynamics of the male self that a more suspicious reading of the love odes would want to critique. Theory that sees gender as a category of analysis makes it possible to understand the asymmetrical relation to temporality of lover and beloved, and thus makes possible the sort of reevaluation of Horace as a love poet that I am attempting here.

For some years now Fetterley's notion of the "resisting reader" has been extraordinarily useful for critics interested in discovering, identifying, and articulating suspicious or resisting ways of responding to the male designs of literary texts. While her book *The Resisting Reader: A Feminist Approach to American Fiction* focuses on a body of writing far removed from Latin poetry, her notion of the "resisting reader" is nevertheless a useful one in approaching any text that calls upon the female reader or critic to identify with the male as a universal subject and against herself. Fetterley argues that what she calls "the pretense that literature speaks universal truths" has had as its effect the belief that "the merely personal, the purely subjective, has been burned away or at least transformed through the medium of art into the representative" (xi). What follows from such a belief is a theory of reading as the pursuit of a kind of identity. As readers, we seek to identify with the universal truths that we find in literature, and what warrants our effort to do this is our certainty that the representations of experience in literature are *representative* of some universal core of humanity. Indeed, the literary critic's embrace of what Fetterley calls the "posture of the apolitical" (xi) is warranted by the assumption that where politics addresses subjective or personal interests, literature instead has transcended such local concerns to offer a view of experience as it really is.

The transcendence literature offers is illusory, though, for Fetterley argues that literature "insists on its universality at the same time that it defines that universality in specifically male terms" (xii). The effect of such gendered universality on a female reader is that "she is asked to identify with a selfhood that defines itself in opposition to her," and she is thus "required to identify against herself" (xii). By showing how universality and male experience are linked, Fetterley is able both to specify the cost to the female reader of identifying with "an experience from which she is explicitly excluded" (xii) and to establish the necessity of what she calls the "resisting reader" as a counter to the cooptation of identity experienced by the female reader who merely assents to male universality: "the first act of the feminist critic must be to become a resisting reader rather than an assenting reader and, by this refusal to assent, to begin the process of exorcizing the male mind that has been implanted in us" (xxii).

What is perhaps most valuable about Fetterley's approach is that it helps to identify both the expectations a text makes of us and the reasons why certain aspects of the text remain blind spots for some critics. To the extent that identifying with the male and with the male as universal is an expectation of Horace's poems and has been the major response of readers and critics, the negative consequences for the beloved (and less obviously for the lover and for how love itself is conceived) implied by Horace's temporal strategies have naturally remained obscured. What Fetterley's approach allows us to see is how a male perspective is often collapsed into a human perspective. In the case of Horace, a resisting reader is in a position to see how gender shapes the poet's particular configuration of time and the erotic. Fetterley shows the cost involved in adopting the male values of the poet as universal, and thus allows us to see the mistake in framing our judgments of Horace's view of love solely in terms of the male lover's perspective.

My own arguments about how the lover's construction of the beloved seeks to surmount the temporality that defines her independent existence are influenced not just by the general strategies of resistance advocated by Fetterley, but also by the more nuanced accounts of how the beloved functions within the dynamics of the lover's desire, which can be found in much recent feminist criticism.[23] A particularly useful example of such work is Jan Montefiore's *Feminism and Poetry: Language, Experience, Identity in Women's Writing*, which draws upon the critique of woman as other, found in such writers as Luce Irigaray, to show how the traditional love poet has as his central concern not the beloved herself, but rather his own identity. Montefiore argues that in what she calls "the great tradition of Petrarch and Shakespeare" (a tradition that could surely include Horace as well), the pursuit of the beloved has as its purpose "not the success or failure of a courtship, but the establishing of an identity through the dialectic of desire and response" (98).[24] Regardless of whether the lover's desire seems to be "for the image of his beloved" or for how his own image is "mediated through her response to him" (98), the beloved functions merely instrumentally, as the occasion for the lover's self-creation.

While the desire for the "image" of the beloved and the desire for the beloved's response may seem to point to different relations the lover has to the beloved, Montefiore argues that in each case the beloved functions merely as an instrument of self-creation, and she thus indicates the fallacy of allowing differing versions of the *lover's* desire to guide interpretive response. While from the perspective of the lover, there might be a significant difference between desiring the beloved as an "image" and desiring the beloved because of her response to the lover, an analysis of the beloved's position would instead indicate that her role as an instrument of the lover's "establishing of an identity" remains unchanged. Thus, Montefiore's point is to show how, from the perspective of gender, an analysis of the functional dynamics of male desire in love poetry can reveal the underlying forces that shape the positions of the lover and beloved in a way that is precluded if the lover's perspective is taken as an unquestioned interpretive frame.

Indeed, for Montefiore the polarity of lover and beloved cannot itself be understood without considering how such roles are themselves the consequences of gender distinctions. She argues that the dynamic of self-definition that can be traced in traditional love poetry itself "implies the masculinity of the lover and the femininity of the other" (109) and shows how this feminizing of the other, while serving as the basis of the lover's creation of his identity, must inevitably lead to a denial that the other's existence has any independent worth: "In a poem where the speaker establishes an identity through his relationship with another person, that person, reduced to a necessary presence, is denied full humanity and is thus feminized in the sense of being rendered negative—made into a blank Platonic mirror" (112).

What Montefiore sees in the traditional love poem confirms what we shall see in Horace's love odes—the centrality of the poet/lover's identity and the sacrifice of the humanity (or more specifically, as I shall discuss it, the temporality) of the female (or feminized) beloved for the sake of the poet/lover's self. The blank mirror of the beloved, in which the lover sees only the possibilities for his own self-creation, functions in Horace as the fantasy of a self removed from time. The beloved is granted a relation to the lover's identity only if she promises to confirm the lover's dream that eroticism can provide an escape from the limitations of temporality, and if she fails to offer such confirmation, the lover's self is sustained only by denying that the beloved has any meaningful existence. By showing so fully how erotic relationship in love poetry serves merely as the vehicle for the lover's self-creation, Montefiore thus provides a powerful rationale for resisting the lover's perspective in our reading of Horace.

However, to argue that the perspective of the lover should not provide the dominant focus of interpretation is not to suggest that we should ignore the particular form that male identity takes in the *Odes*. For while it is certainly true that the poet/lover of the *Odes* seeks through eroticism to discover a version of self, what such a general description seems not to acknowledge is the specific form that such self-creation takes in the *Odes*. As I argue throughout this book, the self that frequently appears as the poet/lover in the *Odes* seems driven by a desire for autonomy, which typically expresses itself through a distanced, ironic stance that seeks to control the temporality of the other. Many critics have recognized this stance, yet few have seen the potentially troubling aspect of that distancing and its relationship to the attempt to control temporality. The following is a fairly typical description of Horace in the love odes:

> In all of his love odes . . . whether he is the observer or the participant, Horace's stance is basically the same as in the first love ode [1.5]: never obsessive like Catullus and the elegists, he is mildly bemused, even detached, and appreciative of the ironies inherent in the situation.[25]

What this sort of description recognizes is what we might call the surface of the love odes: their distanced quality. What it fails to recognize is the problematic nature of the self that so distances desire. The erotic strategies of the *Odes* cannot be fully explored without questioning the function of this surface detachment and its related displacement of desire or, more generally, without attempting to understand the self of the poet/lover.

In searching for such an understanding, I have found the recent work of Nancy Chodorow[26] and Jessica Benjamin[27] particularly helpful. Their use of psychoanalytic theory to show how the male can undergo a pre-oedipal process of differentiation that creates a distanced yet controlling self, and further, Benjamin's specific development of this idea to explain adult erotic domination can help us interpret the poet/lover who is both distanced and controlling with respect to the beloved. My intention in discussing their work is not to give an historical account of a particular kind of male identity nor to psychoanalyze Horace, but rather to find a theoretical framework for explaining the poet/lover's self and the consequences of that self for love.[28] Chodorow and Benjamin offer an approach to the development of the self that may provide us with a model with explanatory power for the strategies of the male poet/lover in enacting his desire.

The theories of Chodorow and Benjamin about the development of the self grow out of the object-relations theory of psychoanalysis, which sees the development of the ego as a relational, social process rather than as a one-way movement away from a self merged with the mother and toward a bounded self. One of the major proponents of object-relations theory, D. W. Winnicott, in his 1958 essay "The Capacity to Be Alone," addresses, as Chodorow puts it, "a certain wholeness that develops through an internal sense of relationship with another." Chodorow goes on to call this " 'capacity to be alone,' [to use Winnicott's words] a relational rather than a reactive autonomy, [which] develops because of a sense of the ongoing presence of the other."[29] Chodorow and Benjamin are particularly interested in the process of differentiation (from the mother), that is, the pre-oedipal process by which the child begins to become a self. This process has consequences for issues of gender because the child develops a gender identity at the same time that he or she is developing a self. For the girl, gender identity is continuous with her identification with her mother; for the boy, gender identity involves a difference from the mother. Failure at successful differentiation produces different results depending on the gender of the child: the girl may experience problems with separation, while the boy may experience an excessive need for autonomy at the expense of the feeling of connectedness or the recognition of the female other. This failure in the male may take the form of domination, "an alienated form of differentiation, an effort to recreate tension through distance, idealization, and objectification."[30] In the sphere of the erotic, according to Benjamin, we reenact these issues of the self arising from the pre-oedipal stage of life.[31]

The work of Chodorow and Benjamin can help us further to understand the self of the poet/lover, which Fetterley and Montefiore would have us resist. By showing how the issues of excessive autonomy and inability to recognize the self of the other can be connected with male gender, and further, how these same issues in conjunction with male gender are played out in the realm of the erotic, Chodorow and Benjamin offer one way for us to explain the distanced, ironic male lover whose way of imagining love ultimately entails denying an essential part of the self of the other. The excessiveness of the poet/lover's need for autonomy precludes his recognition of the very self of the beloved with which he seeks connection. The lover's autonomy in the *Odes* is founded on his struggle to escape time, and such a struggle will be successful only if the beloved offers the possibility of such escape. In this sense, at least, the lover genuinely seeks a relation to the beloved. However, because the relation to the beloved is founded not on the relationship itself, but on how the relationship might confirm the lover's autonomy, any connection with the beloved takes shape as domination—the lover seeks to find in the beloved a confirmation of his own hope for autonomy. What the lover discovers, though, is the intractable otherness of the beloved. In seeking to absorb the beloved into his identity, the lover is confronted with the beloved's own temporality, and in order to preserve the autonomy of his existence, he must seek to deny that such temporality has any relation to his existence. Ironic distance is the form that such denial takes, but the paradox here is that the distance that denies temporality to the beloved precludes the lover from receiving any response to his desire. The beloved, stripped of her humanity, lacks the self necessary for returning love.

What Chodorow and Benjamin finally allow us to see is that the poet/lover's attempt to control the temporality of the beloved is a manifestation of the needs of a *male* who has experienced differentiation in a way that overstresses autonomy and underemphasizes connectedness, and they indicate further why such male desire takes form as ironic distance. But in addition to having explanatory power for understanding the poet/lover in the *Odes*, the patterns of development described by Chodorow and Benjamin may help explain why the poet/lover's attempts to control temporality have remained a blind spot in Horatian criticism. Male critics conditioned by the patterns of development identified by Chodorow and Benjamin would tend to valorize those aspects of the poet/lover's identity that confirm their own sense of what a self should be and would be blind to the significance of the temporality of the beloved as something that would disrupt that same sense of a self. What the strategies of reading proposed by Fetterley and Montefiore and the gendered etiology of desire described by Chodorow and Benjamin each suggest is the danger of allowing such an embrace of the poet/lover's identity to provide the basis for our interpretations of Horace. My own arguments in this book indicate how an analysis of the forces underlying the poet/lover's desire, and in particular the role that temporality plays in conditioning how the poet/lover conceives of the erotic, reveals a Horace whose love poems provide us with a remarkable enactment of the difficulties that the male desire for autonomy must confront. I suggest moments in Horace's poems where the desire for autonomy is itself critiqued, but ultimately conclude that the notion of love as a shared project that could embrace the contingency of time remains elusive in the *Odes*.

TWO

The Temporal

Adverb

My discussion of the temporality of love begins at the level of the word, specifically, the temporal adverb. In each of the following poems—*Odes* 1.25, *Odes* 2.5, and *Odes* 3.7—there is a key temporal adverb that plays a central role in establishing the dominance of the theme of temporality in the particular love situation. In the first two poems, the key temporal adverb begins the poem and helps to set up certain expectations from that point on; in the third, it occurs two-thirds of the way through the poem and makes us rethink what has come before. While these are not the only love odes with what I call key temporal adverbs (cf., for example, *donec* in *Odes* 3.9, *nuper* in *Odes* 3.26, and *diu* in *Odes* 4.1— all of which signal the importance of temporality from the poem's first line), they do show especially well how such an adverb, reinforced by other indicators of temporality, can function as one device by which Horace makes time dominate the erotic situation. Further, as we shall see, this dominance of temporality has consequences for our understanding of the positions of the lover and the beloved.

In *Odes* 1.25 and 2.5, the lover seeks to draw a distinction between himself and the beloved by pointing to how the beloved's experience is determined by time, and this distinction is itself the basis of the lover's effort to control the beloved. Where these poems clearly delineate the roles of male lover and female beloved by distinguishing between the lover's position outside of time and the beloved's temporality, *Odes* 3.7 instead points to a temporal predicament in which lover and beloved seem equally enmeshed. However their differing relationships to time will reveal yet another example of the hierarchical and gendered distinctions between male lover and female beloved.

Odes 1.25

> Parcius iunctas quatiunt fenestras
> iactibus crebris iuvenes protervi,
> nec tibi somnos adimunt amatque
>   ianua limen,
> quae prius multum facilis movebat   5
> cardines. audis minus et minus iam
> "me tuo longas pereunte noctes,
>   Lydia, dormis?"
> invicem moechos anus arrogantis
> flebis in solo levis angiportu,   10
> Thracio bacchante magis sub inter-
>   lunia vento,
> cum tibi flagrans amor et libido,
> quae solet matres furiare equorum,
> saeviet circa iecur ulcerosum,   15
>   non sine questu
> laeta quod pubes hedera virenti
> gaudeat pulla magis atque myrto
> aridas frondes hiemis sodali
>   dedicet Hebro.   20

More sparingly do bold young men shake your joined windows with frequent hurling of stones, and they do not take away your sleep, and the door loves its threshold—the door which earlier moved so much its easy hinges. You hear less and less now "while I, your love, am perishing through long nights, do you sleep, Lydia?" In turn, an inconsequential old woman, you will weep over haughty adulterers in the lonely alleyway, while the Thracian wind rages like a bacchant even more under the moonless sky, when for you blazing love and desire, the sort that maddens the mothers of horses, will rage around your wounded heart, not without complaint that, happy, the youth rejoice in green ivy more than gray myrtle, and dedicate dry leaves to Hebrus, companion of winter.

Parcius, the first word of *Odes* 1.25, establishes a temporal perspective that influences the reading of the entire poem.[1] It sets up a contrast between the erotic successes of Lydia's past, and her present decline, which will only continue. The influence of *parcius* is particularly direct in the first eight lines of the poem. Although all but one of the finite verbs in these lines are in the present tense, there is nevertheless an overwhelming impression of the past.[2] In the first two lines Horace achieves this effect through the choice and placement of the initial comparative adverb. The tense of *quatiunt*, the main verb of lines 1–2, is present. *Parcius*, though, which modifies *quatiunt*, changes the effect of the present tense. Implicit in the comparative degree of *parcius* is the question "more sparingly than when?" This inherent duality challenges *quatiunt* and, read in conjunction with the present tense of the main verb, causes us to be simultaneously aware of both past and present.

The phrase *iuvenes protervi*, highlighted through its postponement to the end of its clause, continues the focus on time by foreshadowing the contrast between youth and age, which becomes more pronounced later in the poem. In the future Lydia will be an old woman (*anus* 9) ignored by the *pubes* (17). The meaning of *protervi* (insolent, bold) underscores the disruptive activity expressed by *quatiunt*,[3] while the prefix *pro-*, combined with the final position of *protervi*, additionally specifies a dimension of urgent, forward movement. The iterative meaning of *crebris* further reinforces the aggressive quality of *iuvenes protervi*, while it contrasts with the controlling temporal adverb, *parcius*. The image created in the first two lines— the picture of the closed windows, the repeated hurling of stones, the violence of the stones hitting the windows, the potential threat to the person inside—is a powerful one, yet having previously absorbed the force of the comparative adverb *parcius*, we know that the activity described is happening less often now, and that the lovemaking that is the goal of this activity belongs increasingly to the past.

The control of *parcius*, though, even in these first two lines, is still more complicated, for *parcius* secondarily modifies the perfect passive participle *iunctas* as well. When *parcius* is seen to affect *iunctas* as well as *quatiunt*, the entire phrase *parcius iunctas . . . fenestras* suggests that Lydia's windows are perhaps not quite as resolutely closed as they appear. Back in the days of Lydia's sexual prime we can imagine that her windows stayed shut. One as sought after as Lydia might not have needed to show her eagerness for love by standing at the window. By qualifying *iunctas* (joined, closed), Horace may be suggesting that while lovers seek out Lydia less often, she is more "open" to their advances. Perhaps we should picture the present-day Lydia degraded by peeking out her window for lovers who now rarely appear. This hint in *parcius iunctas . . . fenestras* of Lydia's movement toward taking the initiative in the love situation becomes fully developed later in the poem when Lydia no longer looks longingly out her windows, but roams the streets filled with a lust that finds no takers. In addition, because of the erotic potential of *iungo* as the "joining" of sexual intercourse, *parcius iunctas* ("joined" less often) links the temporal with the erotic, thus neatly revealing in the poem's first two words the theme of diminishing eroticism.[4]

Despite the violence implicit in impudent youths pelting Lydia's windows with stones, this activity, which belongs increasingly to the past, at least had the positive quality of showing Lydia as an object worthy of erotic attention. Its decline shows that Lydia is no longer as desirable as she once was.

In the first two lines of the poem, then, Lydia's sexual decline is characterized through her status as a less frequent object of aggressive erotic attention. This characterization begins with the phrase *parcius iunctas*, which signals the poem's theme of diminishing sexual attraction. Lydia is established as the former recipient (cf. the passive voice of *iunctas*) of erotic attention. Her sexuality is defined as arising not from within her, as desire, but rather in terms of her desirability. Thus, the sign that she was once desirable is that she was pestered and disturbed by young men, whereas now, her becoming too old for love is signaled through the absence of such attention. In each case, what is constant is her status as an *object* of desire for young men, while her own condition is determined temporally. Who she is in the present is determined by the change from the past, which the present manifests. But that change is itself finally significant only because of the differing reactions that young men (themselves apparently unchanging) have to her; her own despair at this situation is itself the consequence of how her temporality is understood by others.

The blending of past and present continues in *nec tibi somnos adimunt*. Although this statement has its main verb in the present tense, by negating it Horace reveals, as he did through *parcius iunctas quatiunt*, at least as much about Lydia's past as her present. While being deprived of sleep might under other circumstances be viewed as undesirable, in this erotic context it is not. What appears on the surface as potentially pleasant, that rowdy youths are not disturbing Lydia so that presumably now she can sleep, is in fact an indication that she is being ignored.[5] Later in the poem Lydia, kept sleepless not by noisy young men but by her own unsatisfied lust, will resort to wandering the streets at night.

The poem's first seemingly simple statement about present time devoid of any modifier or negative, *amatque / ianua limen*, in fact contains a negative meaning for Lydia. In her situation a closed door implies that no one any longer wants to enter her house. And further, although the personification of the door is a common motif in erotic contexts in Latin poetry,[6] the use of an inanimate subject for the verb *amare*, while not unprecedented in Horace, is striking in this context.[7] While Nisbet and Hubbard miss the full erotic potential of *amatque* and the phrase in which it appears,[8] other commentators have noted the sexually suggestive nature of Horace's language. Catlow points out that Horace is "mockingly transferring to her surroundings the sexually suggestive words which no longer apply to Lydia herself (*iunctas, amatque, facilis*),"[9] while Copley finds the phrase sarcastic, an "unkind reminder to Lydia of her earlier popularity, when she could choose at will among her many lovers those for whom her door would open at a touch, and those to whom it would remain stubbornly closed."[10] To Boyle, the door hugging the threshold is ironic,[11] while Collinge sees wit: "the only hugging at Lydia's house will be between door and threshold."[12]

We may conclude that the door "loving the threshold" certainly suggests hostility on the part of the speaker toward the fulfillment of Lydia's desire and underscores the lack of loving in her present life (*parcius iunctas*). *Amatque / ianua limen* creates a closed circle of loving inhabited only by personified objects and excluding Lydia from the roles of both lover and beloved—of both subject and object of desire. Indeed there is something almost masturbatory about this description of loving—the door loving a part of itself—which further heightens Lydia's exclusion. The door's easy movement of the past, *quae prius multum facilis movebat / cardines*, contrasts with the static image of the door's present. *Prius*, which recalls the opening *parcius*, shifts the temporal perspective from the present time of *amat* to some unspecified time in the past. The imperfect aspect of *movebat* prevents us from focusing on a fixed moment in time and suggests, rather, the duration of Lydia's sexually active past.

Whether *multum* in the phrase *quae prius multum facilis movebat / cardines* should be construed grammatically with *facilis* or *movebat* has occasioned discussion among commentators. Against taking *multum* with *movebat*, Nisbet and Hubbard argue as follows: "Porphyrio takes multum with *movebat* ('often moved'), and he has been followed by some modern editors. It could be argued that on this interpretation the contrast with *parcius* is expressed more clearly. On the other hand it is infelicitous to have two adverbs, *prius* and *multum*, both modifying *movebat*."[13] It is surprising that Nisbet and Hubbard find this "infelicitous" when in the very next line of the poem *audis* is modified by both *minus et minus* and *iam*. There is no reason why *multum* cannot play double duty here as *parcius* does earlier in the poem. But regardless of how one resolves this issue, the temporal effect of *multum* is undeniable. It echoes the iterative meaning of *crebris* and provides additional contrast with *parcius*. Once again, it is by contrast with the past that the poet creates the present.

With *audis* we seem to return to the present. However, *audis* is immediately qualified by *minus et minus iam* which further splits our attention between past and present. The comparative degree of *minus*, which shifts us away from the present, echoes the temporal control *parcius* has exerted since the beginning of the poem. The repetition of *minus*, combined with the reinforcement of the present tense by *iam* strengthens the impression of mixed past and present. The contrast between *audis minus et minus iam* and *me tuo longas pereunte noctes, / Lydia, dormis?* brings to a climax the juxtaposition of past and present in lines 1–8. By directly quoting the words of the shut-out lover, and at the same time undercutting their immediacy by all but relegating them to the past, Horace dramatically illustrates once again the contrast between Lydia's former and present lives. Both the immediacy of the direct address to Lydia (albeit as part of a quotation) and the word order of *me tuo* point to the intimacy sought by the lover. However Horace makes it clear that such desirability is all but a thing of the past for Lydia. *Pereunte*, a common word in amatory vocabulary, ironically foreshadows Lydia's future when, with roles reversed, she will be "dying" not only from lust, but from old age.[14]

The initial antithesis of past and present becomes in the second part of the poem one half of a new antithesis: of then and now (lines 1–8) with future time (lines 9–20).[15] *Invicem* is the pivotal word, which alerts us to a shift both from what has immediately preceded (the shut-out lover's lament) and from the opening temporal distinctions.[16] With *invicem . . . flebis* the poet suddenly unleashes his harsh prediction of Lydia's future, which takes the form of one long sentence filled with language that both echoes and contrasts with that of the first eight lines of the poem. Lydia, having become an old woman (*anus*), will haunt the lonely alleyways,[17] and weep over men who now refuse her.

The future is made more immediately present through the suddenness of *anus* and the placement of *flebis* before the dependent (explanatory) clause *cum . . . saeviet*, which in turn is reinforced by the present participle *bacchante*. Lydia's age (as now projected by the speaker)[18] contrasts with that of her former suitors (*iuvenes*), and the loneliness of the streets is a reminder that the days of her frequent visitors are over (*parcius . . .*).

Lydia now becomes like her former suitors. She is the one seeking companions and lamenting those who are unresponsive (*moechos . . . arrogantis*). Her forays at night (*sub inter- / lunia*) recall the long nights spent by the shut-out lover in front of her closed door (*longas pereunte noctes*). In addition, both the shut-out lover and Lydia lament their lack of success in gaining access to the one(s) they desire. The aggressiveness of Lydia's new actions (her taking on the role of pursuer) is not unlike that of the *iuvenes protervi*. Their implied threat of violence earlier in the poem (1–2) foreshadows the wildness that the poet attributes at first to the wind (*Thracio bacchante magis sub inter- / lunia vento*) but then to Lydia as well (cf. *flagrans, furiare, saeviet, iecur ulcerosum*). The comparative adverb *magis* (11) increases the storminess of the picture and contrasts with *parcius*, which had a controlling effect on the activity implicit in the first two lines of the poem.

While the passage of time creates some similarities between Lydia's situation and that of her former suitors, it ultimately serves to separate Lydia both from her former self and from her past and potential lovers. While her former suitors are described as *protervi* (bold), Lydia is now *levis* (light). The meaning "fickle" may have applied to Lydia in the past, but now the word clearly looks forward to the end of the poem where Lydia's "inconsequentiality" will make her easy to ignore and discard. Another way in which Lydia's situation echoes that of her former lovers is the time at which love (or attempted love) takes place—the night. However, while the *longas noctes* (7) of the shut-out lover's vigil are recalled by *inter- / lunia* (11–12), Lydia's interlunar night has an eerie, displacing quality absent from the shut-out lover's situation.[19] Lydia is not only spatially dislocated to the lonely and dark outdoors; she is located temporally in an in-between time (*inter-lunia*), which further serves to isolate her not only from humanity but at least momentarily from the world of nature (the natural cycles of the moon) as well.

Matres . . . equorum—not, as Nisbet and Hubbard suggest,[20] merely poetic diction for "mares"—continues the emphasis on things temporal. It further develops the impression of Lydia's advancing age (mother versus daughter) and thus underscores the untimeliness of her desire. The attribution to Lydia, a human being, of a *flagrans amor et libido* possessed by mares in heat creates a repulsive picture of Lydia's transformed sexuality as wild and animal-like. From Vergil's comment (*Georgics* 3.266–83) on the proverbially excessive lust of mares (*scilicet ante omnis furor est insignis equarum . . .*) we see that Lydia's comparison to a mare in heat signals not only an animal-like desire, but, more specifically, a desire known for its extremity. The repugnant image of Lydia as mare-in-heat represents the culmination of Lydia's indecorous movement toward desire and away from desirability. A virtually failed object of desire, she becomes a subject of overwhelming desire.

Lydia, however, while possessing the mare's lust, is not even the mare's equal in other important respects. Lydia's likely infertility due to her advanced age contrasts unfavorably with the mare's procreative abilities. In addition, the notion popular in antiquity that mares were sexually stimulated by the wind and could become pregnant by it without mating suggests the mare's further superiority to Lydia; having been aroused, the mare could often become pregnant without unions (*saepe sine ullis / coniugiis*, *Georgics* 3.274–75), while Lydia cannot even find mates (*moechos . . . arrogantis* 9).[21]

The placement of *laeta* before the *quod* of the clause to which it belongs, creates not only the *callida iunctura* of *questu / laeta* but also a momentary ambiguity about what *laeta* modifies; until the reader hears *pubes*, Lydia (the "you" of *flebis*) is what *laeta* ironically seems to modify. This hyperbaton abruptly juxtaposes Lydia's unhappiness and the happiness of the current-day youth. Their enjoyment of fresh ivy rather than somber myrtle (and by extension, young women to aging ones) recalls the increasingly rare visits to Lydia by the *iuvenes* at the poem's outset.[22]

Lydia's devastation becomes complete in the last two lines of the poem where she is casually, but thoroughly, repudiated, a dry leaf tossed to the water, winter's companion. The image of the leaf strips Lydia not only of her power to attract but of her desire as well. The dryness of leaves replaces the wetness of the aroused state (cf. *hippomanes* and *lentum virus*, Georgics 3.280–81). The emphasis on temporality throughout the poem and specifically on Lydia's aging is highlighted a final time by the association of Lydia with winter. Yet even here where a union (and thus at least a sort of love) with death might have been anticipated, Lydia is still kept at a distance from love, for she is dedicated by the youth to the Hebrus, which *in turn* is the companion of winter.[23] Lydia's ultimate isolation, a result of her diminishing sexual attraction, concludes the process begun by *parcius*.

But how are we to respond to this isolation? An obvious possibility is simply to replicate the disgust, as in Collinge's claim that *Odes* 1.25 is "the crudest and nastiest poem in Horace's lyrics."[24] However, if we choose not to succumb to such hysteria, a more sober strategy might be to see in the poem a self-evident truth about the unseemly quality of love and desire beyond the proper time for love.[25] Such criticism would thus see in the male perspective of the poet/lover a "human" perspective—that is, to suppose that we could just as easily substitute a male for Lydia (or a female for Horace, for that matter) without any substantive change in perspective. However, such sobriety fails to recognize how specifically it is *Lydia's* temporality that occasions the disgust. What is evoked by *parcius* is a notion of the beloved as firmly situated within the poet/lover's own idea of what the proper relationship should be between gender and time. Lydia's temporality occasions disgust because it stands outside of what is proper for a woman, but what is crucial to recognize is that such disgust is itself the consequence of a privileging of the male poet/lover's belief that temporality and eroticism cannot be joined. There is no reason that we must share such privileging.

Nondum subacta ferre iugum valet
cervice, nondum munia comparis
   aequare nec tauri ruentis
      in venerem tolerare pondus.
circa virentis est animus tuae   5
campos iuvencae, nunc fluviis gravem
   solantis aestum, nunc in udo
      ludere cum vitulis salicto
praegestientis. tolle cupidinem
immitis uvae. iam tibi lividos   10
   distinguet autumnus racemos
      purpureo varius colore,
iam te sequetur; currit enim ferox
aetas et illi quos tibi dempserit
   apponet annos. iam proterva   15
      fronte petet Lalage maritum,
dilecta quantum non Pholoe fugax,
non Chloris albo sic umero nitens
   ut pura nocturno renidet
      luna mari, Cnidiusve Gyges;   20
quem si puellarum insereres choro,
mire sagaces falleret hospites
   discrimen obscurum solutis
      crinibus ambiguoque vultu.

Not yet can she bear the yoke with neck subdued, not yet equal the duties of her mate, nor endure the weight of the bull rushing into love. Amid the green fields is the mind of your heifer, now relieving the oppressive heat with river streams, now very eager to play in the damp willows with the calves. Take away your desire for the unripe grape. Soon for you autumn, varied in its purple color, will set off bluish clusters of grapes. Soon she will follow you; for cruel time runs on and will add to her the years it will have subtracted from you. Soon with forward brow Lalage will seek a mate, loved as was not fleeing Pholoe, not Chloris, shining with her white shoulders just as the bright moon gleams upon the night sea, or Cnidian Gyges, who, if you placed him in a troop of girls, would wonderfully deceive shrewd strangers, difficult to distinguish, with his loosened hair and androgynous face.

Odes 2.5, like *Odes* 1.25, deals with the effect on love and sexuality of time's passing, although here the focus is shifted from temporality that destroys the beloved's desirability to that which the would-be lover hopes will tame the beloved. Here, temporality appears to hold open the possibility that the beloved's elusiveness in the present will be transformed as she ages, but this hope for fulfilled desire will be defeated by the impossibility of controlling temporality itself. This theme of temporality as that which escapes the lover's control is expressed through the poem's dominant motif, "the inevitable cycle of time."[26] The time sequence *nondum . . . nondum . . . nunc . . . nunc . . . iam . . . iam . . . iam . . .* supports the construction of this motif.

Kiessling-Heinze sees the theme of the poem expressed already in its first word, *nondum;*[27] for Nisbet and Hubbard "in its emphatic position it [*nondum*] sums up the message of the poem."[28] This temporal adverb, which denies something up to and including the present, holds out the possibility of change in the future. The ambiguity of the poem's narrative outcome—that is, whether the addressee will finally be united with the beloved[29]—is anticipated by the open-ended quality of the future suggested by *nondum.* The poem's first word, like *parcius* in *Odes* 1.25, gives us a temporal perspective as soon as the poem begins.

We saw in *Odes* 1.25.1–8 that a combination of comparative adverbs and a negative found in conjunction with the present tense had the effect of creating a temporal perspective broader than the present. Horace's use of *nondum,* a temporal adverb that itself contains a negative, has a similar effect in *Odes* 2.5. Like *parcius,* it has an impact on the verb tenses and the images that follow. Just as *parcius* by its position modified both the participle *iunctas* (which followed it directly) and *quatiunt,* the main verb, so *nondum* influences both *subacta* and *valet. Nondum subacta* suggests that there will be a time when the "subduing" will have been completed, just as *nondum valet* denies a present state but suggests its future reversal. These three words— *nondum, subacta,* and *valet*—in combination open up a vista of past, present, and future in the poem's first line.

The metaphor for mating suggested by *subacta, ferre iugum,* and *munia*[30] becomes overt in the picture of the bull rushing into sexual intercourse: *nec tauri ruentis / in venerem tolerare pondus* (3–4). While some have called it gratuitously "crude,"[31] there is a point to the language.[32] It gives graphic expression to sexual desire and fulfillment, while at the same time, through the control of *nondum* and *nec*, postponing its satisfaction. It provides us with a statement about the impossibility of sexual intercourse in the present, along with the image or fantasy of its attainment.[33]

This tension between what Horace says and what he shows, between literal sense and the impression he makes with words, is a common feature of his poetry. We saw the same contrast between literal meaning and impression in *Odes* 1.25.1–8 where despite the predominance of the present tense, our vision was also of the past. Commager has written of the conflict between Horace's formal attitude and his emotional sympathies: "just as it is the Egyptian queen who steals that poem (1.37), so it is the haunting sound of *rosa quo locorum sera moretur* (1.38.3–4) that beguiles our imagination now. The rose lingers in our memory longer than Horace's renunciation of it."[34] So, in *Odes* 2.5.3–4 (. . . *nec tauri ruentis / in venerem tolerare pondus*) the image of desired intercourse outlasts its denial.

The erotic language in the poem continues, but with a shift in focus to the heifer and her activities (lines 5–9) from which the would-be lover is excluded. The youthfulness of the heifer is mirrored by the object of her interest (*virentis . . . campos* 5–6). The young heifer is interested in the correspondingly young/green fields. While *virentis*, through its appearance before the noun with which it agrees, opens up the idea of youth or greenness in a generalized way, the specific identification between the youth or "greenness" of the heifer and the object of her interest is strengthened by the interlocked word order in lines 5–6: . . . *virentis . . . tuae / campos iuvencae.*

The use of the word *gravem* (6), commonly used in reference to passion,[35] to describe the heifer's heat (*aestum* 7) reinforces the sexual potential of *aestum*. The heifer's ability to relieve her own heat (*fluviis . . . / solantis aestum* 6–7) contrasts with the would-be lover's unsatisfied desire. In addition, the sexual connotations of her intense eagerness[36] to frolic with the young calves in wet thickets (*in udo / ludere cum vitulis salicto / praegestientis* 7–9) once again excludes the would-be lover. The repeated *nunc . . . nunc* (6, 7), although specifically suggesting alternatives (now this, now that), by recalling *nondum . . . nondum* (1, 2), underlines the disparity between the heifer/girl's current activities and those for which her potential lover is eager. In addition, the alternation of relief or rest (*solantis*) and play (*ludere . . . praegestientis*) the heifer experiences shows a satisfaction on her part, which escapes the would-be lover.

The injunction to eliminate desire for the unripe grape, *tolle cupidinem / immitis uvae* (9–10), at first appears to cut off all hope for the potential lover based on the heifer's lack of readiness. (It should be noted that the word *immitis*—which in reference to fruit primarily means "harsh" or "bitter," and in reference to people, "harsh" or "unkind"[37]—suggests lack of interest as another possible reason besides lack of readiness for the separation between the girl and the would-be lover.) The mention of autumn, with its ability to ripen grapes, introduces a possible hope that time will bring her closer to the desiring lover. Yet while autumn is endowing the grapes with their purple/bluish color (*purpureo . . . colore* 12, by transference, and *lividos* 10 modifying *racemos*), suggesting ripeness, the word *lividos* with its connotations of "bruising, envy, and malice" make the picture less pleasant. Reckford has pointed out that "the ironies explored in the fourth stanza may be traced back to the single focal image, *Autumnus*, for autumn, the giver of ripeness . . . is also the twilight season of fading, of oncoming death."[38] *Iam* (10), while initially hopeful for the poet (as a contrast to *nondum*), may ironically mean "all too soon."

Autumn's arrival (*iam tibi . . . colore* 10–12) holds out less hope than it initially seems to; such is the case as well with *iam te sequetur* (13). Nisbet and Hubbard have called *iam te sequetur* "a clear imitation of one of the most famous lines in ancient love-poetry, Sappho 1.21 (καὶ γὰρ αἰ φεύγει, ταχέως διώξει [for if she flees, she will quickly pursue])."[39] However, it is significant that Horace is imitating Sappho with a new twist, for the ambiguity of *sequetur* in Latin ("follow," i.e., "come later than" / "pursue") is not present in the Greek διώξει, which does not have the temporal sense of "follow." Therefore *iam te sequetur* prepares for the ironic explanation (*enim* 13) that time will give to the girl what it takes from the would-be lover. As Reckford observes: "The conceit, that time will add to the girl the years it 'takes from' her lover, shows the fallacy of wishful thinking, for the two will never meet, the one ripening, the other growing younger, in an ideal balance. There will instead be a new and worse disparity. Venus can be very funny—and very cruel."[40] Time's cruelty (*ferox aetas* 13–14), which recalls the negative personification of time suggested by *lividos . . . racemos*, is proven by the lack of evidence that the husband Lalage will boldly seek (*iam proterva / fronte petet Lalage maritum* 15–16) will be the would-be lover.[41] The hurried movement toward an imminent future (*iam . . . distinguet* 10–11, *iam . . . sequetur* 13, and *iam petet* 15–16[42]) with its triple use of *iam* (as compared with *nondum, nondum, nec* and *nunc, nunc*) recedes into memories of the past (*dilecta* 17–24), which bring not fulfillment but merely the dissipation or distancing of desire.[43]

The insistent time sequence begun by the poem's first word, *nondum,* switches in the final two strophes to a reverie on past time, which spins out from the perfect passive participle *dilecta,* modifying Lalage. The pressing movement toward the future is lost as well as the certainties of the indicative mood. Lalage is left behind with questions unanswered. There is no ablative of personal agent with *dilecta,* which leaves unstated by whom Lalage will have been loved. Is it the would-be lover? Is it someone other than the would-be lover? Will she be loved by the would-be lover while she seeks a different mate? Former loves should logically recede in comparison to Lalage, loved more than they were (*dilecta quantum non . . .*). However, while there is a remote quality to these former loves— Pholoe's shyness (*fugax*), Chloris' almost statue-like white beauty, and Gyges' lack of gender-specific features—the expanding tricolon of Pholoe described by one word (*fugax*), Chloris by ten, and Gyges by more than a strophe, makes these past loves the focus of the present. Further, the surprising lack of distinction between Gyges and a girl creates a sense of uncertainty about the very object of desire, miming the uncertainty about whom Lalage will love and for whom she will be the object of desire. While the opening of the poem held out the possibility that the inevitability of time might eventually allow Lalage to be tamed and controlled (she is *nondum* [not yet] available to his desire), the end of the poem shows that the would-be lover, by wanting Lalage's desire to be temporally determined, is placed as well within the uncertainties of time. Not only does time make it impossible to be certain whom Lalage will love; it equally leaves uncertain what will be the focus of the would-be lover's erotic attention.

The many indications of uncertainty—the subjunctive mood in the present contrary-to-fact condition, the use of *fallo* (deceive), and the appearance of *ambiguo*—in the poem's final strophe all contribute to an open-ended conclusion for the poem. The excitation of the poem's beginning and the postponement of fulfilled desire (*nondum*) are curiously gone by the end of the poem. The possibilities about the future opened up by *nondum* are never neatly resolved. Thus, while in *Odes* 1.25 it appeared as if temporality condemned the beloved to be nothing more than an object of lovers who themselves stood mysteriously outside of time, here instead it is temporality that places the beloved in a realm that defeats the would-be lover's own attempt to control time.

Odes 3.7

Quid fles, Asterie, quem tibi candidi
primo restituent vere Favonii
    Thyna merce beatum,
        constantis iuvenem fide,
Gygen? ille Notis actus ad Oricum   5
post insana Caprae sidera frigidas
    noctes non sine multis
        insomnis lacrimis agit.
atqui sollicitae nuntius hospitae,
suspirare Chloen et miseram tuis   10
    dicens ignibus uri,
        temptat mille vafer modis.
ut Proetum mulier perfida credulum
falsis impulerit criminibus nimis
    casto Bellerophontae   15
        maturare necem refert;
narrat paene datum Pelea Tartaro
Magnessam Hippolyten dum fugit abstinens;
    et peccare docentis
        fallax historias movet,   20
frustra. nam scopulis surdior Icari
voces audit adhuc integer. at tibi
    ne vicinus Enipeus
        plus iusto placeat cave,
quamvis non alius flectere equum sciens   25
aeque conspicitur gramine Martio,
    nec quisquam citus aeque

Tusco denatat alveo.
prima nocte domum claude neque in vias
sub cantu querulae despice tibiae,   30
    et te saepe vocanti
    duram difficilis mane.

Why do you weep, Asterie, for Gyges, a youth of constant faith, whom the bright Favonian winds will restore to you at the beginning of spring, rich with Bithynian goods? He, driven to Oricum by the South wind after the rising of Capra's wild stars, spends cold nights sleepless not without many tears. But a messenger from his excited host, Chloe, saying that she is sighing and burning unhappily for your lover, crafty, tests him in a thousand ways. He recounts how Proetus' treacherous wife drove him, credulous, with false accusations to hasten death for too chaste Bellerophon; he tells of Peleus almost given to Tartarus while fleeing, without touching her, from Magnesian Hippolyte, and, tricky, promotes stories teaching him to stray, in vain. For more deaf than the rocks of Icarus he hears the words, faithful up to now. But lest your neighbor Enipeus please you more than is right, beware, although no other equally good at controlling a horse is seen on the grass of Mars' field, nor anyone equally swift swims down the Tuscan river. When night comes, close up your house and do not look down into the street at the song of the plaintive flute, and to him always calling you hardhearted, stay hard to get.

In our discussions of *Odes* 1.25 and *Odes* 2.5 we saw how attending to the implications of an initial temporal adverb revealed both a desire for temporality not to be extended beyond the experience of the beloved to that of the lover, and the impossibility of such a desire being achieved. In each of these poems, a temporal adverb—*parcius* in *Odes* 1.25 and *nondum* in *Odes* 2.5—helped to establish a temporal perspective that affected how both lover and beloved are understood in the entire poem. In *Odes* 3.7 we look once again at a significant temporal adverb. This time, though, it makes its appearance not at the beginning, but two-thirds of the way through the poem. Despite this placement, it plays a role as important as that played by the two initial temporal adverbs already discussed. What we find in this case is that the temporal adverb subtly prepares us for the surprising realization that both lover and beloved are enmeshed in temporality. Thus, while the first two poems struggle to limit temporality to a condition of the beloved, here instead temporality is acknowledged as a predicament involving both lover and beloved. We shall see, though, that even when the lover's relation to temporality is acknowledged along with that of the beloved, she is seen both as more vulnerable than he to the vicissitudes of time and as responsible for ensuring her lover's continuing fidelity.

In *Odes* 3.7 the speaker asks Asterie why she is weeping for her lover Gyges who, unhappily detained on his journey home, will be restored to her at the beginning of spring. Gyges, firm in his loyalty, passes cold, sleepless nights. Although a go-between from his host tells him stories designed to compromise his fidelity, Gyges remains faithful (*adhuc integer* 22).

Adhuc is the first indication that anything might alter Gyges' faithfulness. Whether one interprets *adhuc* as "still" or "so far," its appearance with *integer* adds a temporal potential to our perception of Gyges' fidelity by suggesting that his defenses might someday be broken down. *Adhuc*, which affirms something starting in the past and proceeding up to the present, functions as the opposite of *nondum* (discussed above in *Odes* 2.5), which denies something starting in the past and proceeding up to the present. In both cases, though, a tension is opened up about whether the future will confirm the hopes of the present—in the first case for a fulfillment of the potential lover's desire, and in the second for a continuation of Gyges's fidelity.

The importance of *adhuc* has gone unrecognized by most recent Horatian scholars.[44] Williams, for example, in his commentary on and translation of Book 3 of the *Odes*, makes no mention of *adhuc*; indeed, he even fails to translate it. The remarks of Pasquali, written in 1920, have been largely ignored by later scholars. Having noticed the sense of "evil prophecy" (*cattivo augurio*) introduced by *adhuc*, he questions how long Gyges will remain faithful.[45] The oxymoron *surdior . . ./voces audit* (21–22) with its play on deafness and hearing, positioned directly before *adhuc integer*, prepares the way for an ironic use of *adhuc* with *integer*.

Two previous uses of the word *integer* in the *Odes* provide a further suggestion that we should not take *adhuc integer* at face value. The final strophe of *Odes* 2.4 suggests an ironic interpretation of *integer* in that poem:

bracchia et vultum teretesque suras
integer laudo; fuge suspicari
cuius octavum trepidavit aetas
    claudere lustrum. (21–24)

Uninvolved I praise her arms and face and smooth calves; stop
being suspicious of one whose age has hurried to complete forty
years.

In these lines the speaker seems to say "I praise this girl impartially.
Don't worry about me—I'm too old for love." However, that he
chooses to linger over the details of the girl's beauty, part by part,
using the sensuous-sounding word *teretesque* with its "tactile" di-
mension, leads one to believe that *integer* as "uninvolved," "inno-
cent," or literally "untouched," is other than straightforward. If the
speaker were convincingly beyond suspicion because of age, he
would not make such an issue of it. The placement of *Odes* 2.5
immediately after these lines continues the theme of the problematic
relationship between aging and sexuality. The irony of Horace's use
of *integer* in *Odes* 2.4 suggests that we read his use of it here sus-
piciously. Of course, *integer* appears very prominently as the first
word of *Odes* 1.22 (*Integer vitae*), where its meaning must be revised
in the context of the poem.[46]

In *Odes* 3.7, then, if Gyges' future fidelity cannot be taken for
granted, we must reevaluate the speaker's reassurances to Asterie
about Gyges' return (1–6). The definitive quality of the future tense
restituent (2) is called into question. The description of Gyges as a
young man of steadfast loyalty (*constantis iuvenem fide* 4) sounds less
believable. Williams remarks that "the archaic form of the genitive
fide . . . adds an impressiveness of tone to the assertion of his
constancy."[47] This may be, but the "impressiveness" becomes mock-
serious when read in light of the description of Gyges as *adhuc
integer*.[48]

There is another Gyges in classical literature, who may be signifi-
cant to our understanding of the Gyges in this ode: that of Herodo-
tus *Histories* 1.8–12 and Plato *Republic* 2.359d.[49] Gyges also appears in
Archilochus, fragment 19 West, and Herodotus states that his Gyges
is the same as that of Archilochus. In Horace, Gyges is described as
Thyna merce beatum (3), "rich with Bithynian goods." In the Archi-
lochus fragment the focus is on Gyges' wealth (πολύχρυσος, of much

gold) and power, while in Herodotus (*Histories* 1.14), Gyges sends gold and silver gifts to Delphi. Finally, in Plato, Gyges has a gold ring. The notion of wealth, then, is the first connection with the Gyges of Greek literature. Perhaps more important, though, the stories of Gyges in the *Histories* and the *Republic*, while varying because of the different purposes they fulfill in each work, contain the same basic love plot with negative resonance for the Horatian Gyges, that of the man who kills the king with the help of the queen and takes over the kingdom.[50]

In Plato's version, Gyges, in possession of a magic ring that can render him invisible at his will, seduces the wife of the king and with her help kills him and takes over the kingdom. In Herodotus' story, Gyges is forced by Candaules, the king of Lydia, to do something against his principles, namely, to see the queen naked. (Candaules, possessed of a passion for his wife, thinks she is the most beautiful of women and demands that Gyges see her to confirm this.) Gyges is caught by the queen and given the choice of either being killed or killing the king and marrying her. He chooses the latter course of action.

At the beginning of Herodotus' account, Gyges is portrayed as one of the most loyal men in the kingdom and as a close friend of the king. He is an innocent man (*integer?*) who, to save his own life, kills the king, obedience to whom had earlier required him to do wrong (see the queen naked). In Plato's version of the story, Gyges is not "innocent." He is a man who acts purely from self-interest without any sense of justice. In fact the desire exhibited by Plato's Gyges to possess queen and kingdom is reminiscent of the possessiveness shown not by Gyges, but by Candaules, in Herodotus. (As one critic has noted, Candaules' treatment of his wife as an object to be seen by another man violates the customs of the marriage bond.)[51] Herodotus' Gyges, although initially innocent and loyal to his king, when threatened, accedes to the queen in order to save his own life; unlike Peleus and Bellerophon (13–18), who both reject the advances of their hosts' wives, he does give in to a powerful woman.

In using the name Gyges, Horace calls to mind a well-known figure from the Greek tradition whose acquisition of another's wife (albeit with different motives in the two versions) cannot help but influence our perception of the situation of the Gyges of *Odes* 3.7. The recollection of these two versions of the Gyges story prevents us from having complete confidence in the ability of Asterie's Gyges to resist temptation, the persuasiveness of others, or unjust acts. While it is the Herodotean Gyges whose initial innocence is particularly recalled by *integer* in *Odes* 3.7, the Gyges of Plato is, significantly, set up by Glaucon, who narrates the story, as an example of what both the unjust and the just man would do given no societal constraints. Recollection of these two Gygeses—the one given no real choice but to take up with the queen, the other acting solely out of his own acquisitive interests—clearly reinforces the ironic sense of *adhuc integer* in *Odes* 3.7 and undermines confidence in Gyges' fidelity.

Adhuc integer has another effect besides making us doubt what we have heard so far in the poem. It subtly prepares us for the *para prosdokian* which immediately follows: the speaker's warning to Asterie, who we suddenly discover is a serious candidate for infidelity herself. He warns Asterie not to find Enipeus too pleasing, although there is no better horseman or faster swimmer. He tells her to close up her home as soon as evening comes, to ignore the flute music serenading her from the streets, and to remain "hard to get" (*difficilis*) though she is often called hard-hearted (*duram*).

The speaker's warning to Asterie is not only surprising, but gently humorous. By cataloguing Enipeus' "manly virtues" (riding and swimming), and by claiming that in these he has no equal (*non alius . . . aeque . . . nec quisquam . . . aeque* 25–27), the speaker makes Enipeus quite an attractive figure.[52] Indeed the verb "is seen" (*conspicitur* 26) and the adjective "neighboring" (*vicinus* 23) specifically point to Enipeus' visual appeal and his physical proximity. His frequent contact (albeit verbal) with Asterie (*te saepe vocanti / duram* 31–32), reminiscent of the thousand methods of persuasion (*mille . . . modis* 12) and the words (*voces* 22) used on Gyges by the clever go-between, emphasizes the persistence of Enipeus' courting. Pasquali has rightly noticed that Horace is using language in such a way as to tempt Asterie.[53] The speaker indirectly entices Asterie with his description, while literally telling her to ignore Enipeus' advances. This strategy is reminiscent of the ironic final strophe of *Odes* 2.4 (mentioned above), where the poet's literal message that he praises Phyllis "uninvolved" (*integer*) because of his age is countered by the sensuousness of the language used to describe her.

The go-between in *Odes* 3.7 is described as *vafer* (12) and *fallax* (20) for testing Gyges and for promoting stories teaching him to stray: *et peccare docentis / fallax historias movet* (19–20). The parallel here to the speaker's own role in counseling Asterie suggests that the speaker is himself another deceiver, and that Asterie, perhaps like Proetus, who believes his wife's false accusations of attempted seduction on the part of Bellerophon, is too trusting of false reports (*Proetum . . . credulum* 13). There seems no way to explain how the speaker can know what is happening to Gyges on Oricum, and thus his story seems to exist merely to scare Asterie into believing that Gyges might not remain faithful.[54] Indeed, the statement of Gyges' faithfulness "to this point" (*adhuc integer*) seems a pointed warning to Asterie that somehow her fidelity is required for Gyges to remain faithful.

The assurances Horace offered to Asterie in the beginning of the poem are thrown into doubt. And even if Gyges remains faithful, perhaps Asterie would really prefer Enipeus. Perhaps this is why she is weeping. The simple question that begins the poem—*Quid fles, Asterie?*—is by the end of the poem no longer simple. The situation Horace has constructed creates more questions than it answers, and the primary function of such questions is to cast doubt on whether desire can itself be removed from the uncertainties of time. Indeed, the attempt at closure in the conclusion of the poem confirms the uncertain temporality lurking within the speaker's pledge of Gyges' faithfulness. The final advice to Asterie—*difficilis mane* ("stay hard to get")—while ostensibly paralleling the claim that Gyges is *adhuc integer*, casts doubt on the very possibility of a faithfulness or integrity that stands outside of time. The move from *integer* to *difficilis* encapsulates the impossibility of denying time: while Gyges is said to possess an *integritas* that presumably no temporality would threaten, the uncertain nature of such integrity is revealed by the temporal adverb to which it is attached. In contrast, the advice to Asterie that she remain *difficilis* acknowledges temporality even as it seeks to deny it. By being *difficilis*, by situating her resolve in relation to the demands of others, Asterie would open herself to the temporality and contingency that *integritas* seeks (impossibly) to deny.

Finally, we must note that while Gyges and Asterie both participate in the predicament of temporality, their relation to it is not identical. The male lover is portrayed as resisting temptation alone, while Asterie needs the speaker of the poem to dissuade her from infidelity. Still further, Asterie is expected to function, as her name ("starry one") would suggest, as a beacon for Gyges on his voyage home. Thus her fidelity, rather than having any intrinsic value, is instrumental for ensuring the faithfulness of Gyges. By tempting

Asterie to look at him (cf. "do not look down" *neque . . . despice* 29–30), Enipeus threatens to disrupt Asterie's status as subservient to Gyges. We realize, then, that the danger presented to the erotic by temporality is not shared equally by Gyges and Asterie. It is the female beloved who is seen as both more vulnerable to temptation and as responsible for maintaining both her own and her lover's fidelity.

THREE

Seasonal

Imagery

In the previous chapter, we saw how examining the function of temporal adverbs helps to show how both lover and beloved are determined by their relation to time. In *Odes* 1.25 and 2.5, the male lover seeks, by refusing any shared experience of time, to dominate the very time that defines the beloved. In *Odes* 3.7, even though both lover and beloved are seen to be affected by time, the male lover still dominates the beloved's temporality in that his faithfulness over time is made contingent upon hers. What each of these poems indicates is that the attempt to privilege the perspective of the male lover itself depends upon a prior definition of the beloved as herself existing in a temporality foreign to the male lover. This differing relationship to temporality serves both to distinguish lover and beloved and to ensure that the perspective of the lover will be dominant.

In this chapter, my focus is on another strategy that evades the consequences of temporality for the erotic—the attempt both to contrast the recurring cycle of the seasons with the linear temporality of human experience, and to find an image of that linear temporality in the movement from one season into the next.[1] We shall see that imaging human temporality in terms of nature—which is far from nature being a "moral metaphor," as Commager would have it[2]—serves to justify the denial of the actual temporality of human experience, and more particularly, the denial of the actual temporality of the beloved. Such a claim may seem paradoxical in the light of the first two poems I discuss, *Odes* 1.4 and 4.7, for there the temporality of human experience is explicitly contrasted to the cycle of nature; whatever analogy exists between the seasons and human experience serves to reenforce an awareness of the linearity of human temporality. However, in both poems what seems to be an extraneous turn to the erotic reveals that human temporality is acknowledged only in opposition to eroticism, which itself is imaged in terms of the very seasonal cyclicity that has proved inadequate to define human temporality. What is at stake in the locating of eroticism in the spring will become clear in our discussions of *Odes* 1.9 and 1.23, for there we see that the lover's belief that the spring of eroticism is separable from the temporality of experience warrants the refusal to acknowledge the beloved's own humanity.

Odes 1.4

Solvitur acris hiems grata vice veris et Favoni,
    trahuntque siccas machinae carinas,
ac neque iam stabulis gaudet pecus aut arator igni,
    nec prata canis albicant pruinis.
iam Cytherea choros ducit Venus imminente Luna,   5
    iunctaeque Nymphis Gratiae decentes
alterno terram quatiunt pede, dum gravis Cyclopum
    Vulcanus ardens visit officinas.
nunc decet aut viridi nitidum caput impedire myrto
    aut flore terrae quem ferunt solutae;   10
nunc et in umbrosis Fauno decet immolare lucis,
    seu poscat agna sive malit haedo.
pallida Mors aequo pulsat pede pauperum tabernas
    regumque turris. o beate Sesti,
vitae summa brevis spem nos vetat incohare longam;   15
    iam te premet nox fabulaeque Manes
et domus exilis Plutonia; quo simul mearis,
    nec regna vini sortiere talis
nec tenerum Lycidan mirabere, quo calet iuventus
    nunc omnis et mox virgines tepebunt.   20

Harsh winter is unbound by the pleasant change of spring and Favonian wind, and the machines are dragging down the dry keels, and the flock no longer enjoys the stables, nor the ploughman his fire, nor are the meadows white with hoary frost. Even now Cytherean Venus leads her choruses under overhanging moon, and the charming Graces joined to the Nymphs shake the ground with alternating foot, while burning Vulcan visits the oppressive workshops of the Cyclopes. Now it is fitting to gird glistening heads with green myrtle or with the flowers that the unbound earth brings forth; now it is fitting to sacrifice to Faunus in the shady groves, whether he demands a lamb or prefers a kid. Pale Death strikes with equal foot the cottages of the poor and the towers of kings. O happy Sestius, life's brief span forbids us to commence long hopes. Even now night and the storied Shades and the meager abode of Pluto will press upon you; as soon as you have wandered there, you will not with dice allot the mastery of the wine nor wonder at young Lycidas, for whom all the youth now burn and soon the girls will be warm.

Odes 1.4 is founded upon a series of dualities—life and death, spring and winter, hope and despair, youth and age—which seem designed to suggest an inevitable cycle to human experience. Despite the grim allusion to death and the separation of Sestius from Lycidas' erotic life, the overall purpose of the poem seems to be to suggest that the coming of spring can serve as a powerful symbol for the human experience of time. Set against the inevitability of Sestius' death is a contrasting celebration of the joys of spring, a contrast that serves to establish a consoling rhythm to human experience. From this perspective, the blending in the conclusion of the poem of Sestius' loss of love and life with a re-emergence of life and love's continuing cycle is neither an exhortation to enjoy the moment nor a bleak thought of death's finality, but rather a double-edged acknowledgment that while Sestius' love and life must end, others will continue to live and love.

Unfortunately, such a reading of the poem is able to account for neither the real force of the ambivalence that attends the account of spring, nor for the way in which the erotic scene at the conclusion of the poem is made possible only because love is itself separated from what Sestius is told is most important about human experience—the temporal inevitability of death. The speaker's insistence that Sestius' experience is now defined by his impending death produces a sense that spring's message is mixed—that Sestius' awareness of his mortality should cause him to see spring as a sign of his own (temporal) distance from what he desires rather than as the time when desire itself can be fulfilled. Were Sestius to succeed in seeing things in this way, he would presumably be able to accept that his own mortality would inevitably produce separation from Lycidas.

But such acceptance of temporal inevitability has no role to play in how the dynamic of erotic possession in the spring itself is characterized. In the conclusion of the poem, whatever suggestion there might have been of understanding desire in terms of temporality is abandoned. Instead, as we shall see in the language that describes Lycidas, eroticism is imaged in terms of a now that is separated both from Sestius' mortality and from the imagined future with which the poem ends. What spring offers to Lycidas would appear to be nothing more than his status as an object of desire, a condition that is made possible not only by his own attractiveness, but also by a season that implies that such attractiveness defines who he is. While Sestius' immersion in the reality of temporality would perhaps allow at least the possibility of seeing Lycidas as independent of his own desires, Lycidas' own position within the eroticism of spring allows no comparable independence: rather, he is determined by what others want of him. Thus, those critics who have seen the end of the poem as light in tone[3] or as the subject of trifling matters[4] fail to see that it brings into focus precisely what is at stake in the effort to see eroticism as a brief season of denial of human time.[5]

The element of seasonal change established at the poem's outset is quickly characterized as both positive and negative. The pleasure of the change from winter to spring is mixed with the loss that all change presumably brings. In the first line of the poem, the emphasis is on change, as Horace's choice of the word *solvitur* ("is unbound") indicates. Within short scope subject and agent complete the thought begun by the verb: harsh winter (*acris hiems* 1) is unbound by the pleasant change brought by spring and its accompanying breeze (*grata vice veris et Favoni* 1). The emphasis on change is highlighted by the fact that the agent is literally the change or alteration of the seasons (*vice*) rather than spring itself.

However, the hope that seems to attend the arrival of spring is made more complicated by the way in which Horace introduces through indirection the idea that even pleasing change involves a certain loss.[6] The image of ships being readied for renewed activity is a positive one; yet even the dragging down (*trahuntque*) of the ships for sailing entails something negative, the renewal of strenuous physical activity. So too *neque iam stabulis gaudet pecus aut arator igni* (3) makes us aware that winter, while confining the flocks to the stables and the ploughman to the fire indoors, nevertheless offers to both a kind of pleasure, which must end at the coming of spring. The indirect characterization of spring by negation of winter's features in line 3 continues in line 4 with a dazzling description of winter's white beauty: *nec prata canis albicant pruinis.*[7]

Spring's dual nature is further seen in Horace's juxtaposition of the joyous and carefree activities of Venus' choruses and the dancing Nymphs and Graces with Vulcan's labors. While Venus is associated with the creative, "positive," force of spring,[8] the making of the thunderbolts, the likely activity being supervised by Vulcan, (*dum gravis Cyclopum / Vulcanus ardens visit officinas* 7–8) is a reminder of the season's stormy weather.[9] Although suggestive of the beauty of a moonlit spring night, *imminente Luna* (5) has a menacing quality, which casts a shadow on the happy scene involving Venus.[10] When night returns in the poem as a metaphor for death (*premet nox* 16), it no longer merely threatens love, but instead steals it away. This negative potential for love is adumbrated through the figure of Vulcan, who is continually betrayed by Venus, goddess of love.[11] *Ardens* (8), with its pun ("burning lover," "fiery smith"), while literally fitting the context of his activities at the forge, also evokes Vulcan's role as lover. This suggestion—that the fire of Vulcan's passion still leaves him unable to possess Venus completely—foreshadows both Sestius's own inability to possess Lycidas and the imagery of heat used to characterize Lycidas' desirability. As we shall see, the erotic sense of *ardens* is echoed twice at the conclusion of the poem: initially, by *calet* (19), which characterizes the effects of Lycidas' desirability in the "now" of spring, and finally by *tepebunt* (20), which describes how young women will respond to him in the future. This connection between heat and desire in the poem (*ardens, calet, tepebunt*, and spring itself) allows the loss of fire, winter's joy (line 3), which is occasioned by the change of seasons, to be seen in retrospect as the poem's first suggestion of how eroticism is defined in opposition to the movement of time.

The appearance of *pallida Mors* in line 13 is quite abrupt. Yet features earlier in the poem have prepared for both its negative implications and its relentless pace. The pace is anticipated through the following temporal progression: *neque iam* and *nec* (3–4), *iam* (5), then the repeated, persistent *nunc, nunc* (9, 11), whose placement at the emphatic beginning position of lines 9 and 11 looks forward to the walk of death with its heavy alternating gait (*aequo pulsat pede* 13). What this temporal sequence suggests is a movement from ambivalent anticipation to a specification of what the "now" of spring offers Sestius. Since what is being characterized here is Sestius' temporality, the movement to "now" almost requires an acknowledgment of death. If spring heralds a time when the movement of temporality is replaced by an emphasis on the present, on the "now," it then follows that death would appear as the inevitable counterpart to Sestius' "now." Thus, the mixture within lines 1–12 of both a positive anticipation of what spring might offer, and a recognition that spring, as the season of "now," must also entail loss, makes the abrupt entrance of *pallida Mors* in line 13 less a change of thought than a turn to the feelings evoked for Sestius by the coming of spring.[12]

This transition from (largely) hopeful anticipation to a sense of loss as we arrive at the present is signaled further by the word *impedire* (9), which by its central sound "*ped*" suggests a movement from the festive dancing of the Nymphs and Graces in line 7 (*alterno . . . pede*) to the ominous walk of *pallida Mors* in line 13 (*aequo . . . pede*).[13] The bridge from positive to negative is created not only by the sound of *impedire* but also by its meaning. *Caput impedire* suggests not only the pleasant activity of garlanding the head, but also the negative idea of constriction, associated not with spring (*terrae . . . solutae* 10) but with harsh winter (*Solvitur acris hiems* 1) and death (*premet nox* 16). The dance of the Nymphs and Graces (*alterno terram quatiunt pede* 7) becomes the inexorable pounding of pale Death (*pallida Mors aequo pulsat pede* 13).[14] *Pede* (13) recalls *pede* (7), and both occur in the same metrical position in their respective verses. Further, the onomatopoetic quality of the alliteration of the letter *p* in *pallida . . . pulsat pede pauperum* makes the line embody its sense, merging spring with the ominous sound of death striking equally the homes of all.

The direct address to Sestius follows the message that death comes to all. Its "oracular" quality arises naturally out of the sacrifice to Faunus in lines 11–12 and the message about *pallida Mors* in lines

13–14.[15] The ostensible theme here is advice that life's brief span precludes the formation of long hopes (15).[16] However, this suggestion is rendered somewhat ironic by the sudden shift in verb tense in the lines that follow this advice. Up through line 15 all the poem's finite verbs are in the present tense.[17] However, the description of Sestius' impending journey to the underworld abruptly shifts the dominant tense to the future; of the six verbs in the poem's final five lines, all except *calet* are in the future tense (*mearis*, future perfect), and all except *calet* and the concluding *tepebunt* apply to Sestius. As we shall see, these exceptions are significant, but first we should note how the modification of *premet* by *iam* suggests that the "now" of death, which awaits Sestius, is being pulled into the present: *iam te premet nox fabulaeque Manes / et domus exilis Plutonia.* If the function of "now" is to provide a sense of temporal specificity, then what this portrayal suggests is that what is temporally specific to Sestius' experience is a future that empties his present existence of any meaning. What is thus established is a harsh contrast between Sestius' temporality, which allows at best a satisfied (*beate*) recollection of what has passed, and spring, which announces a "now" from which Sestius will himself be excluded. There is an inevitability to spring, both in terms of its arrival and the eroticism that it represents, but Sestius' own temporality suggests a counter inevitability which resists any hope that the change of seasons might mark a genuine cycle of human experience.

The rapid movement into the future of lines 16–20 provides an ironic commentary on the statement prohibiting long-term expectations. The insistence that the passage of time precludes any formation of "long hopes" (*spem . . . longam*) acknowledges the role that temporality plays in human desire. However, the insistence that spring heralds an erotic "now" which can be projected into the future seems instead to suggest that seasonal change allows an escape from the dismal temporality that defines Sestius. Thus, what the last lines create is a future in which Sestius is quickly left behind and replaced. *Iam . . . premet* makes his death immediate, and *simul mearis* introduces his journey to the underworld. The three lines that follow include Sestius only to describe what he will no longer enjoy once he has gone to the abode of the dead. After *mirabere* (19), he disappears. *Quo calet iuventus / nunc omnis* (19–20), with its present tense reinforced by *nunc*, suggests a contrast between the eroticism that defines Lycidas and the temporality that defines Sestius. While from Sestius' perspective, Lycidas' erotic life will occur in a future from which he is excluded, from Lycidas' perspective, merged as it is with spring, eroticism occurs in a present that only obliquely acknowledges the movement of time.

This contrast between the two is heightened by the verbs that characterize how Lycidas is regarded by Sestius, and by all the young men who desire him: *miror* suggests an almost detached attitude, which positions Lycidas at a remove from Sestius' own desires, while *caleo* instead suggests that Lycidas is defined by the desires he awakens in others. The implication, underscored both by the account of how the desiring young men respond to Lycidas and by the association of that response with the "now" of spring, is that eroticism is opposed not merely to death, but to the human temporality of which death is the conclusion. Further, the account of Lycidas himself as significant in the present because of the erotic responses he provokes suggests strongly that the association of eroticism with the spring is in part a strategy to ensure that the beloved can be safely situated as an *object* of present desire. Where Sestius' temporality stands opposed to both spring and the possession of the beloved, the association of Lycidas with spring seems instead both to deny his temporality and to make him something that can be possessed.

We do not, however, remain in the present for long. The heat and homoeroticism of the present are quickly replaced by a future in which Lycidas will awaken mere warmth rather than heat, and will awaken this in young women rather than young men (*mox virgines tepebunt* 20). The milder *tepebunt* suggests a time when the passion of Lycidas' male lovers will be replaced by the lessened ardor of domesticity.[18] The poem's steady progression of time pushes Lycidas (now *tenerum*) away from the clarity of spring, and into a much more ambiguous eroticism. Where the heat of all the young men determined Lycidas himself as an object that might produce such heat, the mere warmth felt by the young women suggests instead an uncertainty about Lycidas and a corresponding uncertainty about the responses he causes. Projecting this dynamic into the future heightens the sense of erotic ambiguity, for it leaves us unsure whether the movement to heterosexual desire should be seen as an inevitable maturation, or a loss of what the present offers. But in either case, this concluding insistence that Lycidas will himself come to be determined by temporality, that the "now" of spring cannot last, inevitably returns us to the separation of eroticism from temporality, which we saw in Sestius. Just as Sestius' age allowed at least a relative autonomy for Lycidas—as he approaches death, he "wonders at" Lycidas—so now Lycidas' own aging grants him, if not autonomy, at least distance from all the young men who burn for him. But this distance, while perhaps allowing autonomy, is devoid of anything like a relationship to others. Rather, the replacement of "heat" by "warmth" points to a temporal descent which, as the example of Sestius shows us, leads only to the solitariness of death.[19]

🪼 *Odes* 4.7

Diffugere nives, redeunt iam gramina campis
    arboribusque comae;
mutat terra vices et decrescentia ripas
    flumina praetereunt.
Gratia cum Nymphis geminisque sororibus audet   5
    ducere nuda choros.
immortalia ne speres, monet annus et almum
    quae rapit hora diem.
frigora mitescunt Zephyris, ver proterit aestas
    interitura, simul   10
pomifer autumnus fruges effuderit; et mox
    bruma recurrit iners.
damna tamen celeres reparant caelestia lunae:
    nos ubi decidimus
quo pius Aeneas, quo Tullus dives et Ancus,   15
    pulvis et umbra sumus.
quis scit an adiciant hodiernae crastina summae
    tempora di superi?
cuncta manus avidas fugient heredis, amico
    quae dederis animo.   20
cum semel occideris et de te splendida Minos
    fecerit arbitria,
non, Torquate, genus, non te facundia, non te
    restituet pietas.
infernis neque enim tenebris Diana pudicum   25
    liberat Hippolytum,

nec Lethaea valet Theseus abrumpere caro
   vincula Pirithoo.

The snows have fled, now the grass is returning to the fields and the leaves to the trees; the earth makes its changes and the shrinking rivers go along their banks. Grace with the Nymphs and her two sisters dares to lead her choruses nude. Not to hope for immortal things warns the year and the hour that seizes the nurturing day. The cold grows mild with the Zephyrs, summer tramples on spring, about to perish as soon as fruit-bearing autumn will have poured forth its yield; and soon inactive winter returns. However the swift moons recover their heavenly losses: we, when we go down to where reverent Aeneas, rich Tullus, and Ancus have gone, are dust and shade. Who knows whether the gods above will add tomorrow's time to today's sum? Everything will escape the greedy hands of your heir, which you have given to your own self. Once you have died and splendid Minos has made his decisions about you, Torquatus, not lineage, not eloquence, not reverence will restore you. For Diana does not free chaste Hippolytus from the darkness below, nor is Theseus mighty enough to break open the chains of Lethe for his dear Pirithous.

We have seen in *Odes* 1.4 that the association of eroticism with spring produces at best an ambivalent escape from human temporality. In *Odes* 4.7 even ambivalence is abandoned, and instead the eroticism of spring is now seen to offer no conceivable solace once the grim reality of time is acknowledged. Further, we find once more an opposition between how human identity is understood from the perspective of temporality and from the perspective of the erotic. The solitude that follows from an awareness of death is opposed to the relational possibilities of the erotic, but now even erotic relation itself seems to offer little more than the status of a desired object.

The refusal to separate spring from the movement of time begins, in a sense, at the start of the poem, with the indirect characterization of spring by reference to the end of winter: *diffugere nives* (the snows have fled). The movement suggested by the poem's first word, *diffugere*, with its sense of flight underscored by the prefix *dis*, points to the swiftness of the change of season.[20] The sense of return (*redeunt* 1) of the grass to the fields and the leaves to the trees may suggest that the rapidity of change should be seen in terms of a natural cycle, but the emphasis is far more on the sense of sudden change itself. The characterization of nature's changes continues in *mutat terra vices* (3).[21] The rivers' shrinking back over their banks (*decrescentia ripas / flumina praetereunt* 3–4), while descriptive of springtime events, indirectly recalls the time when rivers were swollen with the melting winter snow. That the Grace and Nymphs "dare" to dance naked suggests the chill of winter is still near.[22] Even from the beginning of this "spring" poem, reminders of winter force an awareness that seasonal change is as much evidence of the passage of time as it is a return of what has been lost.

The emphasis on temporal change continues in the striking personification of time: not to hope for immortal things warns the year and the hour that seizes the nurturing day (*immortalia ne speres, monet annus et almum / quae rapit hora diem* 7–8). The year as well as the hour warns us (*monet*) not to hope for immortality; and the hour seizes (*rapit*) the day. *Almum* (nurturing, life-giving, kindly) precedes *diem*, which it modifies, by several words and through hyperbaton is placed before *quae*, which begins the relative clause to which it belongs. *Almum* and *diem* frame the relative clause and both are in the final emphatic position in their respective lines. The attention to *almum* is noteworthy. First, by emotionally coloring *diem*, it heightens the sense of loss involved in the passage of time, when the hour seizes the day. The adjective's meaning of "nurturing" and its association with Venus (cf. *almae . . . Veneris* in *Odes* 4.15.31–32, and *alma Venus* in *De Rerum Natura* 1.2) eroticize the day and hence suggest that eroticism might be the day's compensation for the loss of hope in what is immortal. The relative clause, *almum / quae rapit hora diem*, repeats the sense of the immediately preceding *annus*, adding another subject for *monet*, but through its greater length and further specification of temporal vocabulary (*annus*, then *hora* and *diem*), it expands upon and makes more vivid the bare statement *monet annus*. The juxtaposition of "grasping" *hora* (subject) with *diem* (direct object) makes graphic through word order the characterization of time as rapacious.[23]

In the description that follows of the succession of the seasons from winter back to winter again, Horace's choice of word order, vocabulary, and verb tense all emphasize the rapidity of change. However, because the seasons are described in words that are part of

Horace's erotic vocabulary, a counterplot is suggested in which eroticism might be hoped, if not to defeat time, at least to slow its inexorable movement. However, the actual progression of both the seasons, and the erotic language used to describe them, shows the futility of such a hope.

That the seasons are mentioned in the order of their actual temporal occurrence suggests that change will be the dominant motif: *frigora . . . ver . . . aestas . . . autumnus . . . bruma* (winter, spring, summer, autumn, winter). Each description of a season gives rise to the next and then disappears. *Mitescunt* (9), which describes how winter's cold is growing mild through the breezes of spring, like *almum*, has erotic overtones. It is suggestive of the "gentle" or "favorable" disposition a willing lover is expected to have. (Cf. *Odes* 2.5.10, where *immitis* is used by analogy of one unavailable and possibly uninterested,[24] and *Odes* 1.33.2.) The inchoative aspect of *mitescunt* emphasizes the gradual nature of the transition from winter to spring. However, as soon as spring is actually named, it is trampled underfoot by summer (*ver proterit aestas* 9).[25] The military associations of *protero* reinforce the harshness of the image.[26]

The violence of summer towards spring is quickly undermined by the future participle *interitura* (10), which modifies and immediately follows *aestas* (9), for now we know that summer, too, will perish. The message of summer's future death, occasioned by autumn, is brought closer to the present by the temporal conjunction *simul* (as soon as) (10) and the future perfect *effuderit* (11). *Recurrit* (12) brings us back full circle to winter.[27] *Iners* (12), modifying *bruma* (12), calls the cycle to a halt both through its meaning and its placement in final verse position.[28] Its juxtaposition with *recurrit* creates an oxymoron that calls added attention to both words, with *iners* implying lack of motion and *recurrit* implying the opposite. Yet *iners* has the "final word." The cycle of seasons has led us back to winter, but this time Horace characterizes winter not through temperature (i.e., the cold, *frigora*) but through time (i.e., as the season with the shortest days— *bruma* as superlative of *brevis*).[29] In one sense we are back where we started when winter returns, suggesting the cyclical nature of change. In another sense we are not, for the word for winter has changed, and *bruma* is a reminder of the brevity of the seasons in a way that (*frigora*) was not. *Iners*, which in this poem modifies *bruma*, is elsewhere used quite boldly by Horace to mean "impotent."[30]

> pereat male quae te
> Lesbia quaerenti taurum monstravit *inertem*,
>   cum mihi Cous adesset Amyntas,
> cuius in indomito constantior inguine nervus
>   quam nova collibus arbor inhaeret. (*Epodes* 12.16–20)

> May Lesbia perish badly who pointed out you, an impotent bull, to me, looking, when Amyntas of Cos had been with me in whose unconquered groin an erection stands more firm than a young tree in the hills.

The possible sexual connotation of *iners* extends the overlap of vocabulary fitting both seasonal and erotic contexts, which we have already seen with *almum* and *mitescunt*, and further suggests winter as a metaphor for the end of love's powers.

Thus, while in the cycle of seasons, winter presages the return of spring, the erotic language associated with the change of the seasons instead depicts an irrevocable sexual decline. The significance of contrasting the cycle of seasons with the linear temporality of human eroticism becomes apparent in lines 13–16, where the focus of the poem shifts from describing the cycle of the seasons to contrasting this cycle explicitly with human temporality. Winter leads to thoughts of death—in the world of nature merely a step in a continuing process, but for us, and for eroticism, an irrevocable end. Horace uses the moon's phases as an illustration of nature's rapid progression and regenerative power. The prefix *re-* in *reparant* recalls *recurrit* (12) and underscores the idea of continual rebirth in nature.[31] The losses of nature can be recovered (*damna . . . reparant* 13), while for us death is irreversible.

Lines 13–14 (*damna tamen celeres reparant caelestia lunae: nos ubi decidimus*) and 21 (*cum semel occideris*) clearly recall Catullus 5.4–6:[32]

> soles occidere et redire possunt:
> nobis cum semel occidit brevis lux,
> nox est perpetua una dormienda.

> Suns are able to set and return: for us when once the brief light has set, there is one perpetual night to be slept.

In the Catullan poem the awareness of human mortality as a shared predicament leads to sleepless lovemaking, which forestalls and momentarily banishes from thought one kind of *nox . . . perpetua* (death) and substitutes another (erotic activity).

Catullus' move toward a shared eroticism as a response to a recognition of the temporal inevitability of death is quite different from what we find in Horace. As we saw in *Odes* 1.4, the linkage of eroticism to spring allowed little more than the possibility of the lover's desire determining the identity of the beloved. In *Odes* 4.7, even such minimal hopes for eroticism are withdrawn, and nothing is seen to win out against death: not wealth, not *pietas*, not background, not eloquence. The injunction, then, is to withdraw the self from connections to the world and quite literally to enjoy one's *self* in the here and now: *cuncta manus avidas fugient heredis, amico / quae dederis animo* (19–20), with *fugient* (19) recalling *diffugere* (1).

Where Catullus holds open the possibility that eroticism might offer a shared defiance of temporal inevitability, Horace instead here reduces the predicament of temporality to a kind of onanistic economic triumph. The self that confronts temporality sees only the greed of others, a greed that can be defeated only by the ambiguous eroticism of *amico*. *Amico* is undoubtedly the poet's imitation of the Greek φιλος as "one's own," however the word clearly signals the erotic as well because of the unusualness of this usage in Latin.[33] While the language here may suggest the discovery of a certain self-sufficiency in the here and now, the security that this offers is an extraordinarily bleak response to death.

Elsewhere, in *Odes* 1.11, another poem that sets temporality in opposition to eroticism, Horace's response may seem closer to that of Catullus 5. For here, the speaker does suggest that the experience of time is shared (*quem mihi, quem tibi / finem di dederint* 1–2), and his injunction to "pluck the day" (*carpe diem* 8) includes Leuconoe, the addressee, in a joint response to envious time (*fugerit invida / aetas* 1.11.7–8). However, where Catullus sees eroticism as something that in a sense merges lover and beloved in a defiance of time, Horace, by contrast, makes the terrors of time become a rationale for the rhetoric of seduction. *Carpe diem*, then, points not to a mutual or shared predicament, but rather to what is now to us a familiar eroticism of the present in which the lover's desires might triumph.

If there is at least a suggestion in *Odes* 1.4 that while Sestius' death destroys his erotic hopes concerning Lycidas, desire itself continues as new lovers take his place, in *Odes* 4.7 the feeling of death's finality dominates. However, our sense of the significance of this finality will depend upon our understanding of the two mythological *exempla* in lines 25–28, which are apparently intended to illustrate the inefficacy of love in the face of death:

> infernis neque enim tenebris Diana pudicum
> liberat Hippolytum,
> nec Lethaea valet Theseus abrumpere caro
> vincula Pirithoo.

In considering what is at stake in Horace's examples of Hippolytus and Diana and Pirithous and Theseus, we can begin by noting how both Hippolytus and Pirithous share a common devaluing of women, Hippolytus through distance and Pirithous through attempted domination. Hippolytus is known for his rejection of Venus, his devotion to the chaste goddess Diana, and his resistance to his stepmother Phaedra's sexual interest in him, while Pirithous is famous for trying to steal Pluto's wife, Proserpina, for himself.[34] What is shared here is an assumption that women are defined by their sexuality, which is either something to be denied or something to be possessed. Thus, while there may seem to be a dramatic difference between the chastity of Hippolytus and the lechery of Pirithous, in fact the apparent difference masks a shared assumption about the sexual identities of women, which is itself the basis of the relationships with Diana and Theseus that death has destroyed. Alive, Hippolytus and Pirithous were valued because they mirrored the sexual values of Diana and Theseus; dead, they are mourned because such mirroring has been lost.

What this similarity shows is the quite specific erotic dynamic that the poem tells us death has destroyed. The shared sexual values that brought together Diana and Hippolytus and Theseus and Pirithous had as their basis the hope that the contingencies of desire might be defeated; that through either distance or domination, the sexuality of women might remain at a safe remove from self-definition. What this specificity suggests is that it is simply too easy to argue, as one critic has, that "Hippolytus was *pudicus*, Pirithous was not, but the grip of death is as fast on the lecher as it is on the model of chastity."[35] For what the "grip of death" destroys in this poem is not anything so general as love, but rather a particular form of eroticism defined by a fantasy of self-determination, which is mocked by the temporality of death. Obviously, death destroys any other form of eroticism as well, but it is a mistake to leap from the particular sense of erotic loss that Horace describes to a general claim that eroticism is necessarily opposed to time. Such a leap is mistaken because it ignores how much of the pathos of loss that is described here (and in other odes) is a loss of the possibility of dominance or possession.

This sense of the significance of domination is unintentionally suggested by Minadeo when he argues that "[e]ven the most exquisite affection, whether sacred or profane, has its absolute limits. *Omnia vincit mors.*"[36] What is noteworthy here is the implicit violence with which eroticism is characterized: affection is an (exquisite) assault upon limits whose ultimate success is checked only by death. Putnam makes clear that such erotic success would require a defeat, not merely of death, but of temporality itself: "Even love, that intense attempt to procure ecstasis out of time, whether it be the heterosexual, chaste affair of Diana and Hippolytus or the implicitly homosexual liaison of Theseus and Pirithous, cannot bend the rigidity of mortal death."[37] What should be clear by now is how easily such a view of eroticism as "ecstasis out of time" comes to characterize not a universal experience of love but rather the perspective of the lover who struggles to dominate temporal contingencies that ultimately cannot be controlled. The lesson we draw from "the rigidity of mortal death" might just as easily be that what death destroys is the fantasy of domination; in any case, there is no necessary connection between the inevitability of death and a conception of the erotic as ecstatic escape.

The image of winter's immobility, *iners* (12), might more accurately suggest the fate of eroticism if it is conceived in opposition to time. The depiction of Hippolytus as a prisoner of the dark underworld, and Pirithous caught in the chains of Lethe, where desire is impotent to overcome death,[38] produces a grim commentary on the delusion that the eroticism of spring might triumph over the human experience of time. The poem's emphasis, not on the cycle of the seasons, but rather on the rapidity of seasonal change, points to a briefness of human life that no erotic ecstasis might challenge. Further, while in *Odes* 1.4 there is at least the suggestion that the erotic "now" of spring will itself recur, regardless of what time does to Sestius or Lycidas, here nothing counterbalances the bleakness of death and the end of eroticism. At best, what we are offered is a subtle critique of the hopes invested in erotic possession, but what replaces such hopes is a wintry emptiness that no desire can fill.

Odes 1.9

> Vides ut alta stet nive candidum
> Soracte, nec iam sustineant onus
>   silvae laborantes, geluque
>   flumina constiterint acuto?
> dissolve frigus ligna super foco   5
> large reponens atque benignius
>   deprome quadrimum Sabina,
>   o Thaliarche, merum diota.
> permitte divis cetera, qui simul
> stravere ventos aequore fervido   10
>   deproeliantis, nec cupressi
>   nec veteres agitantur orni.
> quid sit futurum cras fuge quaerere et
> quem Fors dierum cumque dabit lucro
>   appone, nec dulcis amores   15
>   sperne puer neque tu choreas,
> donec virenti canities abest
> morosa. nunc et Campus et areae
>   lenesque sub noctem susurri
>   composita repetantur hora,   20
> nunc et latentis proditor intimo
> gratus puellae risus ab angulo
>   pignusque dereptum lacertis
>   aut digito male pertinaci.

Do you see how Soracte stands white with deep snow, and the laboring trees no longer hold up their burden, and the rivers have come to a halt with penetrating frost? Dissolve the cold, putting wood generously upon the fire, and bring forth quite liberally, O Thaliarchus, the four-year-old wine in its Sabine jar. Leave other things to the gods; as soon as they have leveled the warring winds on the fervid sea, neither cypresses nor aged ash are stirred. Stop seeking what will be tomorrow and consider as gain whatever amount of time Fortune will give, and spurn neither sweet love, boy, nor choruses, as long as difficult old age is remote from you in your youth. Now let the Campus and playgrounds and gentle whispers be sought under night at the agreed-upon hour, and now the pleasant betraying laughter of the hiding girl from the inmost corner and the pledge ripped off her arm or her finger unsuccessfully resisting.

In the two poems we have examined in this chapter, we can see a gathering refusal to hold out any hope that eroticism might provide a counter to the inevitability of time. In *Odes* 1.4 we saw how the hope that Lycidas' erotic spring might be set in opposition to Sestius' winter is at least made dubious by the concluding insertion of Lycidas into the inevitable movement of time. The illusoriness of such a hope is confirmed in the bleak conclusion of *Odes* 4.7, where eroticism is situated in an unrecoverable past and winter finally becomes the dominant seasonal metaphor for human temporality. However, despite what we might call the triumph of winter in each of these poems, there is at least a suggestion that what might allow eroticism to be set against time is the peculiar power that eroticism gives to the lover: the triumph of the lover's desires is like spring in that it allows the lover to forget or to deny the inevitable temporality of all human experience. What is implied here is a particular way of configuring the relation of the lover and the beloved, a configuration in which the lover's hopes for a power over time take the form of dominance over the beloved. In *Odes* 1.9 and 1.23, this hope that the "season" of eroticism might triumph over wintry inevitability becomes the central theme, and this will allow us to see more clearly the fate of the beloved when eroticism functions primarily as the lover's struggle to find an experience that time cannot destroy.

This theme takes shape in *Odes* 1.9 as a movement from the "winter" of old age to an unspecified "season" of erotic triumph.[39] However, as recent critics have noted, the poem does not set up any absolute division between winter and the "season" of eroticism, but rather seems to join the two by situating both within some more general consideration. Thus, one critic argues that there are erotic overtones to several of the words in the first two strophes of the poem, strophes traditionally considered devoid of such references, while another has argued that the poem's erotic close is a recollection of past youthful love which occurs in the present time of the poem (i.e., winter).[40] In each case, what is at stake is how what seem to be discrete emphases in the poem—the frigidity of winter and the injunction not to spurn an erotic present—are related to each other. Emphasizing either the omnipresence of erotic language in the poem or the unifying function of the narrative perspective finally seeks to show that we need not be troubled by the appearance of discord, since each of the discordant elements explains the other. However, from either perspective, emphasizing the continuity of winter with the "season" of eroticism risks ignoring the stark difference between eroticized recollection and symbolic rape.

We begin, however, with those aspects of the poem that would support the claim of continuity, in particular, the omnipresence of erotic language. While there is no direct mention of eroticism in the poem until *nec dulcis amores / sperne puer* (15–16) and the lovers' meeting (21–24), eroticism is anticipated by language in the first two strophes—*candidum, onus, laborantes, gelu, dissolve*, and *frigus*—that foreshadows the poem's erotic close while also portraying a winter scene, which metaphorically suggests old age. *Candidum* can apply to the "fair" beauty of a girl as well as the whiteness of snow or old age.[41] *Frigus* (and perhaps *gelu* in retrospect) suggests lack of passion as well as physical cold, and thus *dissolve frigus* can be seen as an injunction to make love as well as to warm the home.[42] Finally, *laborantes*, a common word in Latin's erotic vocabulary (cf., e.g., *Odes* 1.17.19), looks ahead to the "labors" of eroticism while portraying the trees no longer able to hold up their snowy burden.[43]

This mixed eroticism, suggesting both an anticipation of the sexuality of the poem's conclusion and the declining sexual potency of old age, continues in the third strophe (lines 9–12). The funereal associations of the cypress and "old" ash trees and the technical meaning of *sterno* ("lay to rest," "bury"), suggest that the power of the gods to still the storm is their ability to bring about the calm of death.[44] The adjective *fervidus* ("hot," "seething"), unusual as an epithet of the sea (10), is common in erotic vocabulary. Cupid is called *fervidus* (5) in *Odes* 1.30, a hymn to Venus. In *Odes* 4.13.26, old Lyce, compared to a fire turned to ashes, is mocked by youths described as *fervidi*. In still another love context Horace uses *fervidus* of the warmth-inducing quality of wine (*Epodes* 11.14), while in *Ars Poetica* 116, *fervidus* again has specific reference to youth, (*adhuc florente iuventa / fervidus*). In *Odes* 1.9 the associations of *fervidus* with heat and wine recall the second strophe of the poem, where making a fire and drinking are the means of combatting the cold, while its further associations with youth and love foreshadow both the injunction not to spurn love (15) and the encounter between the boy and girl. The erotic connotations of *fervidus*, contrasted with the calm brought by the gods, suggest that the "seething" quality of the sea is a sign of active sexuality. The apparent *hapax legomenon*, *deproelianis* (11), used of the winds, also anticipates the end of the poem by presaging the violence of the concluding erotic encounter, although there no gods will appear to restore order.[45] While *fervidus* and *deproelior* are suggestive of erotic activity, the cypresses and old ash trees no longer being driven by the wind (*nec cupressi / nec veteres agitantur orni* 11–12) suggest the absence of sexual activity. Because of its sexual connotations,[46] the use of the term *agito* to describe the activity no longer experienced by the trees adds further erotic potential to the language of the storm.

In a sense, what all of this erotic language establishes is the *authority* of the speaker to offer the injunction to which the poem now turns. By using language that establishes himself as complexly aware of how eroticism can endure even within the frigidity of winter, the speaker now has presumably earned the right to insist upon the need for Thaliarchus to establish an erotic present that can itself begin the eroticized temporality evoked in the opening three strophes. Thus, Thaliarchus, if he heeds the speaker's advice, will also be able to use his erotic life as the basis for seeing even the bleakness of winter in terms of sexual desire, and will accordingly be given at least some distance from the cruel actuality of time. Indeed, this authority is heightened by the ambiguity of the actual temporal moment of eroticism. It makes little difference whether the "now" that is opposed to winter is the time in which the erotic memories of the speaker occur, or is rather the moment when Thaliarchus should fulfill the speaker's injunction. In either case the eroticized language of the account of winter is what lends authority to the demand that an eroticized "now" be substituted for the awareness of temporality that winter might cause. Stripped of its eroticism, winter presages only the uncontrollable emptiness of death, but merged with a sexual act that can either be recollected or repeated, that emptiness is, in a sense, filled by the power of eroticism to suggest a different temporal destiny.[47]

This merging of an erotic present with the temporality represented by winter is suggested by the *callida iunctura* of *virenti canities* (17), which occurs near the end of the speaker's injunction to substitute an erotic "now" for thoughts of the future.[48] The whiteness (*canities*) of old age clearly is linked to the gleaming snow of Soracte in line 1 (*nive candidum*), but as we have already seen, *candidum* also can refer to a girl's "fair" beauty, which at least complicates the sense in which winter is an image of old age. While the color imagery here suggests that old age is primarily associated with winter, the eroticizing of winter precludes any clear sense of what this association might mean. Thus, the apparent contrast between *canities* as an image of both winter and old age, and *virenti* as an image of both youth and a "green" season of eroticism, is blurred, with the result that the speaker (despite his older age) seems to merge with the "now" of sexual dominance that he is about to evoke.

Accordingly, while the placement of *nunc* seems designed to evoke a sense of dramatic transition from thoughts of old age to the possibilities of youth (the pause between *morosa* and *nunc* is the only mid-verse full stop in the poem), the use of eroticism to blur the temporal distinction between what is associated with age and what is associated with youth leaves it unclear here what transition *nunc* is supposed to evoke. *Nunc* has been the source of much debate, with one critic arguing that "[l]ine 18 *nunc et campus et areae* and what follows suggest a season wholly different from the severe winter at the beginning. This incongruity cannot be removed by any device of apologetic interpretation."[49] Presumably apology would attempt to show that the apparent incongruity masks some deeper unity, the assumption being that the critical choices are limited to either a defense of the poem's success at unifying what is incongruent, or an attack that the poem fails to achieve such unity. However, as our discussion so far indicates, such a critical procedure must ignore what motivates the poem's attempt to join together the apparently incongruent seasons of winter and eroticism; regardless of whether winter and eroticism are adequately joined, there remains the question of how eroticism is understood if its primary interest is its relation to old age. From this perspective, the ambiguity of *nunc* is significant, since it leaves undecidable whether what is being described is an erotic present to which the speaker has no access, or is rather the present time of the poem itself, in which case *nunc* would refer to a "now" in which the speaker can recollect erotic triumphs of the past.

Despite this ultimate undecidability, however, one critic has argued that a solution to the incongruity can be found by emphasizing the second of the possible interpretations of *nunc*, by seeing it as indicating the speaking time of the poem, and thus reading *repetantur* with *composita . . . hora* as an invitation to recollection "at a tranquil time."[50] Thus, the incongruity between *nunc* and *donec* is resolved by seeing them as designating different (although ultimately compatible) ways that the speaker might understand the temporality of experience: "*nunc* is not equivalent to the *donec* clause, but instead stands in contrast to it. So long as old age is far away do not disdain the dance, but now, in contrast, for me, it is possible to recall, relive, recollect the martial exercises of youth, the wrestling ground, and the lover's meeting."[51] Reading *nunc* as designating the temporal present of the poem would resolve the incongruity by seeing the speaker as suggesting his own ability to "recall, relive, [and] recollect" what he is describing, thus in a sense blurring the temporal change from *donec* "while old age is away" to the *nunc* or "now" of old age by understanding both in terms of an erotic "season" which, by merging memory with the present, denies the inevitability of time.

But what allows such a denial of the inevitable temporal distinction between youth and age? A hint is found in the equation between recollection and reliving found in the passage quoted above: somehow, the particularity of what will now be recollected allows a kind of reliving in which past experience merges with an erotic present. But this particularity cannot be seen if we limit the *nunc* in the way just suggested, for if the eroticism that is now described is collapsed into the speaker's memories, then it functions as little more than a delusionary attempt to situate in the present what is irretrievably lost. The unity between recollection and the present, which was sought by seeing *nunc* as limited to the speaker's temporality, will instead need to be found by seeing *nunc* as merging the speaker's temporality with that of Thaliarchus. Understanding *nunc* as functioning not merely as the speaking time of the poem in which the speaker's recollections take place, but also as the time in which Thaliarchus will fulfill the speaker's injunction, thus allows Thaliarchus to function as a kind of confirming repetition of the speaker's memories. That Thaliarchus is intended to play such a role can in part be seen by the speaker's insistence that he not spurn love while he is young (*nec dulcis amores / sperne* 15–16), which points to an erotic immediacy that is then enacted by the insistent use of *nunc* in the account of eroticism that follows. More important, though, is the implicit connectedness between the demand that eroticism function as a confirmation of the possibility of denying the temporality symbolized by winter, and the configuring of eroticism as a symbolic rape. For what Thaliarchus is in effect being asked to do is show, through his power to dominate the "season" of eroticism, that the speaker's memories that eroticism can defeat time might be confirmed by being relived in the present. Insofar as Thaliarchus is able to transform the speaker's recollections into actual repetition, the linearity of time might be denied. Further, as we shall now see, there is a specific connection between the hope to dominate time and the erotic domination that is its substitute. What allows old age and youth to be merged into a single season of erotic triumph is the way in which such triumph enacts the desire for control and power, which time itself seems to defeat.

But of course, as long as we remain committed to the search for unity, erotic dominance will itself have little specificity; rather, the scene described at the end of the poem will be seen as significant to the extent that it succeeds in joining together what otherwise remains discordant. What I now want to try to do is resist such a reading (in a sense, agreeing that the poem enacts an "incongruity [that] cannot be removed by any device of apologetic interpretation") by showing what conception of eroticism we must accept if we claim that the poem succeeds in establishing a "season" of eroticism that confirms the speaker's hopes to deny the temporality of winter.

We can begin by noting that the poem's final scene, with its furtive and elusive interaction between boy and girl, has an indeterminacy[52] that prohibits any easy closure. Its smallness and intimacy, far removed from the wide vista of Soracte at the poem's beginning, are enigmatic, resisting as much as celebrating the "season" of love. The move into the erotic present, signaled by *nunc*, takes shape through the specification of the subjects of *repetantur*. These four subjects—the Campus, the playgrounds, the gentle whispers, and the laughter of the girl—are each joined to the others by a connective (*et* or *-que*), and the effect is to suggest that each is to be recalled by the speaker and sought by Thaliarchus. But the apparent equivalence between grammatical structure and thematic significance of the four subjects of *repetantur* conceals a significant disparity. While the things to be recalled or sought appear to exhibit a kind of balance by being part of a list, in fact the last item is so extended as to preclude its being absorbed on equal terms with the previous items. In part, this imbalance is simply a function of how the language draws a contrast between the significance of, on the one hand, the Campus, the playgrounds, and the gentle whispers, and, on the other hand, the laughter. *Campus* and *areae* are devoid of modifiers, while the whispers (*susurri*) are modified only by gentle (*lenes*). In each case, what seems suggested is an easy availability for either recollection or seeking; where modifiers might complicate the sense of the status of the subject, here instead the subjects stand ready to be absorbed by the needs of the speaker or Thaliarchus. The situation is quite different with the laughter, the fourth subject of *repetantur*. Here, the determination of the laughter's significance requires an entire strophe, and the language that seeks to describe that significance spins dangerously out of control.

Traditionally critics have sought to deny this imbalance by arguing that the whispers are those of the lover and his beloved, and that the actions at the end of the poem are thus merely a continuation of a sort of erotic hide-and-seek.[53] However, by mistakenly merging the gentle whispers with the final episode involving the girl, we miss the fact that nothing in the scene with the girl indicates gentleness, and thus lose much of the force of what is described. Further, the claim that the final strophe continues action begun in the preceding lines ignores how the repetition of *nunc* before the final connecting *et* in a sense sets apart the scene with the girl from anything that has already been described.

What is perhaps most important about this scene is the way that the convoluted syntax and violent language (e.g., *dereptum*) signal an eroticism that is expressed through an assault upon the beloved, and which thus precludes any possible awareness of the beloved as a person existing independently of the lover's desires. One critic has sought to find a harmony within the violence and convolution, arguing that "the arrangement [of *latentis proditor intimo puellae risus ab angulo*] is carefully studied; the three modifiers are placed together, succeeding each other in the same order as the three nouns which they qualify, which are likewise placed together."[54] (*Gratus*, which serves as another qualifier for *risus*, it should be noted, interrupts the pattern described.) What is missing from this observation, though, is the fact that the studied quality is a feature of the speaker's language and not of the scene it evokes. The placement of all the modifiers before the nouns they modify creates the sense that the qualities or activities of hiding, discovery, intimacy, and pleasantness are more important to the speaker than the specifics they modify— girl, laughter, corner. Still further, the juxtaposition of *latentis* (hiding) and *proditor* (betraying) dominates the specificity of the beloved by imaging her discovery solely through terms by which she is related to the lover. The juxtaposition of *intimo* and *gratus* suggests (from the lover's perspective) pleasure in inmost places, whether of the body or of the landscape.[55] (*Intimo . . . ab angulo* could apply equally to the landscape or the body—an inmost corner outdoors, or an inmost corner of the beloved's body.) The speaker's dislocated language thus creates a sense of mystery about what is occurring, which is able to be known as positive only by adopting his perspective.

The dominance of the lover's perspective is further seen in the absence of specificity with regard to the girl and her desires in the descripion of the theft of the token or pledge. The alternatives given with regard to what is stolen by the boy (bracelet or ring) or indeed what part of the girl's body it comes from (finger or arm) make central not the beloved, but the act of stealing itself (*dereptum*). What is clearly important for the lover is not erotic interaction, but rather his having taken something that belongs to the girl. Indeed, the word *pignus* (pledge) for what the lover steals from the girl recalls the language of finance, seen earlier in the speaker's injunction to count as gain whatever time fate will give (*quem Fors dierum cumque dabit lucro / appone* 14–15).[56] The metaphor of the pledge places the girl in the position of having relinquished to the boy a security on a "debt" that she will have to repay. However, it is worth emphasizing here that it is not only the beloved who is impoverished by functioning merely as an object to be possessed. Indeed, the lack of definitiveness about what part of her body the token comes from indicates an encounter devoid of any interest in or attention to the specifics of the beloved's body. By framing her worth in terms of a kind of erotic exchange—her worth is the financial gain in power that the lover gains from conquering her—the lover blocks himself from receiving any of the relational pleasures that genuine knowledge of her body might give.

What is ignored is the perspective of the beloved. We learn that her laughter betrays her. Traditional readings of this poem have assumed that to mean that a game of hide-and-seek is in progress and that the girl laughingly "gives herself up." However there is no indication in the poem that the girl's laughter is directed toward or shared with the boy, even though presumably it is to him that it is pleasant (*gratus*). In addition, the description of the laughter as "betraying" is that of the speaker. What, then, does it betray? There is no evidence that it betrays her location in a prearranged game, for she is never specified as part of the agreement or complicity implied by *composita . . . hora*. Rather the laughter could just as plausibly be seen as (unintentionally) revealing her existence, and thus making her an easy target for the lover's own designs. Still further, traditional readings have taken the final words of the poem (*male pertinaci*) to mean that the girl is not really resisting, relying on the interpretation of *male* as a quasi-negative almost equivalent to *non*. While such a use of *male* is not uncommon,[57] the adverb's literal meaning, "badly," is significant in this context, for it would suggest not that she puts up hardly any resistance, but rather that her resistance is not very successful.[58] Nevertheless, in either interpretation of *male pertinaci* the dynamic of the beloved as something to be conquered is reinforced.

Clearly the final scene of the poem portrays the "season" or "now" of eroticism as the time to get what one can from the beloved regardless of her interests. The symbolic rape at the end of the poem is a sinister representation of the notion of trying to defeat time. The lover's effort to force the beloved to conform to his own desires ignores all of the circumstances of the beloved's present condition— how she is situated in time and what her own desires are. The eroticism the speaker recommends to Thaliarchus and which he hopes to relive through Thaliarchus' activities is thus an eroticism premised upon the denial that the object of eroticism can have any independent existence. From this perspective, temporality can be seen as that aspect of experience that humans share, and the attempt to use eroticism to deny temporality can accordingly be seen as a denial of shared experience. Thus, if much of the poem struggles to find in recollection or reliving an escape from the awful solitude of winter as a metaphor for human temporality, the concluding eroticism merely affirms the solitude it seeks to escape by precluding any real connection with the experience of others.

Vitas inuleo me similis, Chloe,
quaerenti pavidam montibus aviis
    matrem non sine vano
      aurarum et siluae metu.
nam seu mobilibus veris inhorruit   5
adventus foliis seu virides rubum
    dimovere lacertae,
      et corde et genibus tremit.
atqui non ego te tigris ut aspera
Gaetulusve leo frangere persequor: 10
    tandem desine matrem
      tempestiva sequi viro.

You are avoiding me like a fawn, Chloe, seeking its fright-
ened mother on pathless mountains not without empty fear of
breezes and the forest. For whether the coming of spring has
bristled with its pliant leaves or the green lizards have moved
apart the brambles, it trembles in both knees and heart. But I do
not pursue you like a fierce tiger or a Gaetulian lion to break you:
at last stop following your mother, you who are seasonable for a
man.

We saw in *Odes* 1.9 that the effort to ward off wintry solitude
through erotic domination is futile because of its implicit denial of
the temporality of the beloved. By precluding the recognition of the
beloved as an independent person situated in time, the lover makes
impossible any shared sense of experience that would make eroti-
cism something other than a desperate move to escape the limita-
tions of one's own temporality. In *Odes* 1.23 we see the lover once
again attempting to dominate the temporality of the beloved, but
this time that attempt takes shape not through an overt act of sym-
bolic rape, but rather through a discourse whose seemingly disinter-
ested argumentation is undermined by its emotionally intimidat-
ing content. The beloved's readiness for sexual activity is implied
through her identification with spring, thus making the lover's claim
of her timeliness seem natural. But as we shall see, the poet/lover's
attempt to define the right or "natural" time for love as a justification
for his own desires masks a refusal to acknowledge his own motiva-

tions in establishing such a definition. Implicitly, the poet/lover's argument is that the flowering of desire should be a natural phenomenon of human experience, just as the coming of spring is part of the natural order of the seasons. But this attempt to link desire to a natural order is undermined when we consider how the poet/lover's words seek to produce the very situation he claims is natural. While the language of the poem seeks to describe spring as a natural time of eroticism to which human beings will inevitably conform, in fact such a description of spring functions primarily as a device through which the poet/lover seeks to evade his own erotic feelings.

Although one critic dismisses *Odes* 1.23 as "hardly . . . much more than a pretty little artefact,"[59] many others have given it considerable attention, focusing on various issues of a literary-historical, philological, or structural nature.[60] Nisbet and Hubbard's characterization of the poem as "tender, humorous, and discreetly sensuous" is not untypical.[61] Nielsen, who questions the supposed ingenuousness of the poet's denial of predatory intent, is unusual in recognizing and exploring the sexual tensions in the poem.[62] However, what these interpretations overlook is the way in which the poet/lover's seemingly rational assertion of knowledge about the beloved conceals a refusal to recognize or acknowledge her emotional need. The poet/lover's insistence that his own desires pose no threat (indeed, his refusal to specify precisely what his desires are), far from indicating innocence or selflessness, is in fact a subterfuge designed to preserve both the autonomy and dominance of a self incapable of recognizing the object of its desire as an agent. The dichotomy between the rational discourse of the poem (the arguments that the poet makes) and its emotive power (primarily the figurative language in which those arguments are expressed) thus reveals a version of male desire that seeks an autonomy secured by rational detachment, while exhibiting a dominance over the other, which is the necessary consequence of an extreme assertion of self.[63]

This dichotomy between the rational discourse of the poem and the affective power of its language can be made explicit through an examination of the rational arguments of the poem and the specific ways in which they are undercut. To begin with, the word order of the poem's first line mirrors the conflicting interests of the poet/lover and Chloe, the addressee. While the rational meaning of the simile in the poem's first line—you are avoiding me like a fawn, Chloe—is reflected in the separation of verb (*vitas*), direct object (*me*), and vocative (*Chloe*), it is undercut by word order, at the same time, for the poet surrounds himself (*me*) with "Chloe words" (*inuleo . . . similis*). Furthermore, the apparently rational characterization of Chloe's fears as empty or groundless (*vano*) in the fawn simile is undermined by the emotionally disconcerting tone produced by the presence of the fawn's fearful mother (*pavidam . . . matrem*) and the pathless mountains (*montibus aviis*) through which the fawn flees. Then, in the guise of expanding upon the fawn's empty fears (note the explanatory *nam*), the poet/lover begins to employ images that imply both arousal in Chloe and the fulfillment of his own desire.

Chloe's name (Greek for "green bud" or "shoot"), introduced earlier in the poem, has prepared the reader to associate Chloe with spring, which, as Commager argues, functions as the controlling metaphor of the poem.[64] Indeed, Χλόη appears in Greek as an epithet of the goddess Demeter, because of her connection with the young grain worshipped in Attica.[65] In addition, there is inscriptional evidence of a festival of Demeter Chloe and Kore at Eleusis.[66] Thus through its association with Demeter, the name Chloe suggests simultaneously both female youth (Kore) and female maturity (Demeter), and accordingly evokes the mother/daughter dyad that is itself so important in the story of Demeter and Persephone (Kore). This sense of interchangeability between mother and daughter blurs the distinction between generations, and thus makes Chloe more vulnerable to the poet/lover's claim that she has reached maturity.

Further, the conception of spring that emerges in this association of Chloe with both Demeter and Persephone is one characterized by the (ominous) intrusion of the male (here the poet/lover) upon the mother-daughter dyad. This sense of spring lurks behind the poet's description of the bristling forth of foliage at spring's arrival (*mobilibus veris inhorruit / adventus foliis*), which we associate with Chloe. And through the words *mobilis* (pliant, flexible) and *inhorreo* (shudder, bristle, stand on end/become erect) the poet evokes the symptoms of (Chloe's) physical arousal. Still further, the erotic potential awakened in this description of spring is realized in the vivid image of sexual intercourse suggested by the lizards moving apart the brambles (*virides rubum / dimovere lacertae*). The description directly following, of the fawn's or Chloe's trembling knees and pounding heart, is equally evocative of both fear and desire, thus mingling symptoms that describe the effect the poet/lover presumably desires (namely, Chloe's own desire) with the effect that he describes himself as having on Chloe (namely, fear). As we can see, then, the rational argument that Chloe is avoiding him because of unnecessary fears is radically undermined through word order and suggestive sexual imagery. The figurative power of the language evokes designs the poet/lover has on Chloe, which do not surface in his rational argumentation.

What follows in the poem on the rational level (expressed once again through simile) is the poet/lover's attempt to reassure Chloe that he has no plans to attack her: *atqui non ego te tigris ut aspera / Gaetulusve leo frangere persequor.* Yet through word order that embodies pursuit (*non ego te*) and similes of predatory animals, each made more emphatic with a modifier (*tigris / aspera* and *Gaetulus leo*), the poet/lover undercuts his reassurances. The postponement of *frangere persequor* until the end of its phrase, its lengthy separation from the negative *atqui non*, and its demarcation through its appearance after the metrical pause in the line, all serve to undercut still further the denial of predatory intent. Moreover, it is "pursuit" (*persequor*) with which the phrase concludes.

Frangere, finally, demolishes the poet/lover's seeming reassurances. The "rational negation" of *atqui non* is boldly effaced by the figurative power of *frangere*. Indeed, *frangere* functions as the climax of the poem, for it captures the poet/lover's unacknowledged need to completely overpower Chloe. The choice of *frangere* to embody this climax is particularly effective because of the word's range of meanings, which extends from the rational to the emotional spheres. The word encapsulates the poet/lover's multiple goals of *influencing* Chloe through rational argumentation, *taming* her the way one tames an animal,[67] and *breaking down* her resistance. Indeed, *frangere* (which can be used of breaking down doors or barriers)[68] may even hint at the breaking of the hymen, which would make real, and more specific to Chloe's youthful state, the sexual intercourse earlier suggested through the detail of the lizards moving apart the brambles.[69] Perhaps we can now understand *frangere* as a powerfully evocative expression of the destructive component of a desire that requires a subordination of the other.[70] To be sure, the poet/lover backs off somewhat from the explosiveness of the word *frangere* in the poem's final lines. Yet here, too, the seemingly objective language of *tandem* (at last) and *tempestiva* (seasonable) is undercut by the realization that Chloe's "readiness for a man" has been defined all along solely in relation to the interests of her would-be lover. The poet/lover's defining Chloe as *tempestiva* is the culminating moment in his effort to situate her in a season appropriate for his own erotic designs. In the guise of a rational polemic on the necessity for Chloe to adapt to the "natural order of things," the poet/lover conceals his own impatience and desire.

What we can now see is that the tension between the rational discourse of the poem and its affective power can be explained by the dynamics of a self torn between its desire for autonomy and its need for the other. The particular form of desire that emerges from the Chloe Ode—a paradoxical desire both for control of the other and for recognition by her—is expressed through a combination of rational detachment and emotional suggestiveness. "Reason" allows the poet/lover the appearance of speaking from a dispassionate and uninvolved position, while in fact functioning as a kind of erotic subterfuge, which masks an overpowering desire in the cloak of objectivity.

The ultimate futility of the poet/lover's strategy for evoking a natural season of eroticism is evidenced by the fact that what is absent from the poem is any clear sense of Chloe's will, of Chloe as the subject or agent of desire. We are left with only the surface of Chloe, with a Chloe whose trembling reaction to the poet/lover suggests both her fear and (to the poet/lover) her potential for erotic response. And as a consequence, the lines between seduction, domination, and invasion begin to blur. By denying Chloe agency, the poet/lover precludes the kind of response he presumably wants from Chloe, namely, desire.

Not recognizing the intimidating aspect of the poet/lover's persona entails mistaking the poem for a "sweet" portrait of a girl leaving childhood for the season of love. However, if we replace such a simplistic reading with the sort of reductiveness that sees nothing more in the poem than an uncomplicated expression of male dominance, we make it impossible to understand his desire for Chloe. By interpreting the split between the rational discourse of the poem and its affective power as analogous to the conflicting needs and desires found in a fantasy of erotic domination, we have a way of dealing with the poet/lover's simultaneous distancing of himself from Chloe and his expression of desire, an expression that verges on the obliteration of the object of his desire.

FOUR

Age and

Experience

A recurring theme in the previous two chapters has been the function of temporality in delineating the roles of lover and beloved. In chapter 2, we saw how the temporal adverb points to a structure of temporality that stands opposed to the lover's desires. In chapter 3, the lover's hopes to establish a season of eroticism were set in opposition to the temporality of experience, and we noted in *Odes* 1.9 and 1.23 how this opposition comes to justify a denial of the beloved's humanity. In this chapter, I use *Odes* 2.8, 4.1, and 4.13 to explore in fuller detail the consequences of distinguishing between the temporality of the lover and the beloved. While each of these poems presents a similar theme—the effect of age and experience upon eroticism—the poems vary dramatically in how they understand this theme.

In *Odes* 2.8 and 4.13, the temporality of the beloved is *public*, and the monstrosity or absurdity of an aging woman functioning as an object of desire is accordingly seen as a violation of what is socially proper. In *Odes* 4.1, on the other hand, the lover's temporality, while disturbing, is seen as a merely *private* dilemma. Nothing about the lover's recognition of his own temporality has any relation to how he is seen by others. Thus, while these poems each suggest that aging, the ultimate sign of human temporality, stands opposed to eroticism, the distinction between how aging affects the lover and the beloved will indicate that temporality is understood only illusorily as a universal feature of experience. Instead, the insistence that aging should destroy desire and desirability serves as a means for perpetuating the *public* determination of the beloved's identity (she is determined as either an object worthy of being desired by others, or as an object of desire lacking such worth), while ensuring as well the ultimate privacy of the lover.

🍥 *Odes* 2.8

Ulla si iuris tibi peierati
poena, Barine, nocuisset umquam,
dente si nigro fieres vel uno
    turpior ungui,
crederem; sed tu, simul obligasti   5
perfidum votis caput, enitescis
pulchrior multo iuvenumque prodis
    publica cura.
expedit matris cineres opertos
fallere et toto taciturna noctis   10
signa cum caelo gelidaque divos
    morte carentis.
ridet hoc, inquam, Venus ipsa, rident
simplices Nymphae ferus et Cupido,
semper ardentis acuens sagittas   15
    cote cruenta.
adde quod pubes tibi crescit omnis,
servitus crescit nova, nec priores
impiae tectum dominae relinquunt,
    saepe minati.   20
te suis matres metuunt iuvencis,
te senes parci miseraeque nuper
virgines nuptae, tua ne retardet
    aura maritos.

If any punishment for an oath falsely sworn, Barine, had ever harmed you, if you were becoming uglier by one black tooth or nail, I would believe you; but as soon as you have bound your faithless head in vows, you shine much more beautifully and go forth as the public love object of the youth. It is profitable for you to swear falsely on the buried ashes of your mother and on the silent stars of the night along with the whole sky and on the gods lacking cold death. I say Venus herself laughs at this and the artless Nymphs and wild Cupid always sharpening his burning arrows with the bloody flint. Add the fact that all the youth grow big for you, a new group of slaves grows big for you, nor do the earlier ones leave the house of their impious mistress, although often having threatened to do so. You the mothers fear for their young, you the sparing old men and the unhappy brides, recently maidens, lest your allure slow down their mates.

While Horace several times portrays women as just entering sexual maturity or, on the other hand, as too old for love, *Odes* 2.8 is noteworthy for its presentation of a woman whose sexuality is seemingly—and, for Horace, almost uniquely—unaffected by time.[1] While Barine is clearly quite experienced in erotic activity, she nevertheless exhibits none of the abhorrent characteristics that Horace typically associates with women whose sexuality continues beyond youth.[2] On the contrary, her beauty and magnetic sexual power have not diminished with time, thus making her a constant in a world of change. However, far from such constancy being valued, instead it marks Barine as an alarming violation of the natural process of experience. While public displays of eroticism should be limited to those social rituals of courtship that allow one generation to succeed another, and which thus allow temporal experience to be organized into a natural social rhythm, Barine's public display of uncontrollable sexuality instead shatters the norms of temporal experience. Thus, while we have noted in several other poems how Horace seeks to find in eroticism a secure refuge from the inevitability of time, here instead it is time that offers security and eroticism that poses a disturbing threat. But of course, the difference here is that eroticism is located in an unknowable *female* sexuality, and the inevitability of time provides the sole hope that such sexuality might be tamed.

The protases of the conditional sentence with which the poem begins—the past contrary-to-fact, *ulla si iuris tibi peierati / poena, Barine, nocuisset umquam* (1–2), and the present contrary-to-fact, *dente si nigro fieres vel uno / turpior ungui* (3–4)—establish the terms through which Barine's sexuality will be understood. The speaker's attitude appears to be that, in the natural order of things, Barine's past erotic faithlessness would have been punished, and she would now have aged sufficiently to preclude any current desirability. In a sense, social conventions (which would ensure her punishment) and time (which would ensure that her desirability could not continue indefinitely) together would preserve social stability. It is worth noting that such an attitude conflicts with the proverbial notion (echoed in *Odes* 2.8 by the sympathetic reactions of the gods) that eroticism breaks down the normal conventions of social experience.[3] However, the speaker's dismay with Barine indicates that he receives little solace from such a proverbial notion of love, and thus the opening words of the poem show his unhappiness that the natural order has for some reason failed to operate as it should.

The first protasis emphasizes the absoluteness of Barine's exemption from punishment (*poena*) by using the indefinite adjective *ulla* (any) and the indefinite temporal adverb *umquam* (ever) to describe her situation, and by placing *poena*, *ulla*, and *umquam* all in emphatic positions in their verses (*ulla* and *poena* each first, and *umquam* last). The pluperfect subjunctive of the past contrary-to-fact protasis (*nocuisset*) extends Barine's perfidy into the distant past while the contrary-to-fact statement itself brings her immunity from punishment up to the present. The shift from past unreal to present unreal in the second protasis (*dente si nigro fieres vel uno / turpior ungui*) moves the emphasis from Barine's escape from actual punishment to her seemingly ongoing immunity from temporality. Just as, in the natural order of things, Barine's past transgressions should have resulted in some sort of punishment, so the movement of time should be lessening her desirability, and thus would offer some security to the social world that she threatens. However, as the speaker makes clear, not even a single "black tooth or nail" mars her present attractiveness, and thus Barine stands eerily outside anything that might help the speaker to limit her force.

Indeed, the language of these first few lines makes it clear that the real issue here is not Barine herself, but rather the speaker's inability to control what he describes. Thus, in the first protasis, the placement of the vocative, *Barine*, between *poena* and *nocuisset* emphasizes the hope of the speaker that Barine might literally be situated between punishment and harm. The whole condition concludes with an ironic one-word apodosis, *crederem*, whose laconic nature seems designed to emphasize the speaker's present disbelief. What we can see in this language is how, for the speaker, belief is tied to a desire to position Barine in a nexus of punishment and harm. However, such a desire takes shape here only conditionally; the speaker is left with only the hope that his language will replace the failure of social conventions and time to do what they should.

Indeed, while in the opening lines of the poem, the speaker seeks to understand Barine solely in terms of her lack of conformity to social conventions, in the actual description of her that follows it is society that in a sense conforms to Barine. In the connection between *simul obligasti / perfidum votis caput* (as soon as you have bound your faithless head in vows, i.e., as soon as you have sworn falsely by your very life) and *enitescis pulchrior multo* (you shine much more beautifully), the normal social consequences of making a pledge are replaced by what is almost a causal relationship between Barine's swearing falsely and her increased beauty. The temporal adverb *simul*, by making the increase in her beauty seem to be an immediate consequence of her untrustworthy pledges of love, heightens this sense that increased beauty has replaced the negative judgment that should follow a broken pledge. The consequences of Barine's immunity from judgment begin to be specified in the clause that follows: *iuvenumque prodis / publica cura* (and you go forth as the public love object of the youth). As a "public" object, Barine evokes both desire and concern. The ambiguity of *cura* captures well the social effects of Barine's desirability. Her public appearance occasions desire in young men, but this desire is itself an object of concern, since it threatens what should be the normal ritual of youthful courtship. What the two meanings of *cura* thus suggest is a public world divided by Barine into those who desire and those who are concerned about such desire. (In fact, as the example of the old men will suggest, this division can exist within the lovers themselves.) But in either case, of course, Barine has herself triumphed in that it is her attractiveness that now governs social experience.

Barine's position outside the normal social order is further emphasized by the list of witnesses she is said to call upon for her false oaths—her mother's ashes, the stars and sky, and the immortal gods. The buried ashes (*cineres opertos*) and silent stars (*taciturna . . . signa*) along with the gods who "lack cold death" (*gelidaque divos / morte carentis*) stand immutably outside the transitory social concerns that Barine has so disrupted. That such swearing "profits" Barine is undoubtedly intended ironically by the speaker, but the irony in fact turns against him, since there is at this point no normal social world to set against the presumed absurdity of Barine's appeal to nonhuman forces. The disappearance of social order is even more stark in the description of Venus laughing at the absurdity of Barine's oaths. Here, the speaker's irony disappears and is replaced by something approaching wonder: *ridet hoc, inquam, Venus ipsa* (I say Venus herself laughs at this). The change in tone suggests almost frustration at the impossibility of limiting Barine. Where one might expect divine retribution, instead Venus and her companions are allies of Barine, laughing at her success. The description of the nymphs as *simplices* extends the sense of how Barine disrupts the normal distinctions of eroticism—while Barine's conniving should put her in opposition to the "guileless" nymphs, here instead they share in the delight at what she has succeeded in doing.

In addition to Venus and the Nymphs, wild Cupid (*ferus . . . Cupido* 14)[4] is amused by Barine. Cupid's repeated sharpening of his weapons (*semper . . . acuens* 15) suggests the continuing threat of Barine's erotic power. The love god's burning arrows (*ardentis . . . sagittas* 15) further complicates the earlier separation of the gods from human mortality (*gelidaque divos / morte carentis* 11–12): where in the earlier image, the distinction between the human and the divine was figured as the coldness of death, here instead the divine is connected with human experience by the heat of passion. For Barine, such passion is experienced as power, as the effects that she can produce in her lovers. However, *cruenta* (16), used of the bloody whetstone with which Cupid sharpens his arrows, points to the social consequence of that power, which for the speaker is finally the transformation of society into little more than the "bloodied" victims of Barine.

The next strophe begins oddly, with an attempt to "add" the social effects of Barine's exploits to what has just been described. The use of *adde* implies that the poem is progressing as a kind of indictment of Barine, with each of the particular charges serving to advance the speaker's claim that Barine cannot be trusted. But the previous strophe, while certainly confirming that Barine's vows are not to be trusted from any normal human perspective, has also suggested an unearthly power to that untrustworthiness, which subtly changes the sense of Barine's significance. While the speaker continues to believe that the sole issue that has been raised is Barine's relation to normal standards of human conduct, in fact an equally important issue is now how we are to understand this erotic power that seems to surpass any normal human standards of judgment. That such understanding will be difficult is indicated by the sweeping effects of Barine, who, we are told, has caused an entire generation of young men (*pubes . . . omnis* 17)[5] to develop solely in terms of her erotic power (*servitus . . . nova* 18, a new group of slaves). *Crescit*, the verb used to describe the activity of this new generation, suggests both the normal maturation of young men (they are "growing up"), and their literal sexual response to Barine (they are "growing big"). (The latter, more literal, sense is mimed by the repetition of *crescit* in lines 17 and 18, which imitates in language the build-up of the young men's desire.)[6] This merging of the erotic and the temporal blurs the distinctions upon which judgment might be based; while thè speaker certainly feels that Barine should be denounced for the effect she is having on the young, the poem offers little sense of what the basis of such judgment might be.

Indeed, the accumulation of detail here works against the avowed beliefs of the speaker, as the "build-up" of his own rhetoric mimes the effects of Barine, which he wishes to denounce. The denunciation moves quickly from victim to victim, as though the speaker hoped that the sheer extent of Barine's effects would be sufficient to convict her. But the difficulty here is that Barine's "victims" do not themselves seem to feel victimized; indeed, the temporal progression from one group of admirers to another is disrupted by the fact that the "earlier ones" themselves never leave, despite "often having threatened to do so" (*saepe minati*).[7] So the real source of shock here is nothing as concrete as actual suffering; rather, the speaker seems outraged primarily at the *lack* of such suffering, at the fact that Barine's "house" seems to be a place where the disintegration of social order is neither punished, nor experienced as something that should be punished.

In the final strophe, the focus shifts from those who have succumbed to Barine, to the social wreckage she is supposed to have caused. The fear that Barine's success has produced shatters boundaries of age or gender, affecting mothers, old men, and young brides alike. What produces this fear is not merely the social chaos that Barine has caused, but the starkly sexual origin of that chaos. *Iuvencis*, the term used to describe the young for whom "the mothers fear," is used primarily of the young of animals, and thus heightens the physicality of Barine's influence. (Indeed, the *aura* possessed by Barine can have a specific sexual sense: an emanation arising from sexual arousal.)[8] What the mothers fear losing is an animal-like connection to their young, but such an image reduces social bonds to precisely the inhuman passion that Barine herself represents.

Similarly, the pun in *retardet* (*tardus*, like *lentus*, can mean "slow to become erect")[9] indicates that the unhappy brides are afraid not simply that their husbands may be detained, or even that they may be unfaithful, but that through Barine's impact they will return home impotent. And while the "sparing" older men (*senes parci*) may fear for their sons' financial extravagance in relation to Barine, they also fear for themselves. They are interested in conserving (sparing) not only their financial resources, but their sexual resources as well. They fear that if they visit Barine she will exhaust their already diminished sexual capacities.[10] What we can see in these examples of the fear Barine produces is how her real threat is to the sense of security that normal social roles might offer. To be a mother, a bride, or a father is to occupy a familiar place in the social hierarchy, a place determined in large part by society's structuring of sexuality. Barine's sexuality empties these roles of their normal social function, and the fear that results is thus finally a fear that eroticism itself cannot be contained by the familiar social arrangements of experience.

We noted earlier that the description of Barine as someone whose erotic transgressions are unpunished echoes the proverbial belief that the gods forgive romantic excess. However, where the traditional view seems sympathetic to the idea that eroticism cannot be constrained by social convention, in *Odes* 2.8 such lack of constraint instead is a source of fear. We can see more clearly what is at stake in such fear by considering the parodic relation that *Odes* 2.8 has to the traditional belief that the public ritual of marriage provides a stability that eases society's anxieties about the disruptive potential of eroticism.

Critics have noted that *Odes* 2.8 uses certain elements characteristic of a hymn to a divinity.[11] The poem's hymnic form is suggested by such items as the prayer formula of the final strophe (*te . . . te . . . tua*) and other groups of three, characteristic of hymnic form (*cineres, signa, divos*; *Venus, Nymphae, Cupido*; *pubes, servitus, priores*). One critic, citing the poet's declaration of nonbelief, *si . . . fieres . . . turpior, . . . crederem*, wonders whether the ode is "a hymn in reverse."[12] However, the connection of such hymnic echoes with the poem's account of Barine's disruptive force has largely gone unnoticed. A suggestion for how such a connection might be established was offered by Ensor, who in the early 1900s argued in a short note that the last strophe of *Odes* 2.8 contains specific elements of parody of Catullus 61.51–55 (the hymn to Hymen):[13]

> te suis tremulus parens
> invocat, tibi virgines
> zonula soluunt sinus
> te timens cupida novus
>   captat aure maritus.

> You the trembling parent calls upon for his children, for you the maidens loosen their garments from their girdles, you the new husband timidly listens for with eager ear.

Ensor notes four points of similarity: (1) each clause is introduced by a second person pronoun [sic] *te, te, tua / te, tibi, te*; (2) *matres* and *senes / parens*; (3) *virgines / virgines*; (4) *aura maritos / aure maritus.* He suggests that Horace is "maliciously burlesquing the 'Epithalamium.' "[14] However, the parody of Catullus 61, I would argue, cuts deeper than the malicious burlesque that Ensor suggests. For Catullus, marriage allows both the hope for generational continuity (the *tremulus parens* appeals to Hymen to secure his children's place in the social order) and for controlled (and thus socially acceptable) eroticism (Hymen offers the maidens a proper setting for them to "loosen their garments from their girdles"). This sense of marriage as allowing temporal and social stability is of course precisely what is threatened by the constancy and power of Barine's attractiveness; her unchanging beauty (and its availability to her would-be lovers) challenges the belief that marriage is a necessary counter to the uncertainties of desire and time. Thus, the burlesquing of Catullus serves not to ridicule the celebration of marriage, but rather to insist even more dramatically on the direness of Barine's threat to all that Catullus praises.

Further parallels between the two poems sharpen this sense of the danger that Barine poses to marriage. The striking phrase *prodis / publica cura* (2.8.7–8), used of Barine, ironically recalls the refrain *prodeas nova nupta*, spoken to the bride (92, 96, 106, 113). The contrast here between the public roles of Barine and the bride frames further connections between the two poems. The bride's honorable modesty, which slows her travel to the groom's house (*tardet ingenuus pudor* 79), suggests that the beloved's acceptance of modesty as the form that eroticism should take literally determines how her body will move in public. In contrast, Barine's refusal of social convention, her refusal to limit what her body does, produces anxiety that the recently married young men who visit her will themselves "slow down" (*retardet* 21), and thus fail to fulfill their own roles as husbands. The fear that Barine's sexuality threatens the institution of marriage ironically echoes the claim in Catullus' marriage hymn that the groom will be faithful (97–101). The groom's ability to remain faithful seems dependent on marriage as itself a limitation of eroticism, and thus would have little force against Barine.

What these parallels between the two poems allow us to see is that what finally motivates the speaker's dismay with Barine is nothing so simple as her refusal to fulfill her vows; rather, the speaker sees desire for Barine as in effect producing a kind of worship that denies limitation, and thus denies social order. Here we might contrast Venus' laughing acceptance of Barine with the rather different role she plays in Catullus (61.44–45):

> dux bonae Veneris, boni
> coniugator amoris.

> bringer of virtuous Venus, joiner of virtuous love.

For Catullus, Venus and love become "virtuous" because of the legitimating role of Hymen, suggesting the illicit potential of Venus/ love in the absence of marriage. With this in mind, we can see the allusion to Venus' sympathy for Barine as less an affirmation of proverbial wisdom than a sinister suggestion of the monstrous consequences that would follow from worship of Barine. Catullus celebrates Hymen because of the beneficent social order that marriage allows, while a celebration of Barine would instead implicitly accept the nightmarish fear that governs society in a world controlled by her erotic power.

But it is important to conclude by noting how in both Catullus and Horace what is at issue is the positioning of female sexuality. The fear that Barine produces is structurally identical to the joy that greets the bride's journey to her husband's house. In each case, temporal and social stability are defined in relation to female sexuality; generational continuity can be ensured only if daughters become wives, and public order is possible only if erotic passion is limited to the lawful roles of husband and wife. Barine, however, is immune from both the social and temporal forces that would normally allow female sexuality to be controlled. Her erotic successes mock the belief that only the ordered eroticism of married love can offer enduring satisfaction, and her timeless attractiveness obviates any need to find a husband before aging destroys her erotic value. Such immunity from the normal positioning of the female might suggest an instability that would require a rethinking of the "proper" position for female eroticism to occupy. But the speaker's fear of Barine provides a powerful example of the obstacles such rethinking would face.

Odes 4.1

> Intermissa, Venus, diu
>   rursus bella moves? parce precor, precor.
> non sum qualis eram bonae
>   sub regno Cinarae. desine, dulcium
> mater saeva Cupidinum,   5
>   circa lustra decem flectere mollibus
> iam durum imperiis; abi
>   quo blandae iuvenum te revocant preces.
> tempestivius in domum
>   Pauli purpureis ales oloribus   10
> comissabere Maximi,
>   si torrere iecur quaeris idoneum.
> namque et nobilis et decens
>   et pro sollicitis non tacitus reis
> et centum puer artium   15
>   late signa feret militiae tuae,
> et, quandoque potentior
>   largi muneribus riserit aemuli,
> Albanos prope te lacus
>   ponet marmoream sub trabe citrea.   20
> illic plurima naribus
>   duces tura lyraque et Berecyntia

delectabere tibia
    mixtis carminibus non sine fistula;
illic bis pueri die   25
    numen cum teneris virginibus tuum
laudantes pede candido
    in morem Salium ter quatient humum.
me nec femina nec puer
    iam nec spes animi credula mutui   30
nec certare iuvat mero
    nec vincire novis tempora floribus.
sed cur, heu, Ligurine, cur
    manat rara meas lacrima per genas?
    cur facunda parum decoro   35
    inter verba cadit lingua silentio?
nocturnis ego somniis
    iam captum teneo, iam volucrem sequor
te per gramina Martii
    Campi, te per aquas, dure, volubilis.   40

Venus, are you starting up again battles interrupted for a long
time? Spare me, I beg you, I beg you. I am not as I was under the
reign of good Cinara. Stop, savage mother of sweet Cupids,
prevailing upon me, fifty years old, and now unresponsive,
with your gentle commands; go away to where the flattering
prayers of the youth call you. Winged with your purple swans,
you will carouse in more timely fashion at the home of Paulus
Maximus, if you want to inflame a suitable heart. For this young
man, noble, and handsome and not silent on behalf of his
anxious defendants and skilled in a hundred ways will bear the
standard of your army far and wide, and when he will have
iaughed, more powerful than his lavish gift-giving rival, near
the Alban lakes he will establish you in marble under a citrus-
wood beam. There you will breathe in with your nose much
incense and will be delighted by songs mingled with lyre and
Berecynthian flute, not without the pipe. There twice a day
youths with tender girls will shake the ground three times with
shining foot in the manner of the Salii, praising your power.
Now neither woman nor boy nor credulous hope of mutual
feelings nor contesting with wine nor binding temples with
fresh flowers pleases me. But why, alas, Ligurinus, why does an

occasional tear spread along my cheeks? Why does my eloquent tongue fall amidst my words in a scarcely decorous silence? I, in my night dreams, now hold you captured, now pursue you, swift, through the grass of the Campus Martius, you, hard-hearted, through the unstable waters.

If in *Odes* 2.8 Barine's public status as a kind of timeless object of desire is made to seem monstrous, in *Odes* 4.1 the lover's continuing desire into old age is instead presented as a dilemma with which we should sympathize. The primary difference here is that the lover's resurgence of desire, while surprising and embarrassing, is understood as existing in a private realm, which is immune from the sort of public judgment that the speaker of *Odes* 2.8 sought for Barine. Where Barine's apparent exemption from the aging process and from the constraints of time is understood as a public threat, here instead the lover's recognition that his desires violate the normal temporal order of experience is implicitly applauded. In *Odes* 4.1 the poet/lover presents himself as "knowing" what the right time for love is, but, regrettably, having no control over his ability to conform to what he believes is proper. His lack of conformity to what he sees as the acceptable "season" for love is presented as almost charming in its poignance; the failure of the private struggle to control desire occasions not dismay, but rather admiration for the poet/lover's honesty.

What we can see here is a sharp distinction between how lack of conformity to social standards is viewed in the case of the lover and the beloved. The lover (who is seen only in terms of desire) is forgiven his transgression of the appropriate time for love, while the beloved (who is seen only in terms of desirability) is condemned. Forgiveness is possible for the erotic *subject* who transgresses public norms, because his desires, originating in the privacy of self-determination, are an essential part of his humanity. Such privacy is, of course, denied to the erotic *object*, whose desires are expected to be nothing more than a mirror of the demands of the lover, and thus the condemnation of the beloved for her failure to conform to social expectations is itself the consequence of denying that the beloved has existence outside the desires of the lover. With this in mind, we can see less poignancy in the poet/lover's recognition of his continuing desire than an almost willful reaffirmation of personal power. Defined by nothing but the privacy of his own desires, the poet/

lover has a freedom to transgress temporality, which is denied to any beloved.

This sense of the privacy of the poet/lover's desire is announced in the opening words of the poem.[15] *Intermissa, Venus* (interrupted, Venus), the first words of *Odes* 4.1, introduce the notion that the issue of whether eroticism will have an end is conceived exclusively in relation to the poet/lover's own understanding of his temporality. Both the interruption of desire and the reawakening, which Venus is supposed to have caused, are figuratively described solely in terms of the temporality of the poet/lover; not until late in the poem will we be given any sense of whether the renewal of the poet/lover's desire is connected to any person. *Intermissa*, preceding *bella* (2), the noun it modifies, by several words, and first qualified by *diu*, establishes this dominance of a private temporality, focusing attention not on any actual activities that his recent quietude might have interrupted, but rather on the agent's sense of his own time in relation to the erotic. Indeed, *intermissa*, by seeming, until *bella* appears, to modify *Venus*, produces the sense that it is the poet/lover's relation to Venus (rather than his relation to any actual beloved) that has been interrupted.[16]

Of course, we do not learn until later in the poem that the poet/lover is actually still experiencing desire, but Venus' attempt to enlist him in new battles suggests that the conflict between the poet/lover's desire and his sense of his present situation is what is at issue here. While *diu* indicates that it has been a long time since Venus has assailed the poet, the meaning of *intermissa* (temporarily abandoned) contains the implication that she will return in the future, a future which by the present time of the poem has already arrived. Thus, the encounter with Venus is significant primarily because it forces the poet/lover to confront his own temporality; for the lover, desire poses a threat because it disrupts the comfortable certainty that he knows his place in time.

That place in time is, however, curiously void of any specificity. The poet/lover's request that Venus spare him (*parce precor, precor* 2), made emphatic through the use of alliteration and anaphora, seems almost desperate in its insistence that any change of the present "interruption" would be loss. But the phrase *non sum qualis eram* (3) (I am not as I was), in which the poet/lover contrasts his present self with his self of the past "when Cinara ruled him,"[17] empties the present self of any significance beyond a (negative) relation to the past. This lack of clarity about what, precisely, the poet/lover will lose if Venus fails to spare him heightens the sense of privacy that marks the disruptive appearance of Venus. The poet/lover's identity in the present has meaning only in relation to *his* memories of what he was in the past, and while the plea to Venus suggests that this present identity is something the poet/lover values, that suggestion is undermined by the rhetorical suggestion that the present has meaning only in relation to the mysterious way he once was (*qualis eram*), which has been interrupted.

With *desine . . . flectere* (4–6) the poet/lover extends the sense of *parce* (spare me) by trying to clarify what is at stake in the appearance of Venus. The ominous and seductive power implied by the characterization of Venus as *dulcium /mater saeva Cupidinum* (4–5), when set against the poet/lover's admission that he is fifty years old, seems designed to heighten the pathos of the poet/lover's predicament. The poet/lover seems buffeted by the competing demands of time and desire: his age produces an expectation of declining desire, but this expectation is futile in the face of Venus' sweet savagery. However, this easy evocation of pathos, centered on the plea for Venus to "stop" (*desine*) luring him, becomes complicated if we consider the very different use of *desine* both in *Odes* 1.23.11, when Chloe is urged to stop following her mother, and in *Odes* 3.15.4, when Chloris is told to stop cavorting among the young. In each case, an object of desire is told to stop (*desine*) whatever she is currently doing because her actions conflict with the poet/lover's notion of the socially proper temporal progress of desire. Chloe must stop clinging to her mother because her life has arrived at the time when she should submit to the desires of a man; Chloris must cease her seductions not merely because she is married, but because such a role must now be left to her daughter. In contrast to this sense of a social or public determination of what is temporally proper, in *Odes* 4.1 *desine* evokes only the poet/lover's *own* sense of his temporality. While Venus may be blamed for luring him back to erotic battles, whether he succumbs to that lure is an entirely private matter, standing outside any public judgment of what is proper.[18]

The privacy of the poet/lover's response to erotic feelings remains in force even as he becomes more precise about his own temporal situation. The issue of aging, addressed only in relative terms in *non sum qualis eram*, becomes explicit when the poet/lover explains that he is fifty years old (*circa lustra decem* 6) and thus "unresponsive" to the "gentle commands" of Venus. This insistence that he is too old for love, which concludes with the plea that Venus instead go to the young who are calling for her with flattering prayers (*abi / quo blandae iuvenum te revocant preces* 7–8), initiates the lengthy account (9–28) of why Venus is likely to have more success with the young. But the seeming contrast between the readiness of the young for erotic adventures and the poet/lover's own aging detachment is undermined by the fact that both the poet/lover and the youth are defined by their erotic feelings. We can see this in the way that the *blandae . . . preces* of the youth to Venus repeat the older poet/lover's prayer for Venus to go (*precor, precor*). While the specific relation the poet/lover and the youth have to Venus is clearly different (the youths "flatter" her while the poet/lover pleads to be "spared"), what is common is the centrality of eroticism as itself what determines identity: the difference between the responses to Venus seems less important than the suggestion that both the youth and the supposedly aged poet/lover do in fact understand themselves in relation to the eroticism that Venus represents. This centrality of eroticism blurs the distinction between youth and age upon which the poet/lover bases his own claim that his age makes him powerless to respond to Venus, and thus subtly anticipates the admission in the poem's conclusion than the poet/lover's age is irrelevant to erotic desire.

Nonetheless, the account of Paulus and the worship of Venus that his desire makes possible does insist that the poet/lover lacks the erotic capacity of those to whom Venus is now told to turn. Venus' celebrants will now be young (*teneris* 26) and beautiful (*candido* 27), and Venus will herself find a more suitable reception at Paulus' house than the poet/lover can offer.[19] By placing this worship of Venus in the future, the poet/lover distances himself even further from eroticism, for if he is not now the man he once was, he presumably would be even less so in the future. This distinction between the erotic readiness of Paulus and the poet/lover is emphasized in the language that describes Paulus. The comparative adverb *tempestivius*[20] (9), used of Venus' "more timely" approach to Paulus, heightens the temporal contrast between the poet/lover and Paulus, while the placement of *purpureis* (10), which grammatically modifies *oloribus*, directly after *Pauli*, combined with the alliterative effect of *Pauli purpureis*, joins to Paulus, by association, the ruddy glow of youth.[21] *Puer* (15) further reinforces the temporal appropriateness of Paulus. The extensive military glory Paulus will gain will be in the service of Venus (*tuae* 16), from whose battles the poet has asked to be excused. Finally, the sexual connotations of the words used to describe Paulus' ability to set up a marble statue of Venus (*potentior* 17, more able, potent; and *trabe* 20, beam, penis) suggest that Paulus surpasses the poet/lover in sexual as well as financial resources.[22]

Initially, the shift in focus back to the poet/lover (announced by the prominent position of *me* at the beginning of line 29) seems merely to repeat the claim at the beginning of the poem that the poet/lover is too old for eroticism. The poet/lover's lack of interest in either woman or boy (29) distances him from the boys and girls who honor Venus in the lines immediately preceding (25–28), and his distaste for wine and garlands (31–32) sets him apart from the cele-bratory activities implied by *comissabere* (11).[23] But this emphasis on the flagging desire that presumably comes with age is complicated by *iam nec spes animi credula mutui* (30), which suggests less temporal inevitability than doubt about whether eroticism can be shared.[24] The credulity that the poet/lover says he has lost seems less a result of aging than of actual experiences, but, of course, the poem has offered no sense of what those experiences might have been. Fur-ther, while the contrast between the poet/lover and the young has until now rested on the claim that the young have a capacity for eroticism that the poet/lover has lost, here instead the implicit con-trast is between success and failure at establishing a mutuality of feeling. But nothing in the description of Paulus or Venus' other young worshippers implied such mutuality, beyond the fact that both boys and girls are joined in an ecstatic worship of Venus. What this suggests is that the insistence upon aging as having removed the poet/lover from erotic battles conceals an anxiety about the relation of the poet/lover's erotic feelings to others. While we have noted in other poems how temporality poses a threat to the autono-mous control of the lover, here instead temporality seems to func-tion as a dimension of experience that preserves autonomy, because it allows a position outside the needs or demands of others. Further, this sense of eroticism as posing a demand for mutuality that seems inconceivable prepares for the particular shape eroticism takes in the final lines of the poem, for there the threat of mutuality is met by locating eroticism in a purely imagined space, which is as safely autonomous as old age had promised to be.

This sense of fear at the risks posed by shared eroticism is sig-naled by the substitution of Ligurinus for Venus as the object of the poet/lover's fears. Where the plea at the beginning of the poem for

Venus to "spare him" located the poet/lover's dilemma solely in terms of his own sense of the proper role that eroticism should play in the life of someone his age, now instead the dilemma is focused on the relation of his desires to their object. Venus poses no real threat to the poet/lover's privacy, to his autonomy, because her power to awaken his desire itself merely confirms the essential privacy of his self-understanding. Venus threatens the particular conception the poet/lover has of himself as too old for desire, but leaves untouched his ability to conceive of his life independently of the needs and desires of others.

In contrast, Ligurinus' position outside the poet/lover's own contemplation of desire evokes, at least for a moment, a public world in which the lover's desires are complicated not merely by his own sense of the temporally proper, but equally by the response of the beloved to his desires. The initial response to this threat to the autonomy of the poet/lover's desires is to present the dynamic of lover and beloved as a thoroughly conventional romantic melodrama in which the beloved's position outside the desires of the poet/lover produces tears, lapses into silence, and repeated lamentation (*cur . . . cur . . . cur* 33, 35).[25] But these conventional signs of the lovesick condition, acknowledging even if only negatively the power of the beloved to disrupt the poet/lover's autonomy, are suddenly and dramatically replaced by an erotic dream where quite literally nothing exists outside the poet/lover's desire.[26]

The earlier fear that his age precluded erotic pursuit now dissolves into the timeless simultaneity of a dream, where both possession and pursuit occur in a "now" far removed from actual human temporality: *iam captum teneo, iam volucrem sequor* (38) (I now hold you captured, now pursue you, swift). The pursuit itself recovers for the poet/lover the strength (and implicitly the military might as well) that had previously been seen as the province of the young.[27] Most important, the positioning of Ligurinus as nothing more than an object of desire obviates any need for the alarming mutuality that eroticism had earlier been said to require. In the final line of the poem, even the resistance of Ligurinus participates in the general sense of triumph over the dangers that eroticism poses. The description of Ligurinus as *dure* (40) (hard-hearted), by echoing the earlier characterization of the poet/lover's inability to respond to Venus (*iam durum* 7), suggests a transference from the poet/lover to Ligurinus of anxiety about eroticism. While we are given no sense of what provokes Ligurinus' hard-heartedness, it seems fair to suggest that at least for the poet/lover, the recalcitrance of his beloved, by shifting the onus of erotic doubt from internal uncertainty to external resistance, allows an uncomplicated certainty about his own desires. In the private space of dreams, the mutuality of eroticism troubles only the beloved, and the lover is himself able to discover a certainty about his desires that actual experience had threatened to preclude.

But of course, that certainty is itself conditioned on the privacy of the resolution the dream offers. Whatever suggestion there might have been earlier in the poem that desire is somehow incongruent with the inevitability of aging has disappeared, for the poet/lover finds in the dream a freedom of eroticism that no temporal inevitability can challenge. In a sense, temporality poses the same threat to the autonomy of the poet/lover as mutuality, for in each case his own power of self-determination is challenged by something that lies outside his control. But such a threat, rather than provoking a rethinking of identity, instead occasions little more than ambivalence about whether personal identity should be determined by time or desire. The poet/lover's expression of unease about the continuation of desire beyond what is temporally proper can be seen, at the end of the poem, to be little more than a conflict between his thoughts about the proper course a life should take and his feelings of desire, which challenge such propriety. But in the case of both thoughts and feelings, nothing external to the poet/lover has any real significance. The contrast here to the way in which the temporality of the beloved is typically constructed by Horace is striking. For the beloved, temporality is the dimension of experience that is most fully defined by the desires of the lover, while here instead the poet/lover's temporality serves merely to complicate his own certainty about who he is. The dream is an ideal image of how such certainty might be restored, for in his dream the poet/lover can recover the privacy that time and mutuality threaten and can thus find a place where his desire can triumph over any self-doubt.

 Odes 4.13

> Audivere, Lyce, di mea vota, di
> audivere, Lyce: fis anus; et tamen

vis formosa videri
   ludisque et bibis impudens
et cantu tremulo pota Cupidinem   5
lentum sollicitas. ille virentis et
   doctae psallere Chiae
      pulchris excubat in genis.
importunus enim transvolat aridas
quercus et refugit te, quia luridi   10
   dentes, te, quia rugae
      turpant et capitis nives.
nec Coae referunt iam tibi purpurae
nec cari lapides tempora quae semel
   notis condita fastis   15
      inclusit volucris dies.
quo fugit Venus, heu, quove color, decens
quo motus? quid habes illius, illius
   quae spirabat amores,
      quae me surpuerat mihi,   20
felix post Cinaram notaque et artium
gratarum facies? sed Cinarae brevis
   annos fata dederunt,
      servatura diu parem
cornicis vetulae temporibus Lycen,   25
possent ut iuvenes visere fervidi
   multo non sine risu
      dilapsam in cineres facem.

The gods, Lyce, have heard my prayers, Lyce, they have heard them: you are turning into an old woman; and still you want to seem attractive and you play and drink without shame and drunk you try to arouse an unresponsive Cupid with tremulous song. He stands guard for the lovely cheeks of young Chia skilled at playing the lyre. Indeed, unaccommodating, he flies past dry oaks and flees from you, because yellow teeth, wrinkles, and snowy-white hair disfigure you. No longer do Coan purple and expensive jewels bring back for you the time that winged day has confined in famous annals buried forever. Where has your Venus fled? Alas, or where the beauty and the attractive moves? What do you have of that one, of that one who used to breathe forth love, who had stolen me from myself, who was fortunate after Cinara and a well-known beauty of charming talents? But the fates gave few years to Cinara, intending to preserve Lyce for a long time, equal to the age of an old crow, so that the fervid youth might view her, not without much laughter, as a torch collapsed into ashes.

In *Odes* 2.8 we saw how the public spectacle of Barine's continuing (and even increasing) sexuality and desirability over time, continuing despite her lack of faithfulness to her lovers, was seen as a threat to the social order. Temporality, rather than limiting her behavior, functioned merely as additional evidence of her "disturbing" power. In *Odes* 4.1 temporality is also seen to have failed to control the erotic, but there the failure of such control, because it occurs only privately, is not only removed from disapproval, but is even supposed to elicit sympathy for the plight of the speaker as he struggles with his feelings of desire. In *Odes* 4.13, this distinction between understanding the beloved as defined by public assumptions about temporality and the lover solely in terms of his own desires warrants special attention, for it is central to the speaker's initial certainty that the passage of time has ensured his triumph over the threat that Lyce's desirability once posed to his sense of self. Where Barine's position outside of time robbed the speaker of any secure sense of his identity, here instead Lyce's aging promises to restore to the poet/lover the autonomy that her earlier desirability had threatened. Because Lyce's temporality has meaning solely in relation to the desires of others, her aging now renders her completely vulnerable to public ridicule. On the other hand, such ridicule seems to offer the poet/lover the possibility of surmounting his earlier rejection by Lyce and thus recovering control over his own temporality.

However, this strategy of securing autonomy by envisioning the beloved as defined by public assumptions about the inevitability of time risks losing precisely the immunity from time that the poet/lover seeks. The poet/lover hopes that he will regain his sense of self (and thus free himself from the past) by contrasting the painful desires he once felt with the disgust that she now evokes. But the difficulty with this strategy is its success—if Lyce is really nothing more than an object of scorn because of the effects of time, then the poet/lover's secure (private) sense of himself as a desirer is threatened because he has to see himself *now* in relation to what Lyce has become. Thus, Lyce's age, far from securing the poet/lover's hopes

for a triumph over the past, instead threatens to destroy his auton-
omy by robbing him of certainty about his own capacity to desire.
His difference from Lyce (and thus his triumph over her) will be
established by what time is now doing to her, the assumption being
that he somehow stands outside this process. But his reliance on
Lyce as the source of how he understands himself enmeshes him in
the very temporality that was to have been the basis of his difference
from her, for her present state shatters his certainty about what she
must have been like (and what he must have been like) in order for
desire to have been so powerful.

The difficulty produced by the poet/lover's effort to define himself
in relation to Lyce is thus that while he needs Lyce to age in order to
recover the sense of self that she once threatened, that very aging
causes him to lose as well an essential component of his autonomy,
which is his sense of continuity with the past. His triumph over Lyce
is necessary only if he is himself still the person he once was; how-
ever, his recognition that his connection to his past identity can
happen only through memory leaves him as enmeshed in time as
Lyce, both of them now being defined by temporal difference (his
difference from the past, hers from the desires of others). Realizing
that Lyce's desirability is now only a memory leaves him as vulner-
able to temporality as she is; the only difference is that her vul-
nerability will be played out in a public forum, while his will occur in
the privacy of recollection.

The double temporal perspective that results from this merging of
past and present is established within the first two lines of *Odes*
4.13.[28] The tense of *audivere* (1) immediately introduces the past into
the poem, while its perfect aspect, combined with the vocative ad-
dress to Lyce, establishes the poem in the present. The vows (*vota* 1),
direct object of *audivere*, while made in the past, looked toward
fulfillment in a future that is the present of the poem. The notion of
"becoming" inherent in the meaning of the verb *fio* makes *fis anus* (2)
(you are turning into an old woman) include not only the present,
through its tense, but also, by implication, the past and future.
Thus, the present seems to promise to the poet/lover a time when
his own past desires for triumph over Lyce might be fulfilled, and
what enables such triumph is the contrast between the present as a
confirmation of the poet/lover's vows and the present as a moment
in Lyce's decline. For the poet/lover, the answering of his prayers,
which is signaled by Lyce's decline, allows the temporal progression

of past and present to be replaced by an alternative conception of time as the fulfillment of desire: in a sense, Lyce's immersion in a world of becoming enables the poet/lover to establish for himself what we might call a space of desire uncontaminated by time.

However, the poet/lover's assertion that the formerly desired future has now become the present is complicated by how intertwined his own desires are with the temporality through which he seeks to distinguish himself from Lyce. Past, present, and future are merged for the poet/lover only because the answering of his prayers unifies time in a way that is distinct from Lyce's aging. But such a distinction between the poet/lover and Lyce is undermined by the role that memory plays in establishing Lyce's decline. The poet/lover's mocking words are made possible not only because of what he sees in the present of Lyce's erotic behavior, but, more importantly, because his own memories establish such behavior as a sad perversion of her former ways. This sense of contrast between Lyce as she is now and as she once was is in part established by echoes in *Odes* 4.13 of the description of Lyce as a desirable woman in *Odes* 3.10.[29]

Thus, while in *Odes* 3.10.17 the image of Lyce as "not softer than a rigid oak" (*nec rigida mollior aesculo*) shows her proud ability to resist unwanted lovers, in *Odes* 4.13 the oak is no longer firm but has become mere "dry oak [leaves]" (*aridas quercus* 9–10). When Lyce appears in *Odes* 3.10, she is presented as hard-hearted and unyielding to the ardent poet/lover stretched out at her doorstep. In *Odes* 4.13 the situation is seen as reversed; Lyce, grown older, and forced to encourage sexual response in her potential admirers, is depicted by the speaker as pitifully unsuccessful. At the end of *Odes* 3.10, the poet/lover suddenly declares that he will not put up with being rejected by Lyce forever, and this hope that time will provide the means for surmounting her rejection is now apparently confirmed by the answering of his prayers. But the very reliance upon memories of what Lyce once was as the basis for the poet/lover's present sense of triumph calls into question his separation from the temporality that now destroys Lyce's desirability, for his use of memory as the means of establishing her decline insists upon the temporality of his own experience.

The impossibility of the poet/lover's establishing a clear demarcation between his own experience and the forces that now define Lyce is perhaps most obvious in his comparison of Lyce to Chia.

What is at issue here is the perspective from which this comparison is to be understood. The poet/lover locates his distinction between Lyce—with her yellow teeth, wrinkles, and white hair—and the blossoming, beautiful-cheeked Chia in terms of Lyce's absurd desire to remain beautiful (*vis formosa videri* 3).[30] From the perspective of the poet/lover, Lyce's humiliating refusal to accept her present status confirms his own independence from her. Lyce's inability to comprehend that young women such as Chia have displaced her own erotic centrality serves not merely to diminish any power she might have held over the poet/lover, but also to confirm the poet/ lover's understanding of the present as a time defined by his desire to recover a sense of self, which, we learn later, Lyce had once stolen from him. But the evocation of desire, both negatively in the description of Lyce's appalling physicality, and positively in the account of Chia's talent and beauty, produces a second perspective—that of Cupid— which will itself raise questions about how securely the poet/lover's desires have been separated from Lyce.[31]

Lyce's vain effort to arouse "unresponsive Cupid" (*Cupidinem lentum* 5–6), when set in contrast to Cupid's role of guardian for Chia (*ille* . . . *excubat* 6–8), places Cupid in a position that seems identical to that of the poet/lover—each of them rejects Lyce as an adequate object of desire. But this seeming parallel between Cupid and the poet/lover breaks down when we consider the dramatically different consequences that follow each of their rejections of Lyce. For Cupid, Chia offers the possibility of his performing his function not just as the god of love, but also more graphically as an indicator of desire.[32] The description of *Cupido* as *lentus* ("slow," "limp," "unresponsive") suggests that the aging Lyce no longer arouses physical desire or, more specifically, a quick erection.[33] While *excubat* can mean "keeps watch," befitting either a guardian or an excluded lover, with *Cupido* specifically sexualized and appearing in the context of *lentus* and *sollicito*,[34] both clearly sexual terms, *excubat* (8) also takes an erotic sense. The description of Cupid establishes a contrast between the penis's reaction to Lyce and to Chia. For Lyce, it is limp and needs stimulation; but with Chia, it "remains awake or stands guard" (*excubat*), that is, stays erect merely as a result of being in her presence.[35]

Odes 4.13.6–8 recalls the choral ode to Eros in Sophocles' *Antigone* (783–84):[36]

ὅς ἐν μαλακαῖς παρειαῖς νεάνιδος ἐννυχεύεις

[Eros], you who sleep in a young girl's soft cheeks . . .

However Horace does not translate ἐννυχεύεις into Latin, which would be the simple verb *cubo* ("sleep with"); rather he uses *excubo* ("be vigilant"), which has almost the opposite meaning of the Greek.[37] Horace is clearly interested in recalling the Sophoclean description of Eros, but also in reshaping it with the more pointed sense that desire (or the penis) remains alert (stays erect).

But whose desire? As we saw, for the poet/lover the primary significance of the distinction between Lyce and Chia was not the physicality of response that each might allow, but rather the way in which the distinction itself provided further evidence of time's destruction of Lyce's power. For Cupid, on the other hand, Lyce's decline leads merely to the new possibilities of arousal offered by Chia, producing an almost timeless sense of continuous desire—objects of desire may come and go, but desire itself remains constant. Genuine triumph over Lyce would seem best achieved through such constancy of desire, and thus it is worth considering why the poet/lover retreats from the scorn that was partly enabled by the evocation of Cupid, to the nostalgia and lamentation that mark the remainder of the poem.

The comparison of Lyce with Chia seems designed to situate both women, as objects of desire, in a public realm in relation to which the poet/lover is free to discover a privately determined sense of his own identity. The power that Lyce had over the poet/lover is diminished, not by any actions he might have undertaken, but rather because of the effects of an impersonal temporality upon her desirability. What seems important here is how such impersonal temporality allows the poet/lover an autonomy that real connection with Lyce would preclude—precisely because Lyce inhabits a different realm of experience than his own, the poet/lover can use mockery of Lyce's plight as the basis of his own recovery of self. But such recovery requires a genuine sense of autonomy, of a privacy of self-definition, which the contrast between Cupid and the poet/lover calls into question. For reasons that the poem makes clear, the timeless identity of unmediated desire, which we might associate with Cupid, is unavailable to the poet/lover, who must himself now confront a much more complicated sense than he has yet offered of his relation to Lyce. What is central to this new sense of relation is a change in how Lyce is herself understood. The comparison of Lyce to the young Chia gives way to a contrast between Lyce and her own former self, a contrast that the poet/lover will be forced to see precludes any clear distinction in how he and Lyce are located in time.

The basis of the contrast between Lyce's present and former selves is the poet/lover's admission that Lyce "had stolen me from myself" (*quae me surpuerat mihi* 20), the hope being that the difference between what she once was and what she has become will allow that self to be regained. Indeed, in a sense, the entire poem is an attempt to recover what was once stolen, but where earlier the poet/lover had seen his self as somehow existing completely autonomously from Lyce, now instead that earlier theft of self is imaged as central to any present sense of self that might be possible. The poet/lover wants to regain the self that was once taken from him, but the desire that impels such a want itself depends upon its knowledge of the past, and thus its complicity with time. The very desire to recover what Lyce once stole is made possible only if the poet/lover is himself implicated in the temporality that had promised to free him from Lyce. The poet/lover's gathering recognition that he and Lyce are both creatures of time seems responsible for the shift in tone from bitter triumph over Lyce's diminished status—*Audivere, Lyce, di mea vota, di / audivere, Lyce* (1–2) (The gods, Lyce, have heard my prayers, Lyce, they have heard them)—to nostalgic remembrance. While the repetition of lines 1–2 has a taunting quality, the persistent *quo . . . quo . . . quo . . .* of lines 17–18 has a tone of mixed disbelief and desperation; still further, the repeated *illius, illius* (18) has a mournful, wistful quality enhanced by the imperfect aspect of *spirabat* (19), which has the effect of extending the image of the time during which Lyce was desirable. While the language used to describe Cupid's flight from the older Lyce (*transvolat* 9, *refugit* 10) is echoed in the words used to describe Lyce's lost desirability (*quo fugit Venus . . . ?* 17) and in the characterization of the passage of time as swift (*volucris dies* 16), there is a dramatic difference between Cupid's easy transference of desire to Chia and the poet/lover's almost obsessive attention to time's effect on Lyce. Underlying the entire shift in emotion is an implicit recognition by the poet/lover that he seeks to recover not just a self, but the desire that once defined that self. The laughter of the *iuvenes . . . fervidi* (26), far from confirming the poet/lover's recovery of a self that Lyce cannot steal, instead evokes a temporal distance from Lyce's desirability, which for the poet/lover can be experienced only as loss.

However, it is important to note that the experience of loss that occasions the change in emotional tone does not in any sense produce sympathy for Lyce's plight, nor any genuine sense of recognition of a shared dilemma. The pain that the poet/lover experiences in remembering Lyce has its source only in a private sense of loss that the object that once inspired such passion has been wrecked by the passage of time. The contrast between Lyce and Cinara emphasizes the degree to which the poet/lover's loss is itself immune to the publicly defined effects of time upon a woman's desirability. For women who are objects of desire, the sole alternative to the mockery of the youth, which Lyce now faces, is apparently the early death that came to Cinara, while for the poet/lover there is instead the bitter and melancholy satisfaction of memory. Time functions with a ruthless linearity for objects of desire, while for the desiring self there is instead the solace of remembrance, which at least establishes a realm of experience that stands outside public scrutiny.

The incompatibility of eroticism and temporality presents the woman with a stark fate: either she dies young while her value as an object of desire is secure, or she loses her status as such an object as temporality itself comes to define her experience. But in either case, it is her public status as an object of desire that determines her identity, for in each case, her self is itself the consequence of its position in a temporality defined solely by the desires of others. For the poet/lover, on the other hand, temporality has meaning solely in relation to his own desires. While his own aging obviously implicates him in the very temporality that is the basis of his scorn for Lyce, what is clear in the poem is how protected he is from any public judgment of that temporality. What is judged publicly is desirability, while desire itself remains securely private.

Thus, the poet/lover's separation because of age from the *iuvenes . . . fervidi*[38]—the fervid youth who will laugh at Lyce, "a torch collapsed into ashes"[39]—does not imply a current shared experience of aging with Lyce, but rather indicates only the poet/lover's isolation from his own former experience of desire. Indeed, the laughter of the youth, by renewing the speaker's tone of ridicule earlier in the poem, suggests a unity between the speaker and the youth, whose eroticism will one day presumably become the melancholy of the older poet/lover.[40] Further, the poet/lover's sense of loss (and the corresponding recognition of his own temporality, which it causes) is occasioned not by any real connection with what Lyce has become, but only by a sense that she has changed. What seems important here is that the poet/lover understands Lyce's present condition solely in terms of specific features of her body that are subject to change, but not in any sense as a person who herself has a relation to what she once was. Indeed, his own sense of loss itself depends upon this distinction, for what allows him to indulge his melancholy is a sense of solitude that itself is possible only because Lyce's identity has been so sharply delimited. The poem does indeed invite sympathy with the melancholy of the poet/lover, but such sympathy requires accepting that desire itself is significant only in a private realm that has no real relation to the person who is desired.

FIVE

The Romantic Ideal

and the Domination of

the Beloved

While seemingly far from the *Odes*, the romantic ideal of a never-ending and never-changing love is in fact central to the recurring insistence in the *Odes* that the difficulties of eroticism stem from a failure on the part of lovers to control their own and their beloveds' temporality. We have seen this failure to control temporality appear in various forms in each of the previous three chapters. In chapter 2 we saw the difficulties that result from trying to distinguish between the temporality of the lover and the beloved. In chapter 3 we noted how the effort to establish a "season" of eroticism is little more than a strategy for denying the beloved's own temporality. Finally, in chapter 4, we saw how differently the distinction between youth and age functions in characterizing the eroticism of the lover and the beloved. In each case, the romantic ideal of a timeless love seems on the surface to be rejected in favor of a more ironic or realistic view of the inevitability of time. But in fact, the very characterization of time as a threat to eroticism reinscribes the value of timelessness itself, and as we have seen, that value is most frequently represented as the dominance the lover would gain through defeating time. Thus, insisting on the power of temporality to defeat an idealized view of love produces less a rethinking of love than a bitterness at those elements of temporality—most obviously, the recalcitrant temporality of the beloved—that stand in the way of the lover's triumph over time.[1]

In this chapter I explore the role that such an attitude toward

temporality plays in the construction of the erotic, focusing specifi-
cally on how romantic ideals are joined to the belief that temporality
poses a threat to eroticism. Regardless of whether temporality is
seen to threaten love, or is seen to expose the absurdity of love, in
either case what is at issue is the assumption that the erotic must
itself be understood as seeking an unworldly timelessness.

This notion is clearest in *Odes* 2.9, where we shall see that the overt
message of the poem that a romantic ideal of everlasting love must be
replaced by a more realistic acceptance of temporal change is under-
mined by the way in which the language used to characterize the
realistic view evokes the very ideals that are being challenged. Fur-
ther, the solution that is proposed to the inevitable failure of eroti-
cism—a celebration of Augustus' military triumphs—offers less an
openness to the risks of temporality than a depiction of a scene in
which the lover's dream of dominance can be fulfilled. This sense
that dominance lies at the heart of the romantic ideal also appears in
Odes 1.22, where the seeming parody of the conventions of romantic
love conceals the poet/lover's own desire to use those conventions as
a means of securing his control over the beloved. While both of these
poems reinforce the idea that temporality functions in Horace's love
poetry primarily as a threat to the lover's power, in the final two
poems I examine—*Odes* 1.13 and 3.9—that sense of temporality is
replaced by an alternative conception, which finds in temporality the
possibility of reconceiving the central terms of the erotic. This may
seem a puzzling claim to make about *Odes* 1.13, given how clearly the
poem seems to emphasize precisely the sense of threat to the poet/
lover's identity that we have noted so frequently. However, here this
sense of threat produces not a bitter retreat to a belief that eroticism is
futile, but rather an attempt to rethink what the basis of erotic
relationship might be. Much will depend here on how we read the
final strophe; while most critics read the strophe as offering an
enigmatic appeal to the very timelessness of love that the rest of the
poem seems to question, I shall argue instead that the rich ambiguity
of *irrupta* allows instead a reading that finds an openness to change
that the poet/lover's own rage and despair at his powerlessness over
change would preclude. Finally, in *Odes* 3.9, the entire dynamic of
conceiving eroticism solely from the perspective of the lover is re-
placed by a dialogue in which temporality functions as a medium
through which lover and beloved are able to define their relation-
ship. Here, the romantic ideal of timelessness, which seems finally to

produce only irony or despair, is abandoned decisively and what is suggested instead is a fragile recognition of temporality as the inescapable condition of erotic desire.

Odes 2.9

Non semper imbres nubibus hispidos
manant in agros aut mare Caspium
    vexant inaequales procellae
        usque, nec Armeniis in oris,
amice Valgi, stat glacies iners   5
mensis per omnis aut Aquilonibus
    querqueta Gargani laborant
        et foliis viduantur orni:
tu semper urges flebilibus modis
Mysten ademptum, nec tibi Vespero   10
    surgente decedunt amores
        nec rapidum fugiente solem.
at non ter aevo functus amabilem
ploravit omnis Antilochum senex
    annos, nec impubem parentes   15
        Troilon aut Phrygiae sorores
flevere semper. desine mollium
tandem querelarum et potius nova
    cantemus Augusti tropaea
        Caesaris et rigidum Niphaten   20
Medumque flumen gentibus additum
victis minores volvere vertices
    intraque praescriptum Gelonos
        exiguis equitare campis.

Not always do rains flow from clouds onto rough fields or do variable storms trouble the Caspian sea continuously, nor on the Armenian shores, friend Valgius, does the ice stand immobile through all the months or do the oaks of Mt. Garganus labor under the Aquilonian winds and are the ash trees made bereft of their leaves: you always press on about lost Mystes in mournful ways, nor for you does love cease with the evening star rising nor with it fleeing the rapid sun. But the old man who lived three generations did not mourn for his lovable son Antilochus all the years, nor did his parents or Phrygian sisters always weep for young Troilus. Stop at last your soft laments and let us sing rather of the recent victories of Augustus Caesar and icebound Niphates and the river of the Medes added to the conquered peoples rolling with smaller eddies and the Geloni riding on meager fields within their prescribed area.

Odes 2.9 has traditionally been interpreted as an attack by Horace on the excessive involvement with the beloved, which typifies elegiac poetry, and there is, indeed, much in the poem that supports such a reading.[2] Valgius' loss of Mystes has occasioned a mourning whose real basis is Valgius' belief in the romantic ideal of a beloved who can remain free of temporality, and the speaker, in advising Valgius to abandon his grief, is accordingly rejecting the notion of such an ideal. In place of this ideal, the speaker instead invokes a world defined by the reality of time, and tries to show Valgius how such a world might allow loss to be seen simply as an inevitable feature of human experience.

But what such an opposition of Valgius' deluded romanticism to the speaker's realism misses is how the two perspectives share a basic assumption that desire itself seeks to dominate what is desired. Valgius' loss of Mystes signals his failure to control the temporality of his beloved, and the speaker of the poem chastises Valgius, not for his desire for such control, but rather for his failure to accept that temporality itself cannot be controlled. The acknowledgment of temporality does not, for the speaker, require any rethinking of the desire for control, but rather serves as a necessary reminder of where such control might be sought. Indeed, much of the poem implicitly accepts the validity of Valgius' mourning by proposing alternatives that simply mirror the desire for control, which defines Valgius' own view of love. Thus, as we shall see, the examples from nature and of human mourning fail to address the threat that temporality poses to eroticism, while the description of the world under Augustus evokes a form of dominance that even time seems unable to threaten. In each case, the speaker's advice, far from offering Valgius a genuine alternative to his excessive grief, instead reinforces the idealized view of love as a desire for control, which has produced Valgius' mourning.[3]

The poem begins (lines 1–8) with examples from the natural world (specifically, bad weather—rain on the land, stormy winds at sea, wintry ice, and trees laboring under the wind), which are meant to show Valgius that in nature disturbance does not last forever (*non semper* 1). The comfort these examples offer, however, is deceptive— the notion that because even the upheavals of nature come to an end, Valgius himself should stop what is later in the poem called his soft laments (*mollium . . . querelarum* 17–18)[4] ignores how starkly different human temporality is from the cyclicity of nature. As we noted earlier,[5] the repetition that marks the cyclical changes in nature has no analogue in the linear temporality of human experience.

Indeed, while Valgius is apparently supposed to draw strength from the presumed analogy between his mourning and such natural phenomena as storms or ice, the language of the poem can instead be seen to emphasize how firmly separated he is from such natural occurrences. While natural phenomena are characterized here as functioning within an almost invisible causality of natural necessity—there is certainty that the condition of the stationary ice or the leafless ash trees will improve (*non semper*)—the explicit address to Valgius as "friend" (*amice*) instead points to the fragile contingency of human relations. Natural phenomena have relation only to the impersonal forces that ensure cyclical renewal, while humans are instead defined by the uncertain temporality of their relations to other humans. Valgius can be a "friend" only while both he and the speaker are alive, while the cyclicity of nature instead ensures that even death presages only renewal. Thus, what we can see suggested in the contrast between nature and Valgius as a "friend" is why the appeal to nature as a source of human comfort must fail. The repetition or cyclicity of nature denies the vulnerability of the human being, whose life is linear, and yet it is precisely such vulnerability that has occasioned Valgius' grief.

The personification that marks the examples from nature seems designed to bridge this gap between the human and the natural, but its effect is rather to reinstate the terms of Valgius' mourning.[6] Valgius' grief has been caused not merely by the loss of a beloved, but more importantly by the sense that such loss exposes the futility of erotic love when it is confronted by the changes that temporality inflicts. For Valgius, despair is the sole resource for preserving the erotic love that time has destroyed, and it is thus ironic that the examples from nature—which are supposed to suggest an alternative to Valgius' clinging to what has been lost—replicate precisely this sense of emotional turmoil.

We can begin by noting how the language used in the descriptions of nature seems deliberately to evoke human dimensions of experience. Thus, *imbres nubibus hispidos / manant in agros* (1–2), while indicating the falling of rain upon the fields, is equally evocative of mourning, for *imber*, a common word for rain, is not infrequently used of tears as well.[7] This use of language applicable to both weather and grief continues with *nubibus* (clouds) with its figurative meanings of something that "clouds" one's physical demeanor, like a gloomy expression, or something that "clouds" one's mental state, like sorrow.[8] While the modification of *agros* by *hispidos* literally signifies the roughness of the land, in keeping with the example of stormy weather, Horace is drawing as well upon the most common meaning of *hispidus*: covered with hair, shaggy, rough, hence "bearded."[9] Complementing the double sense of *hispidos* is that of *manare* (to flow, drip, spread), which can be used of rain and tears alike.[10] Rain spreading through the fields completes the weather image, while *manare* as "the flowing of tears" concludes the image of a weeping, bearded face. Since *procellae* can mean "emotions or passions" as well as "storms," *inaequales procellae* suggests an "uneven" emotional state.[11] Still further, *vexant* signifies disturbance both physical and mental, thus allowing *mare Caspium* to be taken both literally as the sea itself, or figuratively, as the sea of the emotions.[12] The image of static ice (*stat glacies iners*) is personified through the use of erotic vocabulary,[13] while the laboring of the oak trees in the wind suggests the "laboring" of love.[14] Finally, Valgius' erotic loss is evoked by the image of the ash trees "bereft" of their leaves (*viduantur*).

But the replication of Valgius' state in the descriptions of nature goes beyond these merely verbal suggestions, for the very effort at establishing a natural temporality that might be contrasted to Valgius' own recoil from temporal change emphasizes precisely the sense of unrecoverable loss that underlies Valgius' despair. Thus, while the negation of the temporal expressions *semper* (1), *usque* (4), and *mensis per omnis* (6) is supposed to indicate an acceptance within nature of the inevitability of change, the actual changes described produce the sense that stasis has overwhelmed the negation that would establish temporality—the distance from the initial *non* of the temporal modifiers that introduce each of the examples has the effect of making the natural occurrences seem permanent. The temporality that the speaker seeks to invoke as a contrast to Valgius' grief recedes as the examples accumulate, and instead the examples themselves testify to the impossibility of temporality providing a solace for loss.

This sense that the examples function primarily as analogues of Valgius' own emotional state is heightened by the curious structure of conjunctions that join the examples. Because the examples are each meant to illustrate the ubiquity of change in nature, what we would expect is for each of them to be conjoined to the next by *nec*, which would establish the required parallelism to the initial *non semper*. But instead, only the example of the ice is conjoined by *nec*—the storms and the trees bent by the wind are conjoined by *aut*, which locates their meaning not in relation to the initial *non semper* but rather in relation to the immediately preceding example. This produces a gathering sense of connectedness among the examples, a kind of crescendo (not unlike the buildup of evidence against Barine in *Odes* 2.8 signaled by *adde quod*)[15] which culminates in the use of *et* to end the list of examples. Here, the conjunction serves not to refer the example back to the temporality of the initial *non semper*, but rather to link it merely aggregately to the previous examples of loss in nature. Thus, the final image of the ash trees bereft of their leaves suggests a solitary emptiness devoid of any temporal connection, an emptiness that seems to replicate exactly Valgius' own sense of loss.

This blurring of the distinction between the natural and the human continues in the final appeal to nature, where the speaker seeks to oppose the cyclical movement of the evening star and the sun to Valgius' resistance to time. He begins by insisting that Valgius' temporality is fundamentally different from that found in nature: where natural temporality is marked by the *non semper* (1) with which the poem begins, *tu semper* (9) instead characterizes Valgius' refusal to accept the passage of time. The distinction between *non* and *tu* would seem to suggest that the solution to Valgius' difficulties would be to open himself to temporality as a kind of negation of his own desires. While Valgius has sought to make his desires the basis of existence, in nature temporal change is itself the determinant of what exists—*tu semper* accordingly establishes the desiring self as immune to temporal change, while *non semper* instead would situate the self and its desires within a temporality that stands outside any control.

However, the implicit acknowledgment in this distinction of the need for desire to recognize temporality is undermined by the eroticism that underlies the description of the evening star and the sun. Valgius' desire for Mystes is supposed to seem unnaturally prolonged in that it fails to cease or "set" (*decedunt*) even when Vesper, the evening star, is rising (*Vespero / surgente* 10–11). But this contrast between Valgius and the evening star ignores how the relation between the evening star and the sun replicates Valgius' own refusal of temporality. *Urges* (9), which was used to describe Valgius' continuing erotic pursuit of Mystes,[16] suggests a view of the beloved as something to be possessed, even when the loss of the beloved has made possession literally impossible.[17] The description of the evening star and the sun, far from providing an alternative to such a model of eroticism, instead evokes the temporality that erotic possession seeks to overcome. Thus the evening star's rising (*Vespero / surgente*) and then fleeing from the rapid (rapacious?)[18] sun (*rapidum fugiente solem*) produces a sense of an unwilling beloved for whom temporality is the sole refuge from the demands of the lover. The evening star's disappearance as the sun appears seems exactly to mime the disappearance of Mystes, for in each case temporality is resisted by a figure that pursues the very thing that time has changed. This final evocation of nature, by representing temporal change as an object to be pursued, thus leaves in place the opposition between the lover's desire for domination and the temporality of the beloved as something that must be controlled, an opposition that is itself the basis of Valgius' mourning.

The poem next turns to examples from human experience that are meant to show Valgius how mourning might accept temporality, but because the examples have no connection to the erotic desire that impels Valgius' grief, they offer him no real alternative to his desire to control time. As epic figures, both Antilochus and Troilus are certainly dignified objects of grief—Antilochus, son of Nestor, dies a heroic death in battle while protecting his father's retreat,[19] while Troilus, son of Priam, is killed by the great hero Achilles.[20] However, the speaker provides no explanation of why Valgius' loss of Mystes should be seen as comparable to the grief caused by the deaths of Antilochus and Troilus, and insofar as Antilochus and Troilus are thought of in terms of epic heroism, it is difficult to see what the comparison might be. There is, however, an alternative way of conceiving the significance of Antilochus and Troilus, which is to point to their status as objects of male desire.[21] From this perspective, what is significant about the account of mourning that the speaker offers is how the difficulties of erotic loss are simply excluded.

In the accounts of both Antilochus and Troilus there are at least hints of their erotic status. The description of Antilochus as *amabilem*[22] (lovable) evokes the relationship between Antilochus and Achilles. In Homer it is Antilochus who brings the news of Patroclus' death to Achilles and who first comforts him,[23] and later writers such as Philostratus[24] make explicit the erotic nature of their relationship. Similarly, the description of Troilus as *impubem* (young, beardless) focuses attention on his lack of maturity, a quality that underlies the depiction of his desirability. Nisbet and Hubbard cite Strato, *Palatine Anthology* 12.191.4, for the use of Troilus as an exemplum for a boy still without a beard,[25] while Phrynicus describes the "light of love" in Troilus' ruddy cheeks, and Statius compares the lost male beloved of Flavius Ursus to Troilus.[26] In light of the sense of *hispidos* (1) as "bearded" discussed above, Troilus' beardlessness is noteworthy—just as the "bearded" image of mourning helped to reinscribe Valgius' mourning, so Troilus' immature body reinscribes the image of the lost Mystes.

But despite these suggestions of eroticism, the speaker's focus on the families of Antilochus and Troilus as appropriate models for Valgius' grief excludes precisely the desire for erotic control that underlies Valgius' feelings. Indeed, the choice of Nestor and Priam as examples of mourners seems deliberately to remove the mourning from any connection with erotic desire. Nestor is typically depicted as being of an age (*ter aevo functus . . . senex* 13–14) beyond sexual passion, while Priam is a standard symbol of worn-out sexuality.[27] This removal from eroticism would seem to underlie the fact that the mourners for Antilochus and Troilus are able to accept temporal limits (*non . . . ploravit omnis . . . annos* and *nec . . . semper*)— the loss of a family member, while tragic, leaves the surviving members of the family still in possession of their own identities, and thus allows them to accept their temporal distance from those who have died. The loss of a beloved, on the other hand, takes from the lover his identity as a self who can possess what he desires. Valgius continues to mourn his loss of Mystes because such mourning presumably allows at least the semblance of erotic possession, while if he were to abandon his grief because of the passage of time (as the mourners for Antilochus and Troilus do), he would be forced to abandon as well the self that can dominate what it desires.

In the final section of the poem (lines 17–24) the speaker proposes to Valgius a specific alternative to continual lamentation for Mystes, an alternative that will allow a recovery of the self that can dominate what it experiences. What the speaker proposes is that Valgius abandon his soft laments (*mollium . . . querelarum* 17–18) and that they both take up in writing the celebration of Augustus' recent victories (*et potius nova / cantemus Augusti tropaea / Caesaris* 18–20).[28] Considering Horace's identification of his talent with the "slender muse" rather than with the "grand muse" of military exploits (cf. *tenues grandia* in *Odes* 1.6.9), it is striking that he includes himself along with Valgius in potentially writing about the *nova . . . Augusti tropaea / Caesaris* (19–20). It suggests that writing can provide a kind of male solidarity in which erotic loss can be replaced by a celebration of military triumph.[29] Where earlier in the poem the speaker had criticized Valgius' mournful ways (*flebilibus modis* 9) as an inadequate response to loss, now songs in praise of Augustus will replace loss with the vicarious thrill of imperialist domination.

What is crucial to note is how this solution to Valgius' difficulties implicitly grants his own desire to exist independently of temporality. In both the descriptions of nature and the examples of mourning for Antilochus and Troilus, the speaker sought to evoke a sense of human experience as itself intertwined with an uncontrollable temporality. We can now see that at least one reason for the inadequacy of this effort at describing how human experience might acknowledge temporality is the speaker's own embrace of Valgius' effort to defeat time. Finally, Valgius is criticized not for his desire to dominate, but rather for the inadequacy of his enactment of that desire. By replacing "mournful meters" with poetry that celebrates military triumph, Valgius will discover not the inevitability of temporality, but rather the proper space for temporality to be defied.

At the poem's end we return to Armenia, but the landscape is now imaged in terms of spatial constriction rather than temporal flow. A frozen mountain, *rigidum Niphaten*, has taken the place of ice that does not last forever (cf. *nec Armeniis in oris, / amice Valgi, stat glacies iners / mensis per omnis* [4–6]). The Euphrates, *Medumque flumen* (21), which recalls the Caspian sea and the images of flowing tears/ rain in lines 1–2, is now humbled, as are its surrounding peoples (*Medumque flumen gentibus additum / victis minores volvere vertices* 21–22). The movement of the nomadic Geloni is restricted now that they ride their horses within a prescribed and reduced area (*exiguis equi-*

tare campis 24). In each case, the unruliness of temporal change has been transformed by military domination, but the speaker's own earlier account of the ultimate changeability of nature makes suspect any real belief in the permanence of such a restricted, domesticated version of the world. Rather than offering a solution to Valgius' failure to control the temporality of his beloved, the speaker replaces eroticism with a curious blending of the military and the poetic, and in doing so merely reinstates the need for the subject to seek power over time. Thus, if the poem does indeed offer realism as a corrective to excessive romanticism, it is worth concluding by noting how fully realism itself leaves in place the lover's desire for domination.

🐚 *Odes* 1.22

Integer vitae scelerisque purus
non eget Mauris iaculis neque arcu
nec venenatis gravida sagittis,
    Fusce, pharetra,
sive per Syrtis iter aestuosas   5
sive facturus per inhospitalem
Caucasum vel quae loca fabulosus
    lambit Hydaspes.
namque me silva lupus in Sabina,
dum meam canto Lalagen et ultra   10
terminum curis vagor expeditis,
    fugit inermem;
quale portentum neque militaris
Daunias latis alit aesculetis
nec Iubae tellus generat, leonum   15
    arida nutrix.
pone me pigris ubi nulla campis
arbor aestiva recreatur aura,
quod latus mundi nebulae malusque
    Iuppiter urget;   20
pone sub curru nimium propinqui
solis in terra domibus negata:
dulce ridentem Lalagen amabo,
    dulce loquentem.

The man virtuous in life and pure of crime does not need Moorish javelins nor bow nor quiver heavy with poison arrows, Fuscus, whether going to travel through the boiling sands of Syrtes or through the inhospitable Caucasus or the places that the legendary river Hydaspes licks. For a wolf in the Sabine forest fled from me unarmed while I was singing of my Lalage and wandering beyond my property line with cares laid aside, the sort of monstrous portent neither warlike Apulia nourishes in its wide oak forests nor the land of Juba bears, dry nurse of lions. Put me in sluggish fields where no tree is refreshed by a summer breeze, the side of the world clouds and unfavorable Jupiter press upon; put me beneath the chariot of the sun too near the earth in land denied habitation: I shall love my Lalage sweetly laughing, sweetly talking.

In *Odes* 2.9, we saw that the move to writing about Augustus' conquests was a vehicle for redirecting Valgius away from his failure to overcome the constraints of time upon the erotic toward activity that could reassert his ability to dominate. Thus, the solution offered for failure to exert control in the area of the erotic was to turn to vicarious domination through writing about military conquest. In *Odes* 1.22 we shall see the military again invoked, but this time not as a source of surrogate power, but rather as a kind of strength that the poet/lover declares he does not need because love or love poetry has provided him with all the protection he requires. While temporality does not itself function directly in the poem as one of the forces against which the poet/lover must be protected, the notion of love as a refuge from the world relies upon the same erotic structure as the romantic ideal of a timeless love, for in each case eroticism is supposed to provide the lover with power over those forces that threaten his autonomy.

In *Odes* 1.22, however, the poet/lover's autonomy comes not merely from his own erotic power, but equally from the beloved who serves as the object of that power. Lalage can save the poet/lover from the world only if she is not herself part of the world, but this suggests an absorption of Lalage into the poet/lover's own identity, which leaves him in precisely the same relation to the world as when he began. The world is frightening because it resists his control, but such fear itself is a result of the assumption that anything that cannot be controlled must be feared. Were Lalage to provide a basis for the poet/lover to understand his relation to the world as reciprocal, then the fear that results from threats to autonomy might be eased. But Lalage could provide such a basis only if her own identity were granted an independence from the poet/lover's desire for security from the world, and this is precisely what the poet/lover does not allow. Thus, what we can see in this poem is how the romantic ideal of a love outside of time is itself motivated by a fantasy of complete security from the world, a security that itself must dissolve if the beloved is recognized as anything more than an extension of the poet/lover's own deluded autonomy.

Several critics have used *Odes* 1.22, as well as *Odes* 2.9, as evidence of Horace's supposedly anti-elegiac stance.[30] Commager, for example, takes this view: "Playing the part of a typical elegiac poet, Horace dramatizes their insulated concept of the world. . . . What Horace parodies here is the same attitude he was to rebuke explicitly elsewhere, the refusal to recognize any emotion or experience that is not amatory."[31] But as Davis has recently pointed out, "[t]he occurrence of the *topos* [of the sacrosanct love poet] in elegy does not *per se* warrant the inference that Horace is here posing as an elegiac *amator*."[32] Rather, he is instead placing himself in the Sapphic and Catullan tradition of love lyric.[33] While working within that tradition, though, Horace makes a significant change by shifting the "I" away from the distraught lover of Sappho and Catullus to a different kind of lover who has a boundary (*integritas*) to his self. This kind of lover recalls not the first-person speaker in Catullus 51 or Sappho 31, but rather the man who with godlike self-possession looks upon the beloved and manages to stay composed. Unlike the Sapphic and Catullan speakers who seem frozen in and immobilized by the moment of desire, the poet/lover of *Odes* 1.22 attempts indirectly to use love and love poetry to overcome the constraints of time. Thus eroticism in *Odes* 1.22, unlike Sappho 31 and Catullus 51, serves not to disrupt the self of the lover, but rather to reinforce his autonomy. We shall see, though, that the very *integritas* that signals the poet/lover's autonomy is what precludes the lover from participating in an eroticism that can acknowledge the beloved.

To understand the nature of the poet/lover's autonomy and his relationship to the world from which he seeks protection, we need to explore the poet/lover's own sense of his self-sufficiency, his construction of the world outside himself, and the position in this distinction between self and world of Lalage, his love object. We can see the poet/lover's position in relation to the world by examining how the poem develops. It falls into three sections (lines 1–8, 9–16, 17–24), each consisting of one sentence extending over two strophes. In each of these sections, the central concern is to establish the poet/lover's *integritas*, which is supposed to function as a source of immunity from the threats posed by the world. In the first section, *integritas* is explicitly named as a quality whose possession produces invulnerability: the man who is *integer vitae scelerisque purus* (virtuous in life and undefiled by crime) can travel without fear wherever he wishes.

The linkage of *integritas* with a kind of boundless travel anticipates the emphasis on boundaries and property, which marks the second section of the poem, although here the freedom from limits seems to come exclusively from an internal rectitude, rather than from the external relation to Lalage, which is emphasized later. The absence of Lalage perhaps explains the curious emphasis on negation here— the poet/lover does not need (*non eget*) such military accoutrements as javelins, bows, quivers, or poisoned arrows, and his *integritas* is partly confirmed by his being pure of crime (*sceleris purus*), suggesting that his virtue lies in what he has not done. As will be the case later in the poem, the world in which the poet/lover finds freedom to travel is bleakly inhospitable, and a tension is thus produced between the putative freedom that the poet/lover's *integritas* is supposed to give him to travel where he wishes, and the absence of any sense of *why* such travel might be desirable. The world outside the poet/lover occasions desire only negatively, as the origin of a need for escape. *Integritas* presumably succeeds in fulfilling such a need because its purely internal status would achieve a much more radical separation from the fearful world than military power, which necessarily remains tied to the world being conquered.

The second section seeks to offer an explanation or proof (*namque*) of this invulnerability, citing the poet/lover's safety from a strange wolf while wandering outside of his property, singing of Lalage (*dum meam canto Lalagen*). The poet/lover's *integritas* is presumably confirmed by his immunity from the wolf, who flees the poet/lover even though he is unarmed. But this sense of self-sufficiency, of an independence from even threatening aspects of the world, needs to be seen in relation both to the description of the world into which the poet/lover ventures, and to the reference to Lalage. We noted how in the opening section the poet/lover's autonomy, his *integritas*, is a result of a purely private self-determination—he is freed from the world because his life is defined by his own choice to live virtuously. But while *integritas* would point to a kind of boundlessness of the self, in the sense that the self is determined by nothing other than its own choices, the connection of the poet/lover's safety here with his "singing of my Lalage" instead situates the self in relation to what it possesses, and thus implicitly makes the self dependent upon those possessions. The world is made safe not because of the poet/lover's autonomous existence apart from the world, but rather because the poet/lover is defined by a possession—Lalage—which is itself some-how separate from the world. Paradoxically, the self-sufficiency of the poet/lover is determined not by his boundlessness, but rather by those boundaries that mark out what is and what is not his property: *ultra / terminum . . . vagor* (10–11). The poet/lover is able to move out into the world not because of any internal *integritas* that leaves him immune from the world, but rather because the world is claimed to have no relation to the boundaries that establish what the self possesses.

This sense of the self as defined by its boundaries is heightened by the allusion to the traditional notion of love as a *cura* (source of concern) in the description of the poet/lover's love as free from care (*curis . . . expeditis* 11). As a *cura*, the beloved would complicate the poet/lover's sense of his own boundaries by causing at least an implicit dependency upon his love object, and thus a dependency upon the world as well. Here, instead, the poet/lover's freedom from the emotional entanglements that eroticism would customarily bring is supposed to allow certainty about his own position in rela-tion to the world. Because Lalage offers an uncomplicated certainty about his own identity, the boundaries that offer the poet/lover security from the world are transferred from the physical to the emotional—in a sense, Lalage now becomes the "property line" that secures for the poet/lover an identity that needs no protection from the world. But this reliance upon his possession of Lalage as a means of securing his own autonomy complicates the poet/lover's hope to establish a boundary that separates his self from the world. Lalage's value as an extension of the poet/lover's "property line" is presum-ably made possible by her own independence from the poet/lover, for if she were merely an extension of his self, she would provide no further protection from the world than the self already can attain. But if Lalage does in fact have such independence, then the poet/

lover's relation to her entails his own dependency upon the world from which he has proclaimed his immunity. Thus, the use of Lalage as part of the "proof" of the poet/lover's invulnerability from the world suggests rather a vulnerability to the very world that the poet/lover seeks to surmount.

The fragility of the poet/lover's independence from the world perhaps explains the language of the final section, where the poet/lover reiterates his protected status in a rather combative fashion, connecting his immunity once again with love: *dulce ridentem Lalagen amabo, / dulce loquentem.* (23–24). The claim that even if the poet/lover were placed in the most extreme of conditions (*pone me* 17, and *pone* 21), his love for Lalage would protect him from harm seems ominous—the lack of specificity about who might place the poet/lover in such conditions produces an unnerving sense of a world whose threat can be met only by challenging it to do its worst. But the grimness of the threat that the poet/lover faces contains its own solution, for the move from what is claimed to be actual recollection in the second section to a fantasized nightmarish landscape of danger in the final section has the effect of dissolving both time and space into the poet/lover's own autonomy. The world outside of the poet/lover has meaning only in terms of what it confirms about his ability to stand outside the limits the world presents. What is continuous despite both the temporal and spatial changes that the poet/lover experiences is the freedom that Lalage gives him to transcend the world, and the necessity of such transcendence is itself established by the unrelenting grimness with which the world is portrayed.

Indeed, the poet/lover's ability to transcend the world seems dependent upon the description of the world as itself desolately removed from the temporality that might challenge the poet/lover's omnipotence. For example, the language used to describe the wolf that flees from the poet suggests that the wolf is able to serve as a *portentum* (portent) in part because of its separation from temporal change—the negation (*neque, nec*) of language associated with nourishment and growth (*alit, generat, nutrix*) removes the wolf from the normal cycle of birth, growth, and death in which even the arid land of Africa, paradoxically, participates (*arida nutrix*). In defining his *integritas* in relation to the threat posed by the portentous wolf, the poet/lover thus succeeds in transcending the world largely because the world has itself been removed from the temporality that ultimately defines human experience. Similarly, the landscape in which the poet/lover boasts that he could be placed unharmed is marked by an absence of temporal change—the wintry terrain experiences no summer breezes, and the hot land is uninhabited because the closeness of the sun precludes seasonal change. In each of these cases, what seems most clear is that the harm from which Lalage will preserve the poet/lover is not the literal physical threat that a wolf or a desolate landscape might pose, but rather a more general threat of a world defined by change. Protected by Lalage, the poet/lover is able to imagine a world free of temporal change, a world in which his own *integritas* is secure because the world itself is composed of nothing more than a kind of static emptiness.

But this effort at escaping into static realms that deny the existence of time, while seeming to offer security, is ultimately deceptive, for the "I" of *amabo* and the self of Lalage, the love object, necessarily involve temporality. The poet/lover seems to be claiming that because of his love for Lalage, the world has itself been transformed into little more than an extension of his own security. But because such transformation itself requires the poet/lover's continued love for Lalage, the very context of human temporality, which the description of the world has denied, is now reintroduced. Continuing love is significant only in a world in which temporality is a defining feature of both lover and beloved, but acknowledging such shared temporality would seem then to preclude the kind of demarcation between self and world upon which the poet/lover's *integritas* depends.

A further complication of the poet/lover's independence can be seen in the paradoxical position of Lalage, who seems to function both as an extension of the poet/lover's own self, and as a part of the world from which the poet/lover seeks protection. The poet/lover appears to believe that he needs protection from any part of the world that is not his possession, and Lalage is supposed to supply that protection. But what is left unexplained is whether Lalage is herself part of the world, or whether she is the poet/lover's possession. If she is merely a possession, then the claim to continuing love is empty, since a possession does not have the independent existence that love itself requires. But if she does have independent existence, then she would seem to be part of the very world from which the poet/lover seeks protection. In either case, the hope that erotic love might offer escape from the world seems doomed to failure.

What we can now see is that the poet/lover's relationship to Lalage epitomizes his paradoxical relationship to the world. The world beyond poses a threat that is blocked only by the talismanic power of his love song for Lalage, which suggests that Lalage's position as an object of love has at best an instrumental value for the poet/lover. Indeed, the poet/lover's effort to control Lalage, that is, to define her in his own terms (*dulce ridentem . . . dulce loquentem*), transforms Lalage into something *intra terminum*, or the poet/lover's own. However, if she becomes part of him, Lalage not only loses her potential threat as part of the alien, potentially dangerous, landscape, but her own identity as well, and such a loss of her identity would preclude her functioning as the talisman that might offer protection from the world. The world threatens the poet/lover because of its threat to his own self-sufficiency, and if Lalage is herself merely an extension of the self that is threatened, then the ominous power of the world is in no way diminished.

On the other hand, the world has its power in large part because of an implicit inadequacy lurking within the self, whose boundaries are meaningful not intrinsically but rather because of the relation they establish to the world. From this perspective, love for Lalage offers the possibility of extending the self's boundaries not by expanding what the self possesses, but rather by relating the self to an other. What this suggests is that the poet/lover's proclamation of his love for Lalage invokes as well a need for the world, which stands in stark contrast to his mania for self-sufficiency, but further that acknowledgment of such need would leave him vulnerable to all those forces in the world that threaten the self. Possession of Lalage keeps the world at a safe remove, but only by denying Lalage the independent existence that would be required if love were to succeed in satisfying the poet/lover's own need for real connection to the world.

The collapse of self found in the lovers of Sappho 31 and Catullus 51 is thus transformed in *Odes* 1.22 into an arming of the self against the world through the agency of erotic domination. While temporality functions only obliquely here as part of what must be dominated, its centrality can be seen in both the account of the world whose safety is secured in part by its absence of temporal processes, and more importantly in the appeal to enduring love as the ultimate guarantor of the poet/lover's *integritas*. What the romantic ideal of a love that can withstand the ravages of time is supposed to offer to the poet/lover is a space within which the boundaries defining his self are literally limitless because they will never change. In a sense, what the poet/lover's possession of the beloved promises is a transference of need from a disturbing and uncontrollable world to an idealized extension of one's self. But this onanistic fantasy is betrayed by its necessary reliance upon a worldly creature—the beloved—whose independence from the timeless boundaries of the poet/lover must finally expose the futility of the dream of a lack of need for the world. Ultimately, the poet/lover's *integritas* is a delusion.

🏺 *Odes* 1.13

> Cum tu, Lydia, Telephi
>   cervicem roseam, cerea Telephi
> laudas bracchia, vae, meum
>   fervens difficili bile tumet iecur.
> tum nec mens mihi nec color   5
>   certa sede manet, umor et in genas
> furtim labitur, arguens
>   quam lentis penitus macerer ignibus.
> uror, seu tibi candidos
>   turparunt umeros immodicae mero   10
> rixae sive puer furens
>   impressit memorem dente labris notam.
> non, si me satis audias,
>   speres perpetuum dulcia barbare
> laedentem oscula, quae Venus   15
>   quinta parte sui nectaris imbuit.
> felices ter et amplius
>   quos irrupta tenet copula nec malis
> divulsus querimoniis
>   suprema citius solvet amor die!   20

When you, Lydia, praise the rosy neck of Telephus, his supple arms, alas, my raging heart swells with angry bile. Then my mind is unsettled and my appearance does not stay the same, and liquid secretly glides onto my cheeks, proving how deeply I am tormented by slow-burning fires. I am inflamed, whether struggles immoderate because of wine have disfigured your white shoulders or the wild youth has pressed with his teeth his telltale mark upon your lips. If you would listen to me sufficiently, you would not hope that he would be forever yours who harms your sweet lips like a barbarian, lips that Venus has filled with a fifth part of her nectar. Happy three times and more are those whom an interrupted bond holds and a love torn apart by serious complaints will not loosen sooner than the final day!

In both *Odes* 2.9 and *Odes* 1.22, the idealized view of love as transcending the limits of the world remains unquestioned, and we have noted how closely aligned this view of love is with the lover's desire for domination. In *Odes* 1.13, the desire for domination remains in place, but the poem itself raises questions about this desire by suggesting both that desire is itself mediated by worldly experiences that cannot be controlled, and by offering a perspective toward love that is responsive to such mediation. The vehicle of domination here is the poet/lover's attempt to demonstrate his erotic knowledge of Lydia—by using both previous experiences and graphic fantasies to suggest a sexual intimacy with her body, the poet/lover attempts to control Lydia by making her an erotic object whose significance comes primarily from her relation to his desires.

However, this struggle to dominate Lydia through a kind of erotic insinuation is complicated by the fact that the poet/lover's desire does not emerge only from his relation to Lydia, but rather is produced by his knowledge of Lydia's sexual involvement with Telephus. The poet/lover's desire, far from being something solely under his control, is in fact largely a *reaction* to Lydia's relationship to Telephus. Thus, his desire is contingent upon something outside of himself and even outside of the beloved's body—it is contingent upon the beloved's erotic relation to a competing lover.[34] Indeed, the repeated naming of Telephus by the poet/lover in the poem's first two lines shows his obsession with an erotic rival he wishes to eliminate. What we find in the poem, then, is an ineradicable tension between two competing structures of desire: the poet/lover seeks to dominate Lydia through language that would force her to grant the centrality of his own desire, but this desire itself emerges only as a consequence of the poet/lover's awareness of Lydia's erotic relation to Telephus. As we shall see, the very centrality of the poet/lover's desire, which domination requires, is inevitably undermined if that desire is dependent upon forces that it cannot control.

From the beginning of the poem, it is the poet/lover's *voice* that serves as the vehicle of his attempted domination. In the poem's opening strophe, Lydia's effort at praise of Telephus' body is undermined by a rhetorical inversion, which substitutes the poet/lover's passion for the more muted attractions offered by Telephus. Lydia's description of the rosiness of Telephus' neck and the suppleness of his arms seems, in the poet/lover's recounting, to reduce him to little more than a sensual plaything, while the contrasting raging heart and angry bile of the poet/lover instead establish him as a troubling source of passion. In the lines that follow, the poet/lover's account of Lydia's effect upon him emphasizes the power of his own desire, but with little sense of why this desire should matter to Lydia. Rather, what he offers is self-description—his mind is unsettled, he is tormented, and so on.

While this litany of internal changes includes many of the traditional symptoms of the lovesick lover—mental upset, change in color, and tears—significantly missing is the "loss of voice," which is the ultimate proof of the beloved's effect upon the lover. Thus, in contrast to the situation in, for example, *Epodes* 11.9–10, where the lover's silence is what proves his status as lover (*amantem languor et silentium / arguit et latere petitus imo spiritus*), here the poet/lover uses his own rhetoric about his symptoms to try to prove (*arguens* 7) his status as a real lover. This ability to speak—to offer arguments for the existence of his own desire—has the effect of placing Lydia in a position subsidiary to the poet/lover's own desires. Where the traditional lover's inability to speak confirms the erotic centrality of the beloved,[35] here instead the voice of the poet/lover is supposed to establish an erotic power that Lydia would presumably be powerless to resist.

The emphasis on voice culminates in the penultimate strophe, where the poet/lover seeks to establish his own words as the authority governing Lydia's erotic behavior (13–15): *non, si me satis audias, / speres perpetuum dulcia barbare / laedentem oscula* (If you would listen to me sufficiently, you would not hope that he would forever be yours who harms your sweet lips like a barbarian). Lydia's status here as auditor comes not merely from the insistence that she listen to the poet/lover, but also from the way in which the poet/lover's words seek to frame her own erotic experience in terms of *his* desires. Her current erotic life is reduced to barbarian harm, and this presumably stands in opposition to the poet/lover's evocation of Lydia's lips as "imbued with Venus' nectar" (*quae Venus / quinta parte sui nectaris imbuit* 15–16). What seems implied here through this graphic fantasy or recollection is that the poet/lover has actual knowledge of Lydia's body (the sweetness of her lips could be known only through tasting), and such knowledge would presumably confirm the authority of his desire, and thus of his words. But this suggestion that the poet/lover's desire is itself mediated by Lydia's actual existence, by his knowledge not merely of his desire but of the body that occasions that desire, has the effect of undermining the very authority the poet/lover had sought to establish in his voice. If the poet/lover's desire depends upon both his relation to, and his knowledge of, an erotic specificity that exists independently of his own words, then his words are themselves meaningful merely in relation to such uncontrollable specificity.

Indeed, when we consider the poet/lover's relation to Lydia's own erotic life, what we find is that the poet/lover's voice, far from articulating an original desire, is rather an ultimately inadequate substitute for his apprehension of an erotic relation over which he has no control. The poet/lover's desire, and the voice that articulates that desire, emerge only from the poet/lover's awareness that the eroticized body of Lydia upon which he gazes has its origin somewhere else. Thus, the marring of her white shoulders (*seu tibi candidos / turparunt umeros* 9–10) and the marks upon her lips (*sive . . . / impressit memorem dente labris notam* 11–12) function as signs for the poet/lover of wild lovemaking (*immodicae mero / rixae* 10–11 and *puer furens* 11), and it is this prior lovemaking that itself occasions the poet/lover's desire. Indeed, the word *memorem*, used literally of the mark Telephus' love bites make upon Lydia's lips, points as well to how the poet/lover perceives Lydia's body not just in terms of its present relation to him, but more importantly in terms of its relation to an erotic past to which he has no connection.

From this perspective, the poet/lover's insistence that Lydia should listen to him functions less as the assertion of his own authority, which I suggested earlier, than as a desperate effort to deny the mediated context of desire that his own words suggest. The opposition between the poet/lover's advice and barbarian harm can thus be seen as itself evading the acknowledgment here of an enduring eroticism from which the poet/lover is excluded. Indeed, the fact that the continuing love the poet/lover warns Lydia not to expect is represented as Telephus repeatedly (*perpetuum*)[36] performing the very activity that arouses the poet/lover's desire suggests an opposition between the static denial of mediation upon which the poet/lover's erotic authority would depend, and the temporally situated *shared* erotic desire of Lydia and Telephus.

The ambivalent status of the poet/lover's desire to dominate comes into sharpest focus in the poem's final lines, where the concluding statement can be read both to support and to undermine the poet/lover's struggle to control Lydia. In considering how the statement might *support* the poet/lover, we can begin by noting that this strophe has been seen as a source of difficulty by Horatian commentators. The seemingly romantic notion found in the traditional translation, "happy are those who have a lifelong love," appears out of place after the poet/lover's suggestion that Lydia give up hopes of a lasting love with Telephus. However, a solution to this difficulty is to interpret the final strophe as ironically counterpoising to the attempted seduction of Lydia the notion of an everlasting love, in which case the poet/lover's evocation of the romantic ideal of a timeless love would serve merely to suggest its near impossibility.[37] Such a perspective would, of course, support the poet/lover's strategy for seducing Lydia, for if lifelong love (with Telephus) is virtually impossible, then a relationship with the poet/lover would be clearly permissible. Indeed, the poet/lover's own position would be enhanced by his possession of a wisdom about love which, presumably, both Telephus and Lydia lack.

However, there is another way of reading the final strophe, which would undermine such irony by insisting upon both the erotic significance of the relationship between Lydia and Telephus and the mediated nature of the poet/lover's own desire. To see how such a different reading might be possible, we need to look closely at the problems presented in translating the final strophe. Traditionally, the language here has been read (whether interpreted ironically or not) as referring to an untroubled, uninterrupted love. However this reading entails two difficulties: translation of the word *irrupta* (18) as "unbroken," which is unprecedented in Latin, and a somewhat awkward, but not impossible, necessity of understanding the negative *nec* twice to get the sense desired. The following is a typical translation of the final strophe:

Thrice blest and more are they whom an *unbroken* bond holds
fast, and whose love, torn apart by *no* bitter quarrels, *will not*
release them before their final day. [emphases mine][38]

However, *irrumpo*, the verb from which the participle *irruptus* is
derived, is formed from the prefix *in-* meaning "into," not the prefix
in- meaning "not," and, according to *The Oxford Latin Dictionary*, the
only occurrence of *irruptus* with the meaning "unbroken" as op-
posed to its normal meaning of "broken into" or "interrupted" is
here in *Odes* 1.13. Yet, despite this uniqueness, commentators and
translators have taken *irruptus* to mean "unbroken."[39] While the
occurrence of a word as an apparent *hapax legomenon* is not a reason
to reject it out of hand, such an occurrence should provide a reason
to examine the word carefully.

My own argument is that reading *irrupta* in its normal sense of
"interrupted" succeeds both in resolving grammatical difficulties
posed by the final strophe and in allowing an interpretation of the
poet/lover's concluding words that is consistent with the ambivalent
status of his own desire, which we have already seen. In the stan-
dard reading of this passage (as we can see in the translation quoted
above) *nec* must be made to function twice as a negative, once with
divulsus or *querimoniis* (torn apart by *no* bitter quarrels, or *not* torn
apart by bitter quarrels), and a second time with *solvet* (will *not*
release). If *nec* did not have such a double function, the reader's
traditional expectation that *felices ter et amplius* refers to a blessed
state would be jarred by the incongruity of lovers "happy three times
and more" whose love is "torn apart by serious complaints" (*malis /
divulsus querimoniis / . . . amor*). Thus, commentators are able to
preserve the traditional force of *felices ter et amplius* by reading an
"*un*broken" (*irrupta*) bond of love which is "torn apart by *no* bitter
quarrels" and which will "*not* release" the lovers until the final day.

However, we can avoid the grammatical ingenuity that this read-
ing requires by translating *irrupta* in the sense it has elsewhere in
Latin (broken into, interrupted) and by using the negative *nec* only
once (which makes better grammatical sense):

Happy three times and more are those whom a bond that has
suffered temporary ruptures holds and whom a love torn apart
by serious complaints will not loosen sooner than the final day.

What this reading suggests is that those whose love can be "inter-rupted" without being destroyed are fortunate in their ability to sur-vive conflict and disruption over time.[40] From this perspective, the ideal of a continuing love must be seen not as a seamless bond that transcends time, but rather as a link that through time can withstand potential erotic interruptions. While an ironic interpretation of the final lines as pointing to the impossibility of timeless love works well for the poet/lover's purposes by minimizing Lydia's relationship to Telephus, the sense of *irrupta* as "interrupted" instead transforms any relationship between Lydia and the poet/lover into an insignifi-cant interlude in Lydia's ongoing, if tumultuous, affair with Tele-phus. Consequently, if the fortunate love signified by *irrupta* . . . *copula* is seen not as "an unbroken bond," but as "an interrupted bond," then the poet/lover unwittingly suggests a version of love that ensures the failure of his own seduction, for if the most success-ful love is that which can withstand ruptures, then choice within the world of the erotic has become more complicated than the poet/lover intends. Lover and beloved have a new possibility: rather than accepting or rejecting an idealized love that denies change and exists unproblematically over time, they can choose a love that continues but which must be continually renewed over time.

The poem's repeated motif of love's battles, intended by the poet/lover to point to problems in Lydia's and Telephus' relation-ship, can now be seen rather as a playful representation of the conflicts an enduring erotic relationship has the capacity to sur-mount. The poet/lover's attempt to characterize the lovers' play (*immodicae mero / rixae* 10–11) as actual combat and his advice that Lydia abandon hope that Telephus will forever engage her in erotic battles (*perpetuum . . . barbare / laedentem* 14–15) have as their aim to persuade Lydia that romantic love is finally impossible. What would remain in place after romantic love has been abandoned is the ag-gressive desire that motivates Telephus' continued "harming" of Lydia, a desire that Lydia herself clearly enjoys. If desire is itself transitory and violent, then the violent physicality of the poet/lover might easily replace the supposed uncertainty of Telephus' love. The poet/lover's ironizing of romantic love would enhance his attempted seduction by eroding Lydia's confidence in her relationship with Telephus while appealing to the same erotic impulses that he be-lieves have defined it.

However, if we see in the final strophe not an ironic commentary on the timelessness of romantic love but rather a vision of how love might acknowledge temporality, then the battles of love that mark the relationship of Lydia and Telephus can be seen as the signs of a love that can withstand the temporary ruptures (*irrupta* and *malis divulsus querimoniis*) that occur over time. Of course, a love that is open to rupture is more likely to allow the poet/lover's erotic feelings for Lydia to receive a response, but such a love also precludes any success for the desire for domination, which was itself the origin of those erotic feelings. Finally, what emerges from such openness to rupture is a love that can withstand even the failure of the romantic ideal of a timeless love, and which thus guarantees that the poet/lover's attempted seduction, insofar as it is based on an undermining of that ideal, must itself fail to achieve the domination he seeks.[41]

🏵 *Odes* 3.9

"Donec gratus eram tibi
   nec quisquam potior bracchia candidae
cervici iuvenis dabat,
   Persarum vigui rege beatior."
"donec non alia magis   5
   arsisti neque erat Lydia post Chloen,
multi Lydia nominis
   Romana vigui clarior Ilia."
"me nunc Thressa Chloe regit,
   dulcis docta modos et citharae sciens,   10
pro qua non metuam mori,
   si parcent animae fata superstiti."
"me torret face mutua
   Thurini Calais filius Ornyti,
pro quo bis patiar mori   15
   si parcent puero fata superstiti."
"quid si prisca redit Venus
   diductosque iugo cogit aeneo,
si flava excutitur Chloe
   reiectaeque patet ianua Lydiae?"   20

"quamquam sidere pulchrior
  ille est, tu levior cortice et improbo
iracundior Hadria,
  tecum vivere amem, tecum obeam libens."

"As long as I was pleasing to you, and no youth more able was giving his arms to your white neck, I flourished happier than the Persian king."

"As long as you did not burn more for another, and Lydia was not after Chloe, I, well-known Lydia, flourished more famous than Roman Ilia."

"Now Thracian Chloe rules me, she who is learned in sweet measures and knowledgeable about the lute, for whom I shall not fear to die, if the fates will spare my love to survive me."

"Calais, son of Ornytus of Thurii, burns me with a mutual flame, for whom I shall die twice, if the fates will spare my boy to survive me."

"What if an old Venus returns and forces together with a bronze yoke those who were led apart, if fair-haired Chloe is driven out, and the door lies open for Lydia, once rejected?"

"Although he is more beautiful than a star, and you more unstable than a cork and more temperamental than the unruly Adriatic, I would love to live with you, willingly I would die with you."

In *Odes* 1.13, we saw how both the ambivalent status of the poet/lover's desire for domination and the ambiguity of the final strophe work to undermine the centrality of the romantic ideal of a love that might transcend time. In place of this ideal, what the poem finally suggests is the possibility of erotic love that can acknowledge the uncertainties of time. As we shall see in the final poem we look at, *Odes* 3.9,[42] a crucial dimension of such acknowledgment is transforming the hierarchical distinction of lover and beloved into a reciprocal erotic relationship in which each of the lovers seeks the recognition of the other. Temporality is a central feature of such reciprocity because it demands an openness to the contingent separateness of the other. Where the romantic ideal allows the desires of the lover to transcend time by reducing the beloved to nothing more than an erotic possession, erotic reciprocity instead requires that the lover's desires recognize how the passage of time mediates the lover's relation to the one he (or she) loves. In reciprocal eroticism, the lover seeks to have desire acknowledged by one whose own identity is constantly changing, and such recognition of change requires that the lover's own desires be situated in relation to such change. Thus, while the romantic ideal presupposes a static conception of identity, where the unchanging desire of the lover reduces the beloved to a mere extension of that desire, erotic reciprocity instead suggests a conception of identity as emerging from one's relationship to the person one desires, a relationship that itself is intrinsically temporal in its recognition of the inevitability of change.

The opposition between the romantic ideal of timeless love and an eroticism that can recognize reciprocity appears in *Odes* 3.9 in the contrast we can see between the temporality of memory, which underlies the first four strophes of the poem, and the temporality of dialogue, which structures the poem as a whole. For both the male lover and Lydia, memory is supposed to demarcate a personal realm of experience from within which the erotic self is free to determine its own identity. Paradoxically, the recognition of the passage of time, which memory requires, can serve as the vehicle of freedom from time—what memory allows is certainty of one's separation from the past, and thus of one's separation from any *present* reminder of what one once was. If a past erotic relationship is firmly established by memory as having meaning solely in the past, and if such past meaning further has meaning in the present solely through the separateness that it establishes, then eroticism itself remains immune to the passage of time. However, such separateness is challenged in *Odes* 3.9 by the way that memory is itself subsumed by the temporal dynamics of the dialogue. Because memory functions here not merely as a private recollection, but more importantly as a means for establishing a position in relation to an other, the privacy of self-determination that is sought through memory is replaced by the reciprocal determination of selves that emerges through conversation.

In their opening speeches, the male lover and Lydia each describe an erotic past where the most significant concern was what the *other* found most pleasing. Thus, the conditional terms that the male lover uses to characterize the past ("*As long as* I was pleasing to you, *and* no youth more able was giving his arms to your white neck, I flourished happier than the Persian king") seek to establish that the male lover's happiness depended upon Lydia's approval of him and his remaining first in her affections. Similarly, Lydia describes the duration of her flourishing as having depended upon the exclusivity of the male lover's erotic attention: "*As long as* you did not burn more for another *and* Lydia was not second to Chloe, I, Lydia, much talked about, flourished better known than Roman Ilia." Indeed, the verbal parallels in their speeches (*donec* introduces each of the speeches, and both speakers use the word *vigui*) seem designed to establish a shared memory of erotic bliss in which the other's desires subsume any personal sense of identity the lover might have.

But these erotic pleasures are remembered at best ambivalently. While each of them claims to have "flourished" (*vigui*) as the object of the other's desires, the sense of erotic well-being seems complicated by the curious displacement of eroticism in each of the speeches from shared pleasure to a kind of defensive narcissism. We can see this narcissism most obviously in the male lover's boast that his own pleasing of Lydia postponed any possibility for a "youth more able," and in Lydia's claim that her relationship to the male lover brought her greater fame than Ilia. But narcissism functions even more significantly in the act of memory itself, for what each of the speakers struggles to establish is an erotic identity that is immune to the contingencies of what it remembers. What is *past*, for each of the lovers, is not desire but the uncertain affections of the one who is desired. The conditionality which opens the speeches may, as I suggested, point to an eroticism that makes the desires of the other central, but it also removes the lover who is speaking from any recognition of how his or her own desire might be related to the one who is desired—the lover's desire is made central by removing it from responsibility for what has happened. The male lover makes his flourishing contingent not on any action he might take, but rather on Lydia's willingness to continue to find him pleasing. Similarly, Lydia's flourishing depends completely upon how strongly the desire of her lover burns, and upon her own temporal priority to Chloe.

While it may seem odd to call such an acknowledgment of dependency on the other narcissistic, the real function of the acknowledgment is not to grant an enduring significance to such dependency, but rather to free the self from such an entanglement. By firmly separating the contingent conditions that ultimately led to the collapse of the relationship from the desiring self that contemplates those conditions, each of the lovers seeks to show how the self that speaks in the present is itself immune from what it describes. From this perspective, the verbal echoes in the two speeches suggest less mutuality than selves removed from relation. Because *donec* and *vigui* have meaning solely in terms of the speaker's *memory* of what occurred, and not in terms of any shared apprehension of the past, the verbal repetition at best evokes a commonality of experience, which is itself shattered by the dramatically different accounts of time and desire that the speakers offer.

But to emphasize in this way the opening two speeches as private statements about the past ignores how the speeches function as *dialogue*. Paradoxically, if the verbal echoes in the two speeches serve only to emphasize the privacy of what is said, the contrasting accounts of desire that are offered will instead begin to bring the speakers in relation to each other. In his opening speech, the male lover's account of his dependency upon Lydia's affections is undermined by his insistence on his own erotic prowess. In the opening line, the speaker uses language that grants the centrality of Lydia's pleasures (*gratus tibi*, "pleasing to you"), but by the second and third lines Lydia's pleasures have been metonymically displaced by her "white neck" (*candidae / cervici*), which is itself valued because its possession gives the male lover supremacy over the "youth" (*iuvenis*) who might replace him. Indeed, the concluding comparison of himself to the "Persian king" (*Persarum . . . rege* 4) indicates clearly how linked eroticism and conquest are for the male lover—he "flourished" not because of his responsiveness to what Lydia found pleasing, but because his possession of Lydia functioned as the erotic equivalent of imperial might. What such possession gives to the male lover is control of his desires, an almost remarkable lucidity about what he seeks in an erotic relationship. In contrast to the indeterminacy of Lydia's pleasures, which is suggested by the opening line of the poem, the male lover's pleasure in erotic possession provides an uncomplicated certainty about his own identity.

In her response to the male lover, Lydia calls into question what we might refer to as the male lover's retreat from mediation. While the male lover portrays his desire as uncomplicatedly centered on possession, and reduces Lydia herself to little more than an object to be possessed, Lydia instead insists that the indeterminacy of the male lover's desire exposes him to an unstable panorama of erotic competition. This occurs most obviously in Lydia's revision of the male lover's description of the eroticism they once shared: while the male lover characterizes himself merely as "pleasing" (*gratus*) to

Lydia and supremely capable (*nec quisquam potior . . . iuvenis*), Lydia's description instead emphasizes *passion: non alia magis / arsisti* ("you did not burn more for another"). This account of the male lover as having once burned with desire allows Lydia to offer a somewhat different account of the social setting of their relationship. While the male lover's hint of other possible lovers for Lydia in *nec quisquam potior* disappears into his own assertion of power, Lydia brings the potential erotic competition into the open by naming names: *neque erat Lydia post Chloen* ("nor was Lydia after [second to] Chloe").

The effect here is not to absolve Lydia of erotic fickleness, but rather to insist that both she and the male lover must recognize how each of their perspectives on the past is mediated by the perspective offered by the other. If Lydia had defended her own constancy of affection, she would have positioned herself outside any relation to the history offered by the male lover, and would thus have precluded any real relation to him in the present. Instead, by insisting upon the male lover's passion and her own competition with Chloe, Lydia emphasizes that desire is itself contingent on the temporal and personal conditions that mediate the relations of lovers. At the conclusion of Lydia's speech, the male lover's boast about the erotic power he once had seems at best a feeble evasion of the complicated passion that Lydia has now offered.

But surprisingly, the male lover's next speech refuses not merely this passion, but any recognition that Lydia has spoken. The Chloe who now rules him seems far removed from the burning desire that Lydia has just described, and indeed, seems removed from the erotic competition that Lydia's own mention of Chloe had suggested. Instead, the male lover evokes an austere, almost scholarly romance where the knowledge of the self and its desires, which Lydia had offered, is replaced by learned Chloe's knowledge of the lute and sweet measures (*dulcis docta modos et citharae sciens* 10). The hyperbolic insistence that this is a love for which he would die is curiously persuasive, given the bleakness of the life that he would lose. Just as, in his opening speech, the male lover's memory of his past relationship with Lydia sought to exclude any acknowledgment of his own relationship to what he had once desired, so here the description of Chloe excludes any mention of what his relationship is to these learned qualities that he claims he values. In each case, the purpose of such exclusion seems to be to leave the self of the male lover immune from either the passage of time or the contingencies of desire, but the immunity that is gained from this exclusion seems finally an immunity to life.

There is, of course, a further exclusion to be noted in the male lover's second speech—the refusal to acknowledge in any way the version of his desire that Lydia had offered in her first speech. Now, in responding to this account of Chloe, Lydia will return to the issues of both passion and reciprocity, which had been the basis of her previous speech: "Calais, son of Ornytus of Thurii, burns me with a mutual flame." The passion that Lydia says Calais offers echoes, of course, the earlier description of the male lover who "did not burn more for another," but what is new about Calais is that Lydia receives the full force of his passion and returns this passion equally— the flame, after all, is "mutual." The male lover's passion, on the other hand, seemed incomplete in Lydia's description (it "did *not* burn more for another") and has disappeared in his own portrayal of Chloe. Insofar as the male lover has anything like a "mutual" relationship to Chloe, its basis is his own abandonment of anything resembling a self, while Lydia instead claims to have found in Calais the possibility of a mutual relationship whose basis is a self defined by its capacity for passion. In her concluding claim that she would die *twice* for Calais, Lydia offers both a parody of the male lover's own hyperbole, but also a subtle insistence on the worth of the life that she has found—the suggestion of a series of lives, each offered for her lover, denudes death of any real force (it is the singularity of death that is terrifying) and thus evokes a passion that seems likely to be unconquerable.

We have only Lydia's words to confirm this passion, though, and the fact that her words function not as description of something in the world but rather as a *response* to what the male lover has just said suggests that we should read the passion that she has evoked as a challenge to the self-description the male lover has offered. In place of the empty autonomy evoked by the male lover in his description of the love he shares with Chloe, Lydia offers a "mutual flame" (*face mutua*) that would require both lovers to see themselves in relation to the passions of the other. (Indeed the root for "change" in *mutuus* suggests that mutuality itself entails the risk of impermanence). In the male lover's first two speeches, such mutual recognition was inconceivable—rather, his evocation of both past and present seemed designed to present a self whose deepest feelings are obscured by a surface placidity about the pleasures of the moment. Despite the underlying rhetoric of possession, which we noted in the first speech, the male lover has so far presented himself as little more than a spectator who observes with a civilized irony his own romantic escapades, and the distanced refusal to grant the presence of his auditor only adds to this sense of a self detached from any of the entangling contingencies of desire. Now, however, the male lover *responds* to what Lydia has said, and in doing so positions himself in a dangerous realm of rhetoric and desire where the self is defined not by its detached autonomy but rather by its relation to what it cannot control.

The rhetorical vehicle through which this new self is announced is a question that abandons any pretense to descriptive truth and instead opens the male lover's self to the contingent separateness of his interlocutor: *quid si . . . ?* ("What if . . . ?"). Each of his first two speeches began with words that delimited the space of experience the male lover was willing to acknowledge. In the opening speech, *donec* had circumscribed the temporal duration of his prior relationship to Lydia, and in the second speech, *me* had even more dramatically limited his focus to his own experiences in the present. Now, instead, "what if" announces an openness to contingent possibilities that would follow not from any deliberate action the male lover might take, but rather from the return of "old Venus" (*prisca . . . Venus*). The replacement of Chloe by Lydia, which would presumably follow the return of Venus, gains erotic force from the transposition that governs the description of Chloe. Previously, Chloe had been described in purely intellectual terms, but now she is instead imaged through the fairness of her hair. While this move from the intellectual to the physical may seem to bring an erotic intensification, in fact the echo of the similar reduction of Lydia to her "white neck" in the male lover's first speech suggests that Chloe is now as far from the male lover's own self as Lydia had earlier seemed to be. Lydia had challenged the reduction of her identity to the token of possession signaled by the "white neck" by insisting on the uncertain passion ("you did not burn more for another") that marks the male lover's relations to women, and now the reduction of Chloe to an insignificant physicality seems to suggest that the male lover recognizes that his relation to Chloe is itself an inadequate setting for the possibilities of passion which Lydia has evoked.

Such a change in the status of Chloe prepares for a similar shift in emphasis in the positioning of Lydia from the object who was "once rejected" to the erotic force who will cause the door to the male lover's passion to be opened. *Reiectae* (20) signals a past that has been called into question by the temporal progress of the poem, for the sense of Lydia as a passive object that can be disposed of at the will of the male lover has been shattered by Lydia's revision of the history the male lover has offered. In place of the initial positioning of Lydia as defined by her past status as a possession, the progress of the dialogue has established both her enduring desirability and the uncertain relation of the male lover to that which he desires. If we take the door that may lie open to Lydia as an image of the male lover's desire, we can see how fully he has felt the force of Lydia's rhetoric. The lover who had the capacity to "burn" is now literally opening himself, as a door might, to the "mutual flame" that Lydia has offered as the possible goal of passion.[43]

In turning to Lydia's final speech, we should begin by noting how it inverts the relations that exist between the two earlier pairs of speeches. As Putnam has noted, the apparent thematic discord of the first two pairs of strophes is undermined by the verbal echoes that tie each of the pairs together, while the apparent concord of the final pair of strophes is challenged by the absence of any rhetorical similarities.[44] However, where Putnam concludes from this that "[t]here is most individuality at the instant where reinforced allegiance would be in order," and argues further that such "individuality" points to a "Horace [who], learned in the nature of human foibles, would have put little trust in the permanence of such a tenuous bond,"[45] I want to argue rather that the inversion of symmetry in the final pair of strophes suggests an eroticism that is content to abandon the delusive search for permanence.

To see how this inversion works, we need to recall that in each of the earlier pairs of strophes, the repetition of the male lover's first word by Lydia does not function to establish a similarity of their viewpoints, but rather to signal a difference in their competing versions of the past and present. In the male lover's speeches, the temporality that underlies *donec* and the version of self suggested by *me* both serve to remove his desire from the instability that would come from recognizing the desire of the other. As long as his past relationship to Lydia and his present relationship to Chloe have no essential relationship to his own identity, then the male lover's own autonomy remains unchallenged by erotic entanglement. Lydia's repetition of *donec* and *me* undermines such autonomy by using these words to suggest that the temporal duration of their past relationship depended upon the uncertain constancy of his own passion ("as long as you did not burn more for another"), and by offering a version of self that can respond to the passion that the male lover seems unwilling to acknowledge (*me torret face mutua*, "burns me with a mutual flame"). What Lydia's revisions of the male lover's perspective accomplish here is to establish the differences (both temporal and erotic) that real relationship must acknowledge. The male lover's transformation of himself into a door that lies hesitantly open to Lydia's passion grants the power of this revisionary account of their relationship, but in seemingly acceding so completely to Lydia's version of the relationship, the male lover risks merely substituting the compelling power of her desire for his own discredited autonomy. The danger here is that in either case an acknowledgment of difference is evaded by defining the erotic relationship solely in terms of the desire that has triumphed.

In her final speech, Lydia recognizes this danger, and refuses the power that the male lover has just seemed to grant her. In beginning her response with *quamquam* (although), she firmly separates her own words, and her own erotic identity, from the version of desire offered by the male lover. Where earlier, an initial repetition had suggested a shared perspective, which was exposed as an illusion by what followed, now an initial difference establishes the separateness that a shared perspective must acknowledge. In his use of *quid si* to frame his announcement of openness to Lydia, the male lover had implicitly offered the possibility of a complete removal from the entanglements of the present. His question, while proposing to Lydia the possibility that his relationship to Chloe might end, offers no real explanation of how or why this might happen, nor is there any suggestion of what the relationship is between what he proposes and the current situation. Against this apparent absence of mediation in the male lover's proposal, Lydia's *quamquam* firmly situates any possible relationship they might share within the contingencies that define each of their identities.

Such acknowledgment of contingency is perhaps less obvious in the first of the two concessive clauses which follow *quamquam*. Here, Lydia's comparison of Calais' beauty to a star seems similar to the male lover's focus on the fair hair of Chloe, for in each case a distance is being created between the passion of the lover and the object of love. Just as the reduction of Chloe to her fair hair had served to distance her from the full range of the male lover's passion, so the comparison of Calais to a star circumscribes his beauty to a remote and inanimate realm far removed from the "mutual flame" that was supposed to have joined him to Lydia. But despite this remoteness, Calais is also acknowledged in a way that Chloe simply is not—the initial *quamquam* establishes clearly that Lydia's own erotic identity is defined in relation to Calais' beauty, and thus shows her unwillingness simply to accede to the ease with which the male lover will apparently abandon any current romance.

This distinction between Lydia's own awareness of how her identity is mediated by what it desires, and the male lover's refusal of such awareness, underlies the second of the concessive clauses— the description of the male lover as *levior cortice* (lighter—or more fickle, in erotic terms—than a cork) and *improbo iracundior Hadria* (more subject to emotional outburst than the untrustworthy Adriatic). In portraying her former lover paradoxically both as a passively bobbing cork and as the actively tempestuous sea, Lydia draws together the accounts she has already offered of both the male lover and herself, and in doing so refuses the easy retreat from the complications of the present, which the male lover has offered. The cork as an image of the male lover's erotic instability recalls the earlier description of their past relationship as having been governed by the conditionality of his desire ("as long as you did not burn more for another"), while the "tempestuous sea" as a metaphor for his unruly passion links her present acknowledgment of the desire she feels for him with the "mutual flame" that she had said she shared with Calais. The male lover's present desire for Lydia is mediated by the instability of his past relationship to her, while Lydia's response to that desire is mediated by her own desire for both passion and mutuality.

In effect, Lydia is insisting that she and the male lover each recognize how their differing erotic histories have shaped their present desires. Her willingness to act upon her desire for the male lover has not occurred because their differing perspectives have magically been joined, but rather because she is able to acknowledge both his difference from her, and how that difference has shaped her own desire. In exchanging the easy, though distant, mutuality that a beautiful star such as Calais might offer for the male lover's instability and unruly passion, Lydia insists that both she and the male lover must recognize the forces that have mediated their relation to the other. The male lover is being asked to recognize not just that his erotic identity is capricious and turbulent, but more importantly that Lydia's willingness to respond to his question comes from her knowledge of that identity.

Similarly, in insisting upon such knowledge, Lydia is announcing her own recognition of the relationship of her desire to what she cannot control—while her final speech says that she would like to join the male lover "although" (*quamquam*) he is capricious and turbulent, the contrast between the remote beauty of Calais and the stormy attractiveness of the male lover suggests rather that she is drawn to the male lover *because* his passion is so uncontrollable. From Lydia's perspective, both she and the male lover must acknowledge that any erotic mutuality that they might share is itself contingent upon the differences that underlie their separate erotic histories. What is new here is not the fact of such differences, but the insistence that they be acknowledged.

But of course, such acknowledgment of difference must itself be mediated by temporality, for what Lydia is offering is not a definitive judgment of their relationship but rather a provisional statement about how their future together might be conceived. Her response to the male lover is thus framed not in the present (as is the question to which she responds [*redit, cogit, excutitur, patet*]),[46] nor in the future indicative (which would suggest certainty or fact), but rather in the less definite "future" of the present subjunctive. This openness to a future that is itself conditioned by the present suggests that the apparent resolution of discord in the poem's final line[47] should not be seen as definitive. The anaphora of *tecum* (with you) and the hyperbole in the willingness to live or to die with the lover recall the rhetoric that proves empty in regard to Chloe and Calais. The asyndeton in *tecum vivere amem, tecum obeam libens* leaves open whether Lydia has a commitment that includes sharing life *and* death or is merely exhibiting a kind of rhetorical casualness about the alternatives of living or dying. The use of *amem* with a complementary infinitive (to like to), rather than in its more erotic sense (to love)[48] merely hints at a passionate commitment. Even the metaphorical interpretation of "dying with a lover" as "making love"[49] would offer only a temporary reconciliation. Yet the very fact of the lovers' continuing conversation suggests, if not a solution to the problem of time and the erotic, at least a shared recognition that temporality is a contingency in which both lover and beloved participate.

CONCLUSION

My goal in this book has been to present a perspective that challenges current notions of Horace as a love poet. I would like to conclude by looking back at the feminist critical perspective I outlined in chapter 1 in order to review how the issues raised by that perspective have been enacted in the poems I have discussed. In doing so, I hope to suggest in retrospect the way in which the theoretical grounding with which I began has enabled my interpretations, and why that theoretical grounding produces a perspective on Horace's love poetry that is unavailable in traditional modes of criticism.

Where traditional criticism has begun by privileging the perspective of the male poet/lover and has derived its understanding of temporality from what that perspective has to say, I have sought, using an approach that breaks free of the gender assumptions that have so frequently guided such criticism, rather to establish that the male poet/lover's perspective is itself a consequence of the role that temporality plays in shaping his desire. In taking this approach, I have tried to show that the perspective on temporality of the poet/lover, far from giving voice to a universal dilemma besetting erotic relationships, is rather the outgrowth of a gendered reaction against the challenge to erotic dominance posed by the contingencies of time.

While my interpretations of individual poems have located this reaction largely in terms of problems internal to the poems being discussed, my very sense of what might count as a problem in the representation of eroticism was enabled by the theoretical accounts of eroticism and gender surveyed in my opening chapter. Thus, in drawing upon the work of Fetterley, Montefiore, Chodorow, and Benjamin, my hope has been to offer an interpretation of Horace which, while focused on specific poems, is informed by a theoretical self-consciousness about the significance of gender in relation to the erotic. Using Fetterley's notion of the "resisting reader," I have attempted in my analyses to resist both acceptance of the values of the poet/lover and acceptance of critical perspectives which, by naively assuming those values to be authoritative, fail to recognize the gendered basis of what is accepted. Montefiore's argument that putatively universal love poetry enacts an effacement of the beloved by the desires of the lover was instrumental for my critique of the perspective of the poet/lover, while her discussion of the feminizing of the beloved provided a framework for understanding the particular ways in which the identity of the beloved emerges solely from its relation to the lover's own conception of eroticism. Finally, Chodorow and Benjamin showed how the attempt by the poet/lover to control the temporality of the beloved should be understood not merely in terms of desire but, more importantly, in terms of the power and domination through which a self seeks to secure its fantasy of autonomy.

I chose to start my analysis, in chapter 2, at the level of the individual word, in order to show how an interpretive procedure as traditional as examining how a specific word gains meaning through the context of an entire poem could lead us to see the critical role that the lover's perspective plays in shaping how temporality is conceived in relation to eroticism. In tracing how key temporal adverbs shape the erotic dynamics of the entire poem, I showed the extent to which lover and beloved were positioned unequally with regard to temporality. Specifically, we saw that the beloved's worth as an object of desire was defined by the lover's own determination of what was appropriate to her temporal condition, while the lover himself somehow remained magically free of the very burden of temporality that proves so decisive in his judgment of the beloved. In each of the poems discussed, the inadequacy of treating the issue of temporality as a universal of human experience became obvious, for in each case the differing experiences of temporality available to the lover and beloved emerge solely from the lover's struggle to dominate and control whatever might threaten his own erotic autonomy. While the fact of temporality is certainly universal, the lover's belief that temporality must determine the worth of his beloved emerges not from some truth of human experience, but rather from the particular, and peculiar, demand that eroticism must somehow allow the lover's desire for autonomy to remain intact.

A similar questioning of the universality of the themes enacted in Horace's love poetry marked my discussion, in chapter 3, of Horace's use of seasonal language in the love odes, for there I argued that the association of eroticism with spring served not as a "moral metaphor," as has traditionally been accepted, but rather as a device that benefited the lover in his quest to define the beloved's seasonability for her. Seeing the seasons as offering metaphors for enduring moral issues of human experience fails to account, I argued, for either the decisive difference in how temporality functions in nature and in human experience, or for how the portrayal of human experience in terms of natural cycles betrays an anxiety about how vulnerable human experience becomes in the face of temporality. While the claim that nature serves as a moral metaphor for human experience presumes that both lover and beloved share a temporal predicament, my own argument showed that the appeal to nature serves largely as a vehicle for the lover's effort to demarcate his own identity from that of the beloved. Rather than portraying a universal "right time," seasonal imagery furthers the lover's desire to define *in his terms* what would constitute the appropriate time for love.

Similarly, in chapter 4, we saw in looking at the effect of temporality upon the erotic how differently lover and beloved are positioned with regard to age. For the beloved, who is seen in terms of her diminishing desirability, aging is a public matter, in the sense that the beloved's status as an erotic object is defined by what are presumed to be shared standards governing the appropriateness of desiring a beloved of a particular age. In contrast to this, the aging lover is allowed to maintain the privacy of his desire, for his position in an erotic relationship is not that of an object scrutinized by public standards, but rather that of a subject who remains free to choose whether his age has rendered erotic conquest inappropriate. Thus, just as in the claim that there is some natural season for eroticism, the claim that there is some natural age when erotic desire or desirability is appropriate serves merely to conceal the lover's desire to dominate the beloved.

Finally, in chapter 5, we saw that Horace's supposed critique of a romantic version of love, while appearing to offer a reversal of that traditional view, does nothing to question the terms upon which it is based. While the transformation of "love must defeat time" into "time must defeat love" appears to undermine decisively the romantic fantasy of a love that might conquer time, what remains constant is the assumption that love and time must be defined in opposition to each other. Thus, the "realistic" idea of love as defeated by time shares with the romantic ideal of a timeless love the notion that temporality is a threat to the erotic, and further joins with the romantic view in seeing the temporality of the beloved as the locus of that threat. As we saw in the final chapter, in neither version of love is temporality seen as a contingency equally affecting lover and beloved or as a factor that those who both love and are loved can incorporate into their evolving senses of themselves. Love as a shared experience that might embrace the contingency of time remains elusive in the *Odes*.

As I have argued, the differing ways in which lover and beloved are made to participate in temporality reflect the male lover's desire to dominate the beloved, and lead, therefore, to a recognition that temporality is not experienced in the *Odes* as a universal feature of experience. To say this, however, is not to leap to any facile dismissal of the *worth* of Horace's poetry. Rather, I think that we can now see poetic worth as emerging precisely from poetry that allows the sort of complex analysis of gender and erotic identity I have tried to offer here. Finally, Horace's love odes offer us a cautionary tale of problematic eroticism as well as a mirror in which to see our own involvement in the constructions of desire that underlie our critical practice. It is difficult to know how poetry could do more.

NOTES

PREFACE

1. See Grassmann, *Die Erotischen Epoden des Horaz: Literarischer Hintergrund und sprachliche Tradition*, for a frank examination of Horace's erotic epodes. On the development of new scholarship that addresses the erotic in an "explicit" and "unembarrassed" manner, see Connor, W.R., "The New Classical Humanities and the Old," 29–30.

2. See Konstan, "What Is New in the New Approaches to Classical Literature," 45.

3. See Johnson, *The Idea of Lyric: Lyric Modes in Ancient and Modern Poetry*, on Horace's "adapting [of] radical hyperbaton as a normal stylistic mode" (126). See also Wender's comment, in *Roman Poetry from the Republic to the Silver Age*, that Horace "does clever things with word order that are irreproducible in English" (61), as well as her discussion (61–62) of the specific difficulties of translating *Odes* 1.5 (the Pyrrha ode).

4. In the following places I have followed the Teubner text of Horace edited by Borzsák (Leipzig, 1984) rather than that of Shackleton Bailey: *Odes* 1.25.6 *et* for *ac*, 9 *invicem* for *in vicem*, 20 *Hebro* for *Euro*; *Odes* 2.5.4 *venerem* for *Venerem*; *Odes* 1.4.8 *visit* for *versat*; *Odes* 1.23.5 *veris* for *ve<p>ris*, 6 *adventus* for *ad ventum*; *Odes* 2.8.3 *uno* for *albo*, 18 *crescit* for †*crescit*†; *Odes* 3.9.20 *reiectaeque* for *reiectoque*.

INTRODUCTION

1. For a critique of this kind of polarization and its gender implications, see, e.g., Cixous, "Sorties: Out and Out: Attacks/Ways Out/Forays" in Cixous and Clément, *The Newly Born Woman*, 63–132.

2. The male beloved, unlike the female, is allowed with age to escape

unscathed from object status and thus to become a desiring subject. Cf., e.g., *Odes* 1.4, discussed in chapter 3, where the male beloved, Lycidas, will one day presumably assume the role of the lover, Sestius. The female beloved, on the other hand, is made grotesque as an older, desiring subject. Cf., e.g., *Odes* 1.25 and *Odes* 4.13, discussed in chapters 2 and 4. On the male beloved in Augustan love poetry, see Murgatroyd, "Tibullus and the *Puer Delicatus*." More generally, on the beloved as feminized, see my discussion of Montefiore in chapter 1.

ONE   Time, Gender, and the Erotic

1. Much of the history of critical attention to Horace has been characterized by interest in his use as a "morally edifying" author. As a consequence, material that did not support this version of Horace was often omitted from texts, commentaries, and translations, and discussion of aspects of Horace's writings in conflict with this version were avoided. (The final chapter of Wilkinson's *Horace and His Lyric Poetry* provides a fascinating overview of interest in Horace and his writings after his lifetime.)

A few examples from a book of Horace's works adapted for the young and published in Boston in 1838 (*Quinti Horatii Flacci Opera: Accedunt Clavis Metrica et Notae Anglicae Juventuti Accommodatae*, B.A. Gould, ed.) will give some sense of the way in which Horace was bowdlerized, specifically with respect to the erotic. The book omits the final two lines of *Odes* 1.4 and lines 5–8 of *Odes* 4.13, presumably for their references to erotic arousal. (See my discussion of both these passages on pp. 50–52 and 98–100). Such odes as 1.5, 1.23, and 1.25 are not included at all. In addition, *Epodes* 8 and 12 are, not surprisingly, omitted.

Even the Loeb Classical Library text of Horace by Bennett (1914, reprinted 1919) omits *Epodes* 8 and 12, providing neither the Latin text nor a translation. Interestingly, Bennett's own edition of Horace (*Horace: Odes and Epodes*, 1901; reprinted by Caratzas Brothers, 1981) does include the Latin text of the two epodes but omits both notes and summary (part of the book's normal structure), giving with each poem the following explanation: "The coarseness of this epode leads to omission of any outline of its contents" (176, 181). While it might be tempting to view such an omission as a curious relic of a more prudish critical practice from the earlier part of this century, it should be noted that Bennett's edition remains influential; it is still used today in many reading courses in Horace for want of more frank editions with sufficient grammatical help for the student.

Even Fraenkel, in his highly influential book *Horace* (Oxford, 1957), devotes little attention to the poems of Horace that deal with love. While there has been a fair amount of recent work on Horace's love poems, indicating a new, or at least revived, interest in Horace as a love poet, blindness to the erotic aspect of Horace's work has not entirely disappeared.

2. Nisbet, "Romanae Fidicen Lyrae: The Odes of Horace," 184.

3. Ibid., 194.

4. Nisbet's view of Horace as a love poet echoes that of Havelock (*The Lyric Genius of Catullus*, 182–83): "Horace's odes . . . are exclusively a work of the intellect, [Catullus' lyrics] were born from the heart . . . [in Horace] only the emotion is absent. But Catullus is all emotion."

5. Nisbet and Hubbard, *A Commentary on Horace: Odes Book 1*, xvi (hereafter *Odes Book 1*).

6. See Eliot, "Tradition and the Individual Talent," and Wordsworth, "Preface to the Second Edition of *Lyrical Ballads*."

7. Eliot, "Tradition and the Individual Talent," 10–11.

8. Richards, *Practical Criticism: A Study of Literary Judgment*, 264.

9. Allen, "Sunt qui Propertium malint."

10. For a recent elucidation of the subtle interplay between art and life, specifically with regard to Augustan poetry, see Griffin, "Augustan Poetry and the Life of Luxury," revised as chapter 1 of his *Latin Poets and Roman Life*.

11. Nisbet and Hubbard, *Odes Book 1*, 71, noted by Griffin, *Latin Poets and Roman Life*, 25.

12. Nisbet and Hubbard, *Odes Book 1*, xvi, 71, xvi, xvi–xvii.

13. Ibid., xvii.

14. Boyle, "The Edict of Venus: An Interpretive Essay on Horace's Amatory Odes," 163 (hereafter "Edict of Venus").

15. Ibid., 164, 167.

16. See Culler, "Beyond Interpretation," in *The Pursuit of Signs: Semiotics, Literature, Deconstruction*: "At its most basic the lesson of contemporary European criticism is this: the New Criticism's dream of a self-contained encounter between innocent reader and autonomous text is a bizarre fiction. To read is always to read in relation to other texts, in relation to the codes that are the products of these texts and go to make up a culture" (11–12).

17. Boyle, "Edict of Venus," 176. For a fuller discussion of *Odes* 1.25, see chapter 2.

18. Ibid., 177. See also Arkins, "A Reading of Horace, *Carm.* 1.25," for a similar blindness to the problem of universalizing Lydia's situation. Arkins fails to realize that what he perceives as Horace's "detached, objective manner" (171) in *Odes* 1.25 is, in fact, the poet's rather insidious way of making a specific situation that he has created, Lydia's demise, seem an inevitable and natural outcome.

19. Boyle, "Edict of Venus," 174–75.

20. A related critical strategy that avoids confronting the specificity of the poet/lover's perspective is that of Lyne (*The Latin Love Poets: From Catullus to Horace*), who not only shares Boyle's universalizing of the perspective of the poet/lover, but also endorses a view that subordinates Horace as a love poet to Horace as primarily a "committed public poet" (203 and passim). Lyne wants us to see Horace establishing the place of love poetry in his *Odes* in the context of his self-comparison with Alcaeus (202–3).

Even if this were an adequate description of how Horace viewed himself as love poet in the *Odes* (and I think that is something we could question), what is problematic in this approach is Lyne's uncritical acceptance of such a description by Horace as authoritative. The problem with treating self-referentiality uncritically has recently been addressed by Culler ("Changes in the Study of Lyric," 52): "In general, self-referentiality does not create a self-enclosed organic unity where a work accounts for itself or becomes the thing that it describes but rather produces paradoxical relations between inside and outside and brings out the impossibility for a discourse to account for itself. A work's self-descriptions do not produce closure or self-possession but an impossible and therefore open-ended process of self-framing."

The question that Lyne's analysis cannot address is whether love in the *Odes* stays as self-contained as Lyne's acceptance of Horace's alleged version of his love poetry would have us believe, or whether there are factors at work in the poems that undermine this description. Lyne's somewhat naive use of Horace as authority on Horace makes him unable to see the potentially disrupting quality of temporality in the *Odes*.

21. See Putnam's articles on Horace in *Essays on Latin Lyric, Elegy, and Epic; Artifices of Eternity: Horace's Fourth Book of Odes* (hereafter *Artifices of Eternity*); and "Horace *Carm.* 2.9: Augustus and the Ambiguities of Encomium."

Kenneth Reckford, both in his article "Some Studies in Horace's Odes on Love" and in his book *Horace*, has offered a similar sensitivity to Horace as a love poet, particularly in his recognition of the poet's ambivalence toward the temporality of love. He sees the complexity of temporality in the love odes and thus describes the poet's response not as a simple acceptance of love's impermanence, but rather as a "flight into the present" (*Horace*, 97). He further recognizes what I discuss in chapter 5 as the attraction for Horace of a romantic version of love: "Again and again, his [Horace's] poems show how much the elegists' dream attracted him; again and again, he gives the lie to his own pose of emotional detachment" (*Horace*, 102). Reckford acknowledges the desire behind the detachment, but does not extend his discussion to develop a critique of that desire.

Davis, *Polyhymnia: The Rhetoric of Horatian Lyric Discourse*, offers an excellent analysis of the ways in which Horace makes persuasive arguments. Included in the book is a plethora of material on the complicated manner in which Horace establishes himself as lyric poet by interacting with other genres. While Davis is not primarily concerned with things erotic, his interest in the ideational level of Horace, especially Horace's interest in time as involving both recurrence and end, produces several nuanced and insightful readings of a number of poems I discuss in this book (e.g., *Odes* 1.25, 2.9, 3.7, 4.1, and 4.7). I regret that my manuscript was virtually complete before I was able to see *Polyhymnia* and that therefore I can cite Davis's book only in this general way.

22. I would like to thank Jeanne Heuving for calling Montefiore's book to my attention.

23. See, e.g., Sedgwick, *Between Men: English Literature and Male Homosocial Desire*. See also Clément, *Opera, or the Undoing of Women*. Clément's feminist analysis of Puccini's *La Bohème*, with its treatment of the themes of love, time, and art, is particularly relevant to our discussion of Horace: "As Muse and inspiration she [Mimi] joins the troop of girls sacrificed by the seducer so he can live in a suspended time" (85). As is the case with the beloved in the *Odes*, her temporality/humanity is sacrificed in order for the poet/lover to gain "suspended time."

24. While Montefiore's focus is the sonnet, her comments are useful for other forms of love poetry as well. For a critique of the status of the beloved in love poetry contemporary with the *Odes*, see Wyke, "Written Women: Propertius' *Scripta Puella*" and "Mistress and Metaphor in Augustan Elegy."

25. Santirocco, *Unity and Design in Horace's Odes*, 33.

26. See Chodorow, *The Reproduction of Mothering: Psychoanalysis and the Sociology of Gender* and "Gender, Relation, and Difference in Psychoanalytic Perspective."

27. See Benjamin, *The Bonds of Love: Psychoanalysis, Feminism, and the Problem of Domination*. Earlier versions of the chapter entitled "Master and Slave" in *The Bonds of Love* appeared as "The Bonds of Love: Rational Violence and Erotic Domination" and "Master and Slave: The Fantasy of Erotic Domination."

28. I am not positing a developmental model to explain actual male development in Roman times, but rather a model that may help to explain the poet/lover in the *Odes* and how he has been perceived by Horatian critics. In fact, Dixon's argument in *The Roman Mother* suggests that such a model would not fit the actual development of the child in the typical Roman family. For other recent discussions of the Roman family, see Dixon, *The Roman Family*; Rawson, *The Family in Ancient Rome: New Perspectives*; Hallett, *Fathers and Daughters in Roman Society: Women and the Elite Family*; and Bradley, *Discovering the Roman Family: Studies in Roman Social History*.

The attempt to account for the erotic dynamics in Horace's poetry through appeal to what little we know of or what we might imagine about Horace's actual life avoids a critique of those same dynamics. For example, Armstrong (*Horace*, 60), despite a curious gesture toward what he calls "the kind of feminist study, in terms of male hostility and fear of feminine sexuality, that has done so much recently for the analysis of the mythology and poetry of early Greece," dismisses the possibility that Horace's poems about "lustful old women" might benefit from such study. Rather, in a move that typifies efforts to remove canonical works from feminist critique, he argues that the problematic eroticism that marks the portrayal of such "lustful old women" should be collapsed into what is finally a kind of fantasy of biography: "*somehow* [emphasis mine] [such portrayals are] connected with Horace's life-long refusal of long-term emotional commitments . . . [and] the result of a fuzzy place in Horace's own human affections." For the problem with using Horace as a source on Horace, see Culler, note 20 above. On the value of a feminist approach to Horace's erotic odes, see my argument throughout this book.

29. Chodorow, "Gender, Relation, and Difference in Psychoanalytic Perspective," 10.

30. Benjamin, *The Bonds of Love: Psychoanalysis, Feminism, and the Problem of Domination*, 68.

31. See Benjamin, "Master and Slave" in *The Bonds of Love: Psychoanalysis, Feminism, and the Problem of Domination*.

TWO   The Temporal Adverb

1. For an expanded version of the following discussion of *Odes* 1.25, which interprets further the identification of Lydia with nature, see my article "Horace *Odes* 1.25: Temporality, Gender, and Desire."

While not "strictly" a temporal adverb, *parcius* (more sparingly) functions as such in this ode.

Syndikus (*Die Lyrik des Horaz: Eine Interpretation der Oden Band 1*, 248) points out the words, including *parcius*, that signal time's inevitable passing: "'Seltener,' 'und nicht,' 'früher,' 'schon immer weniger' sind die Leitworte, die das unabwendbare Weitergehen der Zeit rücksichtslos aufzeigen" ['More seldom,' 'and not,' 'formerly,' 'already less and less,' are the chief expressions that ruthlessly show the inevitable continuing of time]. See also La Penna ("Tre Poesie Espressionistiche di Orazio," 191), who notes the comparative *parcius* at the beginning of the ode and the return of the comparative with *prius, minus et minus*, and *magis*.

2. Most commentators have recognized the combination of past and present in lines 1–8. Boyle ("Edict of Venus," 176) sees strophes 1–2 as a distinct temporal unit concerned with the past and present. Pöschl speaks of the present and the remembrance of the past ("Horaz C. 1,25" 188–89). Catlow ("Horace *Odes* I,25 and IV,13: A Reinterpretation," 815) aptly states that "the first two stanzas imply a whole history and define the poem's immediate context." Kiessling-Heinze's temporal description of strophes 1–2 indicates an awareness of the opposition between past and present: "Die beiden ersten Strophen schildern das Jetzt und zugleich den Gegensatz des Einst" [Both of the first two strophes describe the present and, at the same time, the contrast of the past] (*Q. Horatius Flaccus: Oden und Epoden*, 109). Collinge (*The Structure of Horace's Odes*, 114), however, defines lines 1–8 as "the present—Lydia's fading powers of attraction," thus missing the careful mingling of past and present in these lines.

3. A further sense of violence may be latent in *protervi* through the influence upon it of *protero* (trample down). See Ernout and Meillet, *Dictionnaire*

Étymologique de la Langue Latine, under *protervus*. For the connecting of *pro-terve* with *protero* as well as a meaning for the verb denoting what a bull does *in appetitu coitus feminarum* [in his desire for sexual union with females], see Donatus on Terence *Hecyra* 503, as quoted by Maltby, *A Lexicon of Ancient Latin Etymologies*, under *protervus*.

4. For *iungo* as a term used to denote the "joining" of sexual intercourse, see Glare, *The Oxford Latin Dictionary*, under *iungo* 3b, "to unite sexually"; and Adams, *The Latin Sexual Vocabulary*, 179. For another example of this sense of *iungo* in Horace, cf. *Odes* 1.33.8 (*iungentur capreae lupis*). Cf. also *iugum* of the sexual bond (at least metaphorically) in *Odes* 2.5.1 (*ferre iugum*) and *Odes* 3.9.18 (*Venus / diductosque iugo cogit aeneo*).

5. Porter ("Horace, *Carmina*, IV,12," 77) points out that the unbroken sleep of Lydia in *Odes* 1.25.3 and 7–8 contrasts ironically with the *perpetuus sopor* of Quintilius in the preceding ode (1.24.5).

6. Cf., e.g., Plautus *Curculio* 147–55 (*pessuli, heus pessuli, vos saluto lubens . . .*). On the personification of the door in the *exclusus amator* motif in Latin love poetry, see Copley, *Exclusus Amator: A Study in Latin Love Poetry*, 28–42; for the representation of the door in terms more appropriate for a woman, see also Hallett, "*Ianua iucunda*: The Characterization of the Door in Catullus 67." Pucci, "Lingering on the Threshold," discusses the significance in Propertian elegy of the *limen* as that which is to be transgressed.

7. For the erotic overtones of Horace's use of *amare* with an inanimate subject elsewhere in the *Odes*, cf. *Odes* 2.3.9–11: *quo pinus ingens albaque populus / umbram hospitalem consociare amant / ramis?*; and *Odes* 3.16.9–11: *aurum per medios ire satellites / et perrumpere amat saxa potentius / ictu fulmineo.*

8. Nisbet and Hubbard (*Odes Book 1*, 293) translate *amatque* as "keeps to," saying "Horace uses an expression appropriate to a chaste woman."

9. Catlow, "Horace *Odes* I,25 and IV,13: A Reinterpretation," 815 (hereafter "Horace *Odes* I,25 and IV,13").

10. Copley, *Exclusus Amator: A Study in Latin Love Poetry*, 59.

11. Boyle, "Edict of Venus," 177.

12. Collinge, *The Structure of Horace's Odes*, 52.

13. Nisbet and Hubbard, *Odes Book 1*, 294.

14. See under *perire* in Pichon, *Index Verborum Amatorium*, 230–31.

15. I follow the bipartite division of the poem (1–8 and 9–20) made by Collinge (*The Structure of Horace's Odes*, 114) and Boyle ("Edict of Venus," 176). Others divide it into three parts: 1–8, 9–16, and 17–20, as, e.g., Kiessling-Heinze (*Q. Horatius Flaccus: Oden und Epoden*, 109); Syndikus (*Die Lyrik des Horaz: Eine Interpretation der Oden Band 1*, 250), who nevertheless acknowledges that the sentence structure divides the poem in two; and Pöschl ("Horaz C. 1,25," 188–89).

16. Boyle ("Edict of Venus," 176) sees *invicem* as the key word in the ode, "with its overt promulgation of the inevitability of change." He also recognizes its structural importance as the word that divides the two parts of the poem. In my view, *parcius*, with its initial position in the poem and its

comparative degree, is even more important than *invicem*, for it sets up a temporal perspective that affects the entire poem. The effectiveness of *invicem* is due in part to the preparation *parcius* provides.

17. Here, as earlier in the poem, emotional content is carried by words that reflect on Lydia's condition but are grammatically construed with her surroundings (*in solo . . . angiportu*).

18. Catlow rightly remarks ("Horace *Odes* I,25 and IV,13," 814) that Horace is projecting his desires for Lydia into the future rather than reacting to "an accomplished fact."

19. Cf. the disquieting effect of *imminente luna* in *Odes* 1.4.5.

20. Nisbet and Hubbard, *Odes Book 1*, 297.

21. Catlow's point is well taken that *matres equorum* implies procreative value to the horse's sexuality, something presumably no longer available to Lydia at her advanced age ("Horace *Odes* I,25 and IV,13," 816).

22. Fresh ivy, gray myrtle, and dry leaves parallel three stages of life: youth, maturity, old age. Cf. Strato *Palatine Anthology* 12.215 for these periods represented by spring, summer, and the stubble (of old age). The *pubes* prefer ivy, which is evergreen, even to myrtle, which is associated with Venus (cf., e.g., Vergil *Georgics* 1.28). For dry leaves (old women) they have no use at all. In *Odes* 1.25 Horace shows Lydia's progression from youth (in the past) to maturity (in the present) to old age (in the future). In the dramatic time of the poem (the present), Lydia is already at the "myrtle" stage; by the end (which lies in the future), she will have reached old age.

I take *atque* (18) as "than," not "and." For discussion of this issue, see Nisbet and Hubbard, *Odes Book 1*, 298.

23. I think my interpretation of the poem works with either reading (*Hebro* or *Euro*), however, following Lee, "Horace, Odes 1.25: The Wind and the River," I see no need for the emendation to *Euro*.

24. Collinge, *The Structure of Horace's Odes*, 52. For a critique of the sort of approach to a text that focuses on what is represented in the text to the exclusion of the literary purpose or function of that representation, see Suleiman's comments on Andrea Dworkin's criticism of Bataille's *Histoire de l'oeil* in "Pornography, Transgression, and the Avant-Garde: Bataille's *Story of the Eye*." Suleiman's own strategy is summed up as follows: "a feminist reading of Bataille's and other modern male writers' pornographic fictions must seek to avoid both the blindness of the textual reading, which sees nothing but *écriture*, and the blindness of the ultrathematic reading which sees nothing but the scene and its characters" (129–30).

25. See, e.g., Commager, *The Odes of Horace: A Critical Study*, 247–49 (hereafter *Odes of Horace*), and Boyle, "Edict of Venus," 174–78. Boyle, while acknowledging Lydia's specificity ("the poet's . . . presentation of the terrible consequences of time's passing upon one specific, and especially vulnerable, human individual"), concludes that "Horace's concern in I.25 is not so much with vituperation (although the mode of presentation is vituperative) as with change and the human consequences of change—hence the explicit nature

symbolism of the final stanza, which places the personal devastation to be suffered by Lydia within the context of a universal law of nature" (176, 177). It is this leap of Horace's to the universal which, while aptly described by Boyle, remains unexamined. Catlow ("Horace, *Odes* I,25 and IV,13") recognizes the speaker's personal stake in the situation of the poem, which undercuts his own (and most commentators') attempts at universalizing his and Lydia's situation: "To interpret this poem, with Commager, as a moral statement about the unseemly futility of defying the decorum of nature and change is to ignore its mood, structure and the assumptions with which we are clearly intended to approach it, for it is vital to remember that Horace is not disgusted with an accomplished fact but himself wills this moral and physical depravity on a woman who, we are to understand, has formerly rejected him. The development of this poem sheds as much light on the emotional state of a rejected lover as on the moral disaster wrought b[y] untimely sexuality" (814). For a critique of Boyle's alliance with Horace's universalizing, see chapter 1 (pp. 10–12).

26. Boyle, "The Edict of Venus," 180.

27. Kiessling-Heinze, *Q. Horatius Flaccus: Oden und Epoden*, 180.

28. Nisbet and Hubbard, *A Commentary on Horace: Odes Book 2*, 80 (hereafter *Odes Book 2*).

29. There are two distinct but related issues concerning *Odes* 2.5 that have attracted scholarly attention. First is the issue of whether *Odes* 2.5 is addressed to Horace himself or to someone else who remains unnamed. (See Nisbet and Hubbard, *Odes Book 2*, 77, who state that "the primary problem of this poem was already posed by pseudo-Acronian scholia: '*incertum est quem adloquatur hac ode, utrum amicorum aliquem an semet ipsum*'" [It is uncertain whom he addresses in this ode—one of his friends or himself].) The second concerns the poem's outcome, specifically, whether the would-be lover finally gets together with the girl. I am inclined toward taking the poem as a soliloquy, that is, as the poet addressing himself. Boyle ("Edict of Venus") points out in support of this view the fact that *Odes* 2.5 "is the only amatory ode in which the name of the addressee is not mentioned" (179). However to preserve the ambiguity about the addressee, I have chosen to refer to the "would-be lover" or the "potential lover" rather than the poet/lover. As for the poem's outcome, I agree once again with Boyle, who finds the outcome intentionally unresolved: "[The] realization of the unbridgeable gulf between Lalage and himself produces the ambiguous final statement (15–16), in which *maritum* ('spouse') is purposefully vague; it is no longer obvious, as was implied in the first supporting statement (10–12), that Lalage's husband will be himself" (180). This view and the view that completely rejects an outcome of union between Lalage and the would-be lover depend in large part upon not taking *tibi* (10) as a dative of advantage, allowing for the ambiguity of *sequetur* (13), not interpreting the statement about time in lines 14–16 as favorable to Horace, and not assuming that *maritum* (16) refers to Horace.

A different approach to the poem has been taken by Quinn (*Horace: The Odes*, 205–8), who takes the poem as addressed to a husband who, married to quite a young girl, must be patient until she is sexually more mature; and by Fantham ("The Mating of Lalage: Horace *Odes* 2.5"), who takes the poem as "addressed to a man betrothed or contemplating marriage, and concerned not with the readiness of the girl for sexual congress, but with her maturity for breeding" (48).

30. For discussion of these expressions as erotic, see Adams, *The Latin Sexual Vocabulary*, 155–56 and 207 on *subigo*, 207–8 on *ferre iugum*, and 164 on *munus*; cf. also Nisbet and Hubbard, *Odes Book 2*, 80–81. On *iugum*, see also the discussion above of *iunctas* in *Odes* 1.25.1, and *iugo . . . aeneo* (*Odes* 3.9.18). There is an echo of *Nondum subacta ferre iugum . . .* (2.5.1) in line 2 of the ode that immediately follows (*Cantabrum indoctum iuga ferre nostra . . .*); in 2.6, however, the context has switched from sexual to political.

31. See Nisbet and Hubbard, *Odes Book 2*, 81 on *ruentis in venerem*.

32. Minadeo ("Sexual Symbolism in Horace's Love Odes," 410), points out the use of *ruo* in *Odes* 1.19.9, where the poet is (figuratively speaking) the object of Venus' sexual assault (*in me tota ruens Venus*).

33. For other examples of the imaging of the fulfillment of desire in the context of its denial, see my discussion of *Odes* 1.23 below.

34. Commager, *Odes of Horace*, 117–18.

35. Cf., e.g., Horace *Epodes* 11.2: *amore percussum gravi*.

36. On *praegestientis*, Minadeo ("Sexual Symbolism in Horace's Love Odes," 402) points out both the intensive aspect of *prae-* and its temporal suggestion of "beforehand."

37. See Jones, "Horace, Four Girls and the Other Man," 34; see also Glare, *The Oxford Latin Dictionary*, under *immitis*.

38. Reckford, "Some Studies in Horace's Odes on Love," 28.

39. Nisbet and Hubbard, *Odes Book 2*, 86.

40. Reckford, *Horace*, 104.

41. Nisbet and Hubbard assume the husband will be the addressee: "Though the mate is unspecified, *te* must be implied" (*Odes Book 2*, 89), as does Cairns (*Generic Composition in Greek and Roman Poetry*, 86), who sees *Odes* 2.5 as a particular variant on the "threat-prophecy" in which "the speaker can say that the addressee will grow to an age to feel the same sentiments as the speaker but with happy outcome." See note 29 above, for further discussion of this issue.

42. The manuscripts are divided on the reading; either *petet* or *petit* works well. *Petet* continues the pattern of *iam* plus the future tense; *iam . . . petit* suggests that "the future has already arrived."

43. Cf. the end of *Odes* 1.25 where Lydia's desire is forgotten by the *pubes* and the end of *Odes* 4.1 where fulfillment is found only in dreams.

44. However, Porter (*Horace's Poetic Journey: A Reading of Odes 1–3*, 175) acknowledges that *adhuc* (and *difficilis*) "seem not to rule out entirely the possibility of passing flirtations"; and Quinn (*The Odes*, 260) suggests that

adhuc integer "[d]oesn't so much imply that he may yet give in to Chloe, but that this is Gyges' first port of call and further temptations can be counted on to follow." Owens (*"Nuntius Vafer et Fallax*: An Alternate Reading of Horace, *C* 3.7," 163) cites Pseudo-Acro on the possibly ominous implications of *adhuc*: "adhuc integer: adhuc continens tamquam eum demonstret trahi posse in posterum, si diutius moretur" [as if "holding back to this point" shows that he could be led astray for the future, if he were to delay longer].

45. Pasquali, *Orazio Lirico*, 466.

46. See my discussion of *Odes* 1.22 below.

47. Williams, *The Third Book of Horace's Odes*, 69.

48. Boyle's comments ("Edict of Venus," 185–86) on the "comic morality-play aspect" of lines 5–22 indirectly support the idea that *adhuc integer* cannot be taken at face value.

49. Kiessling refers to the wealthy Gyges of Archilochus in the second edition of his commentary (1890), a reference later deleted by Heinze. Cf. Harrison, "Horace, *Odes* 3.7: An Erotic *Odyssey*?" 186, and Mutschler, "Eine Interpretation der Horazode *'Quid fles Asterie,'* 127, note 9. See also Mutschler, 128, note 19, on the relevance of the Herodotean Gyges.

The other appearances in the *Odes* of the name Gyges—2.5.20, discussed above (page 35), and 2.17.14 and 3.4.69 (both references to the mythological giant *centimanus Gyges*)—do not seem relevant to this poem.

50. For discussion of the Gyges story in Herodotus, see Dewald, "Women and Culture in Herodotus' *Histories*," 107–09, and Konstan, "The Stories in Herodotus' *Histories* Book I," 11–13.

51. Konstan, "The Stories in Herodotus' *Histories* Book I," 13.

52. The significance for the poem, if any, of the name Enipeus is not obvious. There may be an intended recollection of the attractive river-god Enipeus with whom Tyro is in love; cf. Homer *Odyssey* 11.235–59. Cf. also, Propertius *Elegies* 3.19.13–14 (*testis Thessalico flagrans Salmonis Enipeo, / quae voluit liquido tota subire deo.*), where Enipeus is the object of great lust.

53. Most commentators have missed the tongue-in-cheek nature of Horace's warning to Asterie. Copley, *Exclusus Amator: A Study in Latin Love Poetry*, sees Horace throughout the poem in the role of "interested bystander, the old family friend" presenting the "claims of the accepted moral code" (66). Although Bradshaw in "Horace and the Therapeutic Myth: Odes 3.7; 3,11, and 3,27," recognizes the "sensual image" of Enipeus, he maintains that Horace "adopts the tone of a stern uncle in addressing Asterie" (159, 156). Cairns, *Generic Composition in Greek and Roman Poetry*, defines *Odes* 3.7 as an inverse komos because, in his opinion, the poet is working against the interests of Enipeus, the excluded lover (208–11). At least two commentators, though, have noticed the seductive (and therefore somewhat ironic) undercurrent of Horace's warning to Asterie. Owens, in a paper entitled "The Go-Between: An Interpretation of Horace, Ode 3.7," sees the poet as an agent, like the clever slave in New Comedy, sent from Enipeus to seduce Asterie. (An expanded version of this thesis appears in Owens's *"Nuntius*

Vafer et Fallax: An Alternate Reading of Horace, C 3.7.") Of particular interest is his suggestion that the end of the poem can be read as an injunction for Asterie to not look down on, i.e., reject, Enipeus (*despice*), but (with a comma placed between *difficilis* and *mane*) to wait (*mane*) and hear him out ("*Nuntius Vafer et Fallax*," 166–67). Pasquali (*Orazio Lirico*, 466–67) has noted several examples of how Horace admonishes Asterie to be faithful, but with words that seem intended to emphasize more than necessary the degree of temptation ("ma con parole che sembrano studiarsi di mettere in rilievo anche piu del necessario quanto forte sia la tentazione" [467]). Concerning the poet's advice not to find Enipeus pleasing *plus iusto* (more than is right), he asks "qual é il iustum? [what is the right amount?]" (467). He sees the poet helping Enipeus to victory both through the *quamvis* clause enumerating his virtues and, at the end of the poem, by mischievously eliciting sympathy for him from Asterie.

54. Bradshaw's view in "Horace and the Therapeutic Myth: Odes 3,7; 3,11, and 3,27" is that the poet, through the use of mythological stories, attempts not to reassure Asterie, but to scare her into maintaining the proper behavior befitting a Roman wife, i.e., being faithful. He calls this kind of persuasion (which he also sees in *Odes* 3.11 and 3.27) the "therapeutic use of myth."

THREE   Seasonal Imagery

1. The use of nature as an analogy for human temporality has a tradition in classical literature extending as far back as Homer's famous simile of the generations of leaves and the generations of men in *Iliad* 6.146–49. On the connection of nature, age, and love, cf., e.g., *Palatine Anthology* 5.20.

2. On nature as a "moral metaphor," see Commager, *Odes of Horace*: 235–54.

3. Fraenkel, *Horace*, 420–21.

4. Quinn, *Latin Explorations*, 24.

5. *Odes* 1.4 has been written about at length. Among the discussions I have found most useful are: Babcock, "The Role of Faunus in Horace, *Carm.* 1.4"; Commager, *Odes of Horace*, 266–69; Fraenkel, *Horace*, 419–21 (discussed with 4.7); Lee, *Word, Sound, and Image in the Odes of Horace*, 65–70; Quinn, *Latin Explorations*, 14–28 (discussed with 4.7); Sylvester, "A Note on Horace 'Odes' 1,4"; and Woodman, "Horace's Odes *Diffugere niues* and *Soluitur acris hiems*" (discussed with 4.7).

6. As I have already suggested in my discussions of *Odes* 1.25 and *Odes* 2.5, indirection is a technique favored by Horace.

7. Sylvester ("A Note on Horace 'Odes' 1,4," 262) also sees positive features in winter (lines 3–4) and thus loss involved in winter's end.

8. Cf. the invocation to Venus in Lucretius *De Rerum Natura* 1.1–49 and Ovid *Fasti* 4.125–32.

9. Cf. Lucretius *De Rerum Natura* 6.365–79 for the prevalence of thunderstorms in spring and autumn.

10. Babcock ("The Role of Faunus in Horace, *Carmina* 1.4," 14–15) argues that while *imminente Luna* is usually interpreted "with the moon hanging overhead," it may also contain a sense of threat which, combined with the concept of the waxing and waning of the moon, reminds us both that winter will return and that death is not far off.

11. See Sylvester, "A Note on Horace 'Odes' 1,4," 262.

12. Ibid., 262.

13. Commager, *Odes of Horace*, 268.

14. Several commentators have noted this; see, e.g., Commager, *Odes of Horace*, 268.

15. Babcock, in "The Role of Faunus in Horace, *Carmina* 1.4," discusses the relevance of Faunus' oracular role to the pronouncement about death in lines 13–14, which he takes to be Faunus' actual oracular response.

16. Cf. *Odes* 4.7.7–8 and 1.11.6–7.

17. See chapter 2 for my comments on Horace's success in evoking the past while using the present tense in *Odes* 1.25.1–8.

18. Woodman ("Horace's Odes *Diffugere niues* and *Soluitur acris hiems*," 775–76) credits J. Bramble for having noted (in a proposed article that does not seem to have appeared in print) that *tepeo* can mean both "to be warm" and "to cool off," citing Ovid *Amores* 2.2.53–54 and *Remedia Amoris* 7. In these two passages the latter meaning is applicable, for *tepeo* is contrasted with *amo*. I do not think the *virgines* of 1.4 should be seen as "unloving," but their lessened heat, as compared with that of the *iuventus*, is noteworthy. (Cf. Stinton, "Horatian Echoes," 163, for a modified position by Bramble.) Considering the seasonal aspects of *Odes* 1.4, it is interesting that Horace uses *tepidus* elsewhere in the *Odes* to indicate "mild" winters (2.6.17–18). Stinton ("Horatian Echoes," 162–63) suggests that *tepebunt* means that Lycidas will soon be too old for the love of girls as well as men.

19. Minadeo (*The Golden Plectrum: Sexual Symbolism in Horace's Odes*, 66–69) finds greater sexual symbolism in 1.4 than I can accept; nevertheless his bold interpretation of the sacrifice to Faunus deserves mention. He sees the necessity of sacrificing to "the great phallic god of the wild" (68) as an exhortation to Sestius that he perform a sexual "sacrifice," i.e., that he should sexually initiate Lycidas. Minadeo offers useful criticism of several of the odes and rightly helps to increase our awareness of their erotic potential, nevertheless I do not find his reductive use of Freud to argue for a consistency of sexual symbolism in Horace convincing.

20. *Fugio* also appears in other temporal/erotic contexts in the *Odes*. Cf. *fugerit invida / aetas* (*Odes* 1.11.7–8) in the love poem to Leuconoe; *fugit retro / levis iuventas et decor* (*Odes* 2.11.5–6); *quo fugit Venus, heu, quove color, decens / quo motus?* (*Odes* 4.13.17–18) for the fleeing of youth and grace; *fuge quaerere* (*Odes* 1.9.13).

21. Cf. *vice veris* (*Odes* 1.4.1).

22. Woodman ("Horace's Odes *Diffugere niues* and *Soluitur acris hiems*," 772) sees the nudity of the Graces as a sign of their uninhibited and happy nature as compared with the more reserved *Gratiae decentes* of *Odes* 1.4.6.

23. On the extensive personification of nature and time in this poem, see Putnam, *Artifices of Eternity*, 135–36. For a recent study of the use of word order to underscore meaning, see Lateiner, "Mimetic Syntax: Metaphor From Word Order, Especially in Ovid."

24. See my discussion of *immitis* in *Odes* 2.5 (chapter 2).

25. See my discussion of *protervi* in *Odes* 1.25 (chapter 2).

26. Putnam (*Artifices of Eternity*, 136–37) notes the appearance of *protero* in Horace only here and at *Odes* 3.5.34 as well as its sole occurrence in Vergil at *Aeneid* 12.330 (*agmina curru proterit*), where Turnus tramples the enemy with his chariot. In *Odes* 3.5.31–36 Regulus comments sarcastically on the chances of a captured Roman soldier again becoming a good warrior:

> si pugnat extricata densis
>   cerva plagis, erit ille fortis,
> qui perfidis se credidit hostibus
> et Marte Poenos *proteret* altero,
>   qui lora restrictis lacertis
>   sensit iners timuitque mortem.

If the deer fights, loosened from the close nets, then will he be brave who entrusted himself to a perfidious enemy, and will he trample the Carthaginians in another war, who impotent felt the straps on his arms drawn back and feared death.

Interestingly, *iners*, which appears three lines from *proterit* in *Odes* 4.7, occurs near *proteret* in *Odes* 3.5 as well (line 36).

27. For the simple verb *curro* used elsewhere of time in the *Odes*, cf. 2.5.13–14: *currit enim ferox / aetas*.

28. Commager (*Odes of Horace*, 278) notes the deadly impact of *iners*, which falls at the end of a cataleptic line and is followed by the silence of a full stop.

29. See Putnam, *Artifices of Eternity*, 137: "Cowardly winter can hurry back only because her unrelenting enemy, spring, is momentarily displaced. But as the etymology of *bruma* implies, such happenings are only momentary." For *bruma* as derived from the superlative of *brevis*, see Glare, *The Oxford Latin Dictionary*, under *bruma*.

30. Putnam's rendering of *iners* as "cowardly" in the previous note, while fitting the military sense of *proterit*, misses the word's possible sexual connotations. Cf. also *iners* as "impotent" in Ovid *Amores* 3.7.15.

31. See Commager's remarks (*Odes of Horace*, 81–82) on Horace's use of the moon in *Odes* 2.18.16: "In a sense the moon mediates between eternal and transient, and Horace found both aspects peculiarly evocative. *Novaeque pergunt interire lunae* (16): the line is both epitaph and promise of continuity. The moon's

changes (*pergunt interire*) predict the mortality of all sublunar nature, but *novae* separates the persistence of nature's changes from the finality of human death." (Commager footnotes *Odes* 4.7.13–16 for these remarks as well.)

Babcock ("The Role of Faunus in Horace, *Carmina* 1,4," 14–15) connects the sense of threat in *imminente Luna* (*Odes* 1.4.5) with the warning of *Odes* 4.7.13–16.

32. Several commentators point this out, including, e.g., Nisbet and Hubbard, *Odes Book 1*, 60; Commager, *Odes of Horace*, 280; and Putnam, *Artifices of Eternity*, 141–42.

33. Glare, *The Oxford Latin Dictionary*, cites "one's own" as the apparent meaning of *amicus* in this passage and cites no other examples of the usage in Latin.

34. See Hyginus *Fabulae* 79.2 and Vergil *Aeneid* 6.392–97.

35. Quinn, *Latin Explorations*, 26.

36. Minadeo, *The Golden Plectrum: Sexual Symbolism in Horace's Odes*, 87 (hereafter *Golden Plectrum*).

37. Putnam, *Artifices of Eternity*, 141.

38. Cf. *Odes* 3.4.79–80 (*amatorem trecentae / Pirithoum cohibent catenae*).

39. *Odes* 1.9 has received much critical attention. Useful discussions include: Cameron, "Horace's Soracte Ode: (*Carm.* 1.9)"; Clay, "Ode 1.9: Horace's September Song"; Commager, *Odes of Horace*, 269–74; Lee, *Word, Sound, and Image in the Odes of Horace*, 25–28; Pöschl, *Horazische Lyrik*, 30–51; Rudd, "Patterns in Horatian Lyric," 386–92 and passim; Wilkinson, *Horace and His Lyric Poetry*, 129–31; Peter Connor, "Soracte Encore"; Striar, "Soracte Reconsidered: The Burden of Youth and the Relief of Age in Horace *Odes* I.9"; Springer, "Horace's Soracte Ode: Location, Dislocation, and the Reader"; Segal, "Horace's Soracte Ode (C. I,9): Of Interpretation, Philologic and Hermeneutic"; Murray, "Horace's Soracte Ode (C. I,9): The Hermeneutic Response"; Palmer, "Horace's Soracte Ode (C. I,9): Philosophical Hermeneutics and the Interpretation"; Edmunds, *From a Sabine Jar: Reading Horace, Odes 1.9* (with extensive bibliography).

40. See Striar, "Soracte Reconsidered: The Burden of Youth and the Relief of Age in Horace *Odes* I.9" (hereafter "Soracte Reconsidered"), and Cameron, "Horace's Soracte Ode: (*Carm.* 1.9)."

41. See Glare, *The Oxford Latin Dictionary*, under *candidus* 5, "fair (usually implying beauty)," and 4b "(of hair, a sign of old age)."

42. See ibid. under *frigus* 6, for coldness in regard to affection.

Striar ("Soracte Reconsidered," 207) comments on the erotic sense of *solve* as the loosening of a girl's girdle.

43. Striar ("Soracte Reconsidered," 207) mentions that *onus* can evoke "not only snow but also leaves and/or ripening, immature, pale green fruit."

44. Cf. Commager, *Odes of Horace*, 271. Wilkinson (*Horace and His Lyric Poetry*, 130–31) also sees the calm as the calm of death. On the funereal associations of the cypress, cf. Vergil *Aeneid* 3.64 (and Servius' commentary *ad. loc. inferis consecrata*); *Aeneid* 6.216; and Horace *Odes* 2.14.23. Cunningham ("Enarratio of Horace *Odes* 1.9," 101), however, argues that the cypress as evergreen represents youth as opposed to age (the old ash trees) in line 11 and that the *silvae laborantes* of line 3 are evergreens.

45. Cf. *Odes* 1.6.17–18 for *proelia* in another love context: *proelia virginum / sectis in iuvenes unguibus acrium.*

46. On *agito* as a sexual term, see Adams, *The Latin Sexual Vocabulary*, 194. Cf. Horace's use of the verb in an explicitly sexual sense at *Satires* 2.7.50.

47. *Odes* 1.4, 4.7, and 1.11 share this movement from thoughts of death to thoughts of love.

48. Lee (*Word, Sound, and Image in the Odes of Horace*, 25–28) discusses the *callida iunctura, virenti canities*, and its importance to the poem.

49. Fraenkel, *Horace*, 177.

50. Cameron, "Horace's Soracte Ode: (*Carm.* 1.9)," 153.

51. Ibid., 151–55.

52. I borrow the term "indeterminacy" as applied to *Odes* 1.9 from Nielsen and Solomon, "Soracte and Sacred Space: Centuries of *carpe diem*," who note that in *Odes* 1.9 "[l]ove-making offers no illusions of permanence and immutability" (824). They see, too, the "negative resonances to the poem's easy hedonism" (824).

53. See, e.g., Quinn, *Horace: The Odes*, 142.

54. Bennett, *Horace: Odes and Epodes*, 214.

55. See Minadeo (*Golden Plectrum*, 21), who quotes Gilbert Murray: "I am not sure that there is not something in 'intimo gratus'—'delightful in the deep'." (*The Classical Tradition in Poetry* [New York, 1957], 150). Minadeo continues: "I am certain that there is, especially seeing that *intimo* modifies the symbolic *angulo.* Finally, rarely does Horace achieve so fine a blend of delicacy and drama in his symbolic effects as in the final two images. Symbolically, both bracelet and ring are vaginal. By suggestion, then, the young lady is weak to resist the surrender not merely of pledges, but of love itself" (21–22). While I find rather reductive Minadeo's narrowly symbolic reading of *angulo* and the circular *pignus*, I do agree that *angulo* is sexually suggestive.

56. The financial and legal associations of the word *pignus* (pledge) have been noted by Vessey ("From Mountain to Lovers' Tryst: Horace's Soracte Ode," 37).

57. See Glare, *The Oxford Latin Dictionary*, for the range of meanings for *male*.

58. That Horace is interested in the literal meaning of words that can have transferred meanings as well is apparent at *Odes* 1.9.13. While *fuge* functions as a negative with the infinitive *quaerere*, the literal meaning of fleeing or escaping is also clearly significant in a poem concerned with the "flight" of time. Cf., also, *fuge suspicari* (*Odes* 2.4.22). So, too, the literal meaning of *male* cannot be ignored.

59. Fraenkel, *Horace*, 184.

60. See, e.g., Nisbet and Hubbard, *Odes Book 1*, 273–74 and 276–77, for discussion of the poem's Anacreontic models and problems with and suggested emendations for *veris inhorruit adventus*. I agree with Commager (and others) that "Bentley's attempt to amend *veris . . . adventus* (5–6) to *vepris . . . ad ventum* ignores the Ode's controlling metaphor, which is a seasonal one" (Commager, *Odes of Horace*, 238). On the poet's use of simile and metaphor, see Lee, "Horace *Carm.* 1.23: Simile and Metaphor"; on simile, as well, and logical structure, see Estevez, "Chloe and the Fawn: The Structure of *Odes* 1.23."

61. Nisbet and Hubbard, *Odes Book 1*, 274. See also Lyne, *The Latin Love Poets: From Catullus to Horace*, who comments on the poem's "charm and discretion" (215) and calls the "message [of the poem] essentially complimentary—but [one that] needs sensitive handling" (216).

62. Nielsen, "Horace Odes 1.23: Innocence." While I do not agree with all of Nielsen's conclusions, her exploration of the nature of Chloe's fears and her recognition of the poet/lover as a possible threat show an interest in and a sensitivity to Chloe's perspective, not common in the scholarship on this poem.

63. See Ancona, "The Subterfuge of Reason: Horace, *Odes* 1.23 and the Construction of Male Desire," for an expanded version of this argument, which utilizes Jessica Benjamin's discussion of the fantasy of erotic domination to explain the dichotomy between the rational discourse and the emotive power of this ode. (For Benjamin's work, see the Bibliography.) My interpretation of the Chloe ode presented in the article cited above was challenged by Ernst Fredricksmeyer in a paper delivered at the Advanced Placement Latin session of the 1992 meeting of the Classical Association of the Middle West and South. Regrettably, I cannot respond to this challenge since I have been unable to obtain a copy of the paper from Professor Fredricksmeyer.

64. Commager, *Odes of Horace*, 238.

65. Cf. Pausanias 1.22.3.

66. Cf. *Inscriptiones Graecae* 2².949.7,35, as cited in Liddell and Scott, *A Greek-English Lexicon*, under χλόϊα, τά.

67. For the purpose of my argument, Rose's interpretation ("Some Passages of Latin Poets") of *frangere* as requiring "mule-colt" rather than "fawn" for the animal to which Chloe is compared is not of consequence. For it makes little difference whether the poet/lover in the tiger/lion simile is (as Rose argues makes sense with Chloe as "mule-colt" but not as "fawn") "an actual or potential owner, not eater, running after a creature which he wants to use for his business or pleasure" (3). The dominating attitude of the lover is equally apparent even if Chloe is merely "owned," not "eaten"!

68. Cf. *quis nostras sic frangit fores?* (Plautus *Asinaria* 384 and *ianua frangatur* (Horace *Satires* 1.2.128).

69. Of course the desire to break down a barrier to gain access to a beloved takes conventional literary form in the *paraklausithyron/exclusus amator* motif. The need to overcome or violate another's boundaries imaged in this motif is central to the fantasy of erotic domination under discussion. For references to this motif in the *Odes*, see Henderson, "The Paraklausithyron Motif in Horace's Odes."

70. On *frangere* as "epexegetic inf. after *persequor* implying *desire* [emphasis mine]," see Page, *Q. Horati Flacci: Opera*, 225.

FOUR Age and Experience

1. Esler, "Horace, Barine, and the Immortality of Words (*Odes* 2.8)," also discusses Barine's unusual atemporality and suggests that Barine represents

"Woman." She states in note 12, page 108, that her reading of Barine has a number of points in common with Fredricksmeyer's reading of Pyrrha in "Horace's Ode to Pyrrha (*Carm*. 1.5)." Esler presents an excellent discussion (110–12) of Barine's rhetorical powers as attractive to Horace as poet.

2. These characteristics include: discolored teeth (*Epodes* 8.3, *Odes* 4.13. 10–11); excessive drinking (*Odes* 3.15.16 and *Odes* 4.13.4–5); wrinkles (*Epodes* 8.3–4 and *Odes* 4.13.11–12); withered skin (*Epodes* 8.5; *Odes* 1.25.19, where *aridas frondis* stands metaphorically for Lydia; and *Odes* 4.13.9–10, where *aridas quercus* functions the same way in relation to Lyce); excessive lust (*Odes* 1.25.13–15, where Lydia's lust is compared with that of a mare, and *Odes* 3.15 generally). For the theme of the aging beloved in Greek epigram, see, e.g., *Palatine Anthology* 5.204, 5.21, 5.273. For discussions of Latin invective against old women (especially Horace *Epodes* 8 and 12) and Horace's sexual satire, see Richlin, *The Garden of Priapus: Sexuality and Aggression in Roman Humor*, 109– 16 and 174–85.

3. For sources on the ancient literary convention that the gods pay no attention to lovers' vows, see Nisbet and Hubbard, *Odes Book 2*, 122–23.

4. *Ferus*, used of Cupid, foreshadows the focus on the animal-like side of human sexuality.

5. For the sexual meaning of *pubes*, see Adams, *The Latin Sexual Vocabulary*, 76.

6. Minadeo (*Golden Plectrum*, 53) has also recognized the phallic excitation suggested by the repeated *crescit*. For *cresco* used elsewhere in an erotic sense, see, e.g., Vergil *Eclogue* 10.54 (where it is also repeated) and 73. In both passages from Vergil the "increase" of love is associated with the growth of trees which, particularly in the latter passage, seems to have a phallic sense. For evidence that such a word play is not alien to Horace, see the sexual pun on his own name in *Epodes* 15.12: *nam si quid in Flacco viri est. . . .*

7. These earlier lovers of Barine recall the *gracilis puer* of *Odes* 1.5, who has difficulty ending his attachment to Pyrrha. Pyrrha, like Barine, remains desirable over time to the same individual(s), even though she does not remain (or never was) available for exclusive use by one partner. See the references to other scholars who have noted similarities between *Odes* 1.5 and *Odes* 2.8 in Esler, "Horace, Barine, and the Immortality of Words (*Odes* 2.8)," 105, note 2.

8. Cf. *aura* in *Odes* 1.5.11. For Vergil's use of the term *aura* for the odor given off by a mare in heat, cf. *Georgics* 3.250–51: *nonne vides, ut tota tremor pertemptet equorum / corpora, si tantum notas odor attulit auras?* See also my discussion in chapter 2 (*Odes* 1.25) of Lydia's comparison to a mare in heat.

9. For *lentus* used of a "slow" lover, cf. Propertius 2.15.8. Columella *De Re Rustica* 10.109 uses *tardus* of "slow" husbands who need an aphrodisiac: *Excitet ut Veneri tardos eruca maritos.*

10. See Pichon, *Index Verborum Amatoriorum*, 226, "Sed *parca* libido est moderata," who cites Ovid *Ars Amatoria* 1.281. See my comments in chapter

2 on the erotic potential of the phrase *parcius iunctas* (*Odes* 1.25.1). McDermott ("Greek and Roman Elements in Horace's Lyric Program," 1642) points out a nonerotic pun on *parcus* at *Odes* 2.16.39.

11. Cf. Campbell, *Horace: A New Interpretation*, 221; and Lee, *Word, Sound, and Image in the Odes of Horace*, 111.

12. Lee, *Word, Sound, and Image in the Odes of Horace*, 111.

13. Ensor, "Notes on the Odes of Horace."

14. Ibid., 110.

15. See Putnam (*Artifices of Eternity*, 33–47) for an excellent discussion of *Odes* 4.1. Other useful treatments of the poem include Fraenkel, *Horace*, 410–14; Commager, *Odes of Horace*, 291–97; Lefèvre, "*Rursus bella moves?* Die literarische Form von Horaz, c. 4,I," 166–89; Habinek, "The Marriageability of Maximus: Horace, *Ode* 4.1.13–20," 407–16; Bradshaw, "Horace, *Odes* 4.1," 142–53.

16. See my discussion in chapter 2 of *Odes* 1.25, in which *laeta* (17) first appears to modify *pubes*, and *parcius* (1) affects both *iunctas* and *quatiunt*.

17. Cinara's name reappears in *Odes* 4.13, discussed below, in connection with matters of youth and age. There Cinara is spared the "indecorous older age" of Lyce through her premature death (*sed Cinarae brevis / annos fata dederunt* 22–23).

18. The use of *desine* in the speaker's injunction to Valgius (*Odes* 2.9) to stop his laments (*desine mollium / tandem querelarum* 17–18) does not indicate the judgment that Valgius' status as a beloved has changed, but rather that his continuing activity as a lover should end. Thus, the temporal issue for Valgius, because of his status as lover, not beloved, remains a private one, as it does for the poet/lover in *Odes* 4.1.

19. A similar comparison is made in *Odes* 4.13, when Lyce is compared unfavorably with a younger woman more suitable for love. (See my discussion of *Odes* 4.13 below.) Bradshaw ("Horace, *Odes* 4.1") and Habinek ("The Marriageability of Maximus: Horace, *Ode* 4.1.13–20") argue that the specific kind of love for which Paulus is more suitable is marital love; they see *Odes* 4.1 as a poem in praise of Paulus' qualities as a potential spouse for Marcia, relative of Augustus. Habinek, in addition, suggests that "the poem presents a contrast between alternative visions of love . . . one permanent, aristocratic, Roman, married; the other fleeting, promiscuous, demi-mondaine, and bisexual—with neither giving way to the other" (413–14).

20. See my discussion of *tempestiva* in *Odes* 1.23 (chapter 3).

21. Cf. *lumenque iuventae / purpureum* (Vergil *Aeneid* 1.590–91) of the enhanced beauty given to Aeneas by his mother Venus.

22. Babcock ("*Si Certus Intrarit Dolor*: A Reconsideration of Horace's Fifteenth Epode," 414) takes *potiori* (*Epodes* 15.13) as sexual and, in addition, lists several other erotic uses of *potior* and related words in Horace (414, note 27). *Trabs* is used by Catullus for "penis" in 28.10. *Trabs* in *Odes* 4.1, especially within the context of Venus' worship, must carry a phallic sense beyond its primary meaning of "roof-beam."

23. Cf. *Odes* 1.4.17–19, discussed in chapter 3, where Sestius is told that death will take him away from banqueting and love.

24. The other three occurrences of *credulus* in the *Odes* also appear in erotic contexts (*Odes* 1.5.9, *Odes* 1.11.8, *Odes* 3.7.13).

25. For tears, awkward silences, and continual laments as conventional symptoms of the *miser amator*, cf. Catullus 51, *Epodes* 11.9, *Odes* 1.13.6–7, and *Odes* 2.9, in which the speaker tells Valgius to cease his perpetual lamenting. See also Pichon, *Index Verborum Amatoriorum*, 181–82 on *lacrimae*. The poet/lover's lapse into indecorous silence (cf. Paulus as *decens* 13) is highlighted by the hypermetric line 35 with its elision of *decoro inter* and the caesura after *cadit* (36), which underscores the meaning of the verb and through its pause anticipates *silentio*. While the description of his own silence as "indecorous" might seem to indicate the possibility of some kind of public negative judgment, the poem in no way suggests that this lapse into silence occurs anywhere but in private.

26. For another erotic dream in Horace, specifically a wet dream, cf. *Satires* 1.5.83–85.

27. *Gramina Martii / Campi* (39–40) picks up the military/erotic metaphors earlier in the poem (*bella moves* 2, and *late signa feret militiae tuae* 16). For both the Campus Martius and the Tiber as sites for the exhibition of the prowess of young males, cf. *Odes* 1.8.3–8 and *Odes* 3.7.25–28 (discussed in chapter 2). For time as "winged" or "swift," cf. *volucris dies* in *Odes* 3.28.6 and *Odes* 4.13.16.

28. The discussions of *Odes* 4.13 I have found most useful are: Commager, *Odes of Horace*, 291–302; Minadeo, *Golden Plectrum*, 36–40; Quinn, *Latin Explorations*, 90–99; Fraenkel, *Horace*, 415–16; Putnam, *Artifices of Eternity*, 219–35.

29. Although we cannot assume that each time a particular name occurs in the *Odes* it must have the same referent, it is useful to identify the Lyce of *Odes* 4.13 with the Lyce of *Odes* 3.10.

30. Lyce's wrinkles (*rugae* 11) are anticipated by *aridas / quercus* (9–10), dry oak [leaves]. See chapter 4, note 2, on stereotypically abhorrent characteristics associated with older women.

31. Putnam (*Artifices of Eternity*, 222, note 2) cites Horace's use of *excubo* with an abstract subject (its first occurrence in Latin) as evidence of the personification of *Cupido* as the god of love.

32. For other abstract nouns that take on the concrete sense "penis" in Latin, see Adams, *The Latin Sexual Vocabulary*, 57.

33. See chapter 4, note 9, on *lentus* used of the lover slow to respond.

34. For *sollicito* meaning to stimulate sexually, cf. Martial 11.46.4 and Lucretius 4.1196.

35. For another Horatian example of an older woman who must work to stimulate her partner (specifically by fellatio) because her ugliness has left him cold, see *Epodes* 8, especially 19–20.

36. This has been noted by, e.g., Kiessling-Heinze, *Q. Horatius Flaccus: Oden und Epoden*, 453; and Quinn, *Latin Explorations*, 94.

37. This revision of Sophocles' lines has not to my knowledge been noted by other commentators. The only other example in Horace of a word related to *excubat* is *excubiae* (*Odes* 3.16.3), which occurs in the Danae ode, the beginning of which Henderson has rightly recognized as a *paraklausithyron* ("The Paraklausithyron Motif in Horace's *Odes*," 64).

38. *Fervidi* (26) recalls *aequore fervido* (*Odes* 1.9.10) where the seething of the sea had erotic overtones in contrast with the calming of the storm. See my discussion of *Odes* 1.9 (chapter 3).

39. See Porter, "The Recurrent Motifs of Horace, *Carmina* IV," 217–220, on the motif of fire and light in Book 4 of the *Odes*, and 218, on this motif specifically in *Odes* 4.13.

40. Cf. young Lycidas (*Odes* 1.4), who will one day, as time moves on, be in Sestius' place, as well as Ligurinus (*Odes* 4.10), whose unhappiness when one day he will have lost his youthful good looks, the speaker predicts. Cf. also the speaker's anticipation of disillusionment for the *puer* in *Odes* 1.5 and the rival in *Epodes* 15.

FIVE   The Romantic Ideal and the Domination of the Beloved

1. Quinn (*Latin Explorations*, 144–66) argues that Lucretius' attack on love in Book 4 of *De Rerum Natura* permanently affected the kind of love poetry the Romans could write, specifically, that romantic love poetry in the Catullan manner was dealt a serious blow. My view here differs from that of Quinn (154–55), who writes in regard to what he has called "Horace's assault on love elegy": "What seemed to him [Horace] really silly was the fuss they [the elegiac poets] made when their mistresses deserted them. A man *could* be expected to have enough sense to know love does not last, and accept the fact, instead of carrying on. . . ." This seems to me a reductive reading of Horace as a love poet, for it fails to recognize the ways in which Horace's apparent antiromanticism in fact reinstates the ideal of romantic love.

For an interesting argument that attempts to correct the view presented by Quinn, and others, of Lucretius as "anti-love," see Nussbaum, "Beyond Obsession and Disgust: Lucretius' Genealogy of Love." To summarize a highly nuanced discussion, Nussbaum concludes that Lucretius is attacking romantic love, which precludes recognizing the beloved as a self, but valuing marriage, which can entail mutual recognition. A brief version of Nussbaum's discussion of Lucretius also appears in Nussbaum, "Therapeutic Arguments and Structures of Desire," 46–66.

2. See, e.g., Commager, *Odes of Horace*, 239: "The elegiac poets tended to move exclusively in the world created by their own emotional fiat. To so insulated a view Horace was instinctively opposed, and in an Ode to the poet Valgius (*C.* 2.9) he sets out to alter it."

3. Putnam, "Horace *Carm.* 2.9: Augustus and the Ambiguities of En-comium," makes a persuasive argument that the poem's invitation to joint encomium reflects an ambiguous stance toward Augustus. While the per-spective from which Putnam examines the poem differs from mine, I agree with him not only on many individual points of interpretation, but also on the problematic status of the alternatives presented to Valgius. Where I have focused primarily on how the content of the alternatives in fact reinforces Valgius' current values, Putnam's analysis is particularly useful for its exam-ination of the ambivalent attitudes implicit in the speaker's suggestion to write in praise of Augustus. Minadeo (*Golden Plectrum*, 141–42) calls atten-tion to the phallic domination reflected in the speaker's description of the world subdued by Augustus.

4. On *querela* here as a techical term for elegy, see Saylor, "*Querelae*: Propertius' Distinctive Technical Name for his Elegy." For an excellent dis-cussion of the term *mollitia* (often translated as "softness" or "effeminacy") in Roman discourse, see Edwards, *The Politics of Immorality in Ancient Rome*, 63–97.

5. See my discussion in Chapter 3 of the appeal to the cyclicity of nature.

6. Putnam ("Horace *Carm.* 2.9: Augustus and the Ambiguities of En-comium," 219–21) also recognizes the reinstatement of Valgius' mourning through personification.

7. See Glare, *The Oxford Latin Dictionary*, under *imber*, 3a.

8. Ibid., under *nubes*, 8a and b.

9. Ibid., under *hispidus*, 1 and 2.

10. Ibid., under *mano*.

11. Ibid., under *procella*, 2b.

12. Ibid., under *vexo*.

13. Cf. *Epodes* 12.17, where *inertem* means "impotent," and *Odes* 4.7.12, where I have suggested in my discussion above (pp. 55–56) that *iners* has erotic connotations as well.

14. On the sexual sense of *laborare*, see Adams, *The Latin Sexual Vocabulary*, 157.

15. See my discussion of *Odes* 2.8 above.

16. Cf. the erotic sense of *urget* in *Odes* 1.5.2.

17. Minadeo (*Golden Plectrum*, 140) comments on lines 9–12 that "[t]he unnaturalness of Valgius' pertinacity is . . . vastly heightened by the hint that it actually enacts an unconscious prolongation of his intimacy with Mystes," while Putnam ("Horace *Carm.* 2.9: Augustus and the Ambiguities of En-comium," 230) discusses Horace's use (lines 10–12) of the description in Vergil *Georgics* 4.464–66 of Orpheus' lamentation for his lost Eurydice.

18. Nisbet and Hubbard (*Odes Book 2*, 145) comment on the connection between *rapidum* and *rapio*.

19. See Rose, *A Handbook of Greek Mythology*, 239, with ancient sources, 251; and Nisbet and Hubbard, *Odes Book 2*, 146.

20. A vivid portrayal of his death appears at *Aeneid* 1.474–78, in the

passage describing the artwork in the Temple of Juno at Carthage. For other sources, see Hammond and Scullard, *The Oxford Classical Dictionary*, under Troilus.

21. Nisbet and Hubbard (*Odes Book 2*, 137) note that they were both καλοὶ παῖδες [beautiful male beloveds]. While Nisbet and Hubbard discuss the homoerotic overtones in the examples of Antilochus and Troilus and note their relevance to Valgius' relationship to Mystes, they fail to see how these overtones in some sense must undermine the effectiveness of the examples.

22. Cf. *amabilem* used of Pyrrha in *Odes* 1.5.10 along with *urget* (see note 16 above), used of her young lover's pursuit.

23. *Iliad* 17.652–701 and 18.1–34.

24. *Imagines* 2.7.1 and 2.7.5, quoted in Nisbet and Hubbard, *Odes Book 2*, 147.

25. Nisbet and Hubbard, *Odes Book 2*, 147.

26. Phrynicus frag. 13 N (quoted) and Statius *Silvae* 2.6.30ff. (cited), in Nisbet and Hubbard, *Odes Book 2*, 147–48.

27. See, e.g., their depiction in Juvenal (6.325–26): ". . . guaranteed to warm the age-chilled balls of a Nestor or a Priam" (. . . *quibus incendi iam frigidus aevo / Laomedontiades et Nestoris hirnea possit*), as translated by Green, *Juvenal: The Sixteen Satires*, 139. For Priam, specifically, cf. Martial 6.71.3–4.

28. Nisbet and Hubbard (*Odes Book 2*, 135) cite the anonymous panegyrist on Messalla for the idea that Valgius was capable of political eulogy: "*est tibi qui possit magnis se accingere rebus / Valgius; aeterno propior non alter Homero*" [You have Valgius, who can equip himself with great matters; there is not another closer to Homer] (lines 179–80).

29. See Minadeo, *Golden Plectrum*, 141–42 (cited above, note 3). For the negative implications of this proposed move toward military celebration, see Putnam, "Horace *Carm*. 2.9: Augustus and the Ambiguities of Encomium," 226–27.

30. See, e.g., Commager, *Odes of Horace*, 239 (cited above, note 2).

31. Commager, *Odes of Horace*, 132.

32. "*Carmina/Iambi*: The Literary-Generic Dimension of Horace's *Integer Vitae* (*C*. I, 22)," 68, note 4. Davis argues that *Odes* 1.22 should be seen in generic terms as a rejection of invective, the genre of Horace's earlier career, and as an affirmation of love lyric in the Lesbian tradition. He sees the fleeing of the portentous wolf, traditionally used as symbol of the writer of invective and/or his victim, as emblematic of the banishment of invective. The fact that the love poet needs no weapons, he argues, further distances him from invective, the genre of attack, and links him with love poetry, in which lovers are often opposed to fighters.

Davis discusses Horace's rejection of invective primarily in terms of iambic invective. However, as I have argued elsewhere, the self-referentiality in *Odes* 1.22, which consists of numerous direct and indirect allusions to *Satires* 1.9, suggests that satire, as well as iambics, should be understood as part of the invective Horace rejects. The most obvious of these allusions is the presence through the word *Fusce* (line 4) of Aristius Fuscus, the figure who appears in *Satires* 1.9, as the ode's addressee. The themes of loquaciousness/song and danger mark additional links between the satire and the ode. Finally, the loquaciousness, which is dangerous in the satire, when subsumed under the poet's song—and thus made subject to his control— becomes a talisman in the ode (see Ancona, "A Further Literary-Generic Dimension of Horace's *Integer Vitae* [*Odes* 1.22]"). However, see my discussion below for the problem with Lalage functioning as a talisman.

Although much of Davis's argument about *Odes* 1.22 is persuasive, his positing of a "metonymic bond" (69) between Lalage and the poet/lover obscures the more problematic relationship between the two I discuss below.

33. *Odes* 1.22 is written in the Sapphic meter, which recalls not only Sappho but Catullus, who uses this meter just twice, in Poems 51 and 11, which treat the so-called beginning and end of the Lesbia cycle. Horace's catalogue of wanderings in *Odes* 1.22 (lines 5–6 and 17–24) recalls the places to which Catullus' friends are said to be willing to accompany him in Poem 11.1–12. *Dulce ridentem* (*Odes* 1.22.23) recalls Catullus 51, Catullus' translation and adaptation of Sappho 31. In addition, *dulce loquentem*, which Horace takes without change and Catullus eliminates, recalls directly the Sapphic original.

34. Girard, *Deceit, Desire, and the Novel*, discusses the triangle (not unlike that found in this ode) that is constructed from the lover, his model, and the beloved. In this triangle the lover imitates the model by desiring what he desires. The beloved is desirable because someone else desires her. The bond between the lover and his model, the rivals in love, is as important as that between lover and beloved. See also Barthes's discussion of identification in *A Lover's Discourse*, 129–31. Sedgwick, *Between Men: English Literature and Male Homosocial Desire*, extends Girard's version of the triangle by revealing the gender arrangements that normally underlie the triangularity of desire. She examines the way in which the woman as beloved functions in the establishment of bonds between men.

35. For the traditional lover's inability to speak, cf., e.g., Sappho 31.7–9 and Catullus 51.7–9.

36. While in my translation of this ode I have rendered *perpetuum* as an adjective, I would suggest that it may alternatively be taken as an adverb (repeatedly, continually) modifying the participle *laedentem* (harming). Taking it in this way (you would not hope for him to continuously harm like a barbarian your sweet lips) profitably heightens the overlap between the specific nature of Telephus' erotic behavior with Lydia and their continuing relationship over time. In support of this interpretation of *perpetuum* as an adverb, see the separate entry under *perpetuum* (adv.) in Glare, *The Oxford Latin Dictionary*. Since neuter forms of adjectives are commonly used as adverbs in Latin, I think we should consider the above interpretation even though the authors cited for *perpetuum* as an adverb postdate Horace. In addition, the fact that *laedentem* is already modified by another adverb (*bar-*

bare) should not dissuade us, since Horace elsewhere uses two adverbs as modifiers. (See my discussion on page 27 of *multum* as a second modifier for *movebat* in addition to *prius*.)

37. Pavlock, "Horace's Invitation Poems to Maecenas: Gifts to a Patron," 86.

38. Commager, *The Odes of Horace: A Critical Study*, 155.

39. Interestingly, the reading in Holder's edition of Porphyrio (*Pomponi Porfyrionis Commentum in Horatium Flaccum*, 22) is *interrupta*, although Porphyrio's commentary does not reflect this. Meyer's edition (*Pomponii Porphyrionis Commentarii in Q. Horatium Flaccum*, 19) reads *inrupta*. Porphyrio's commentary on *interrupta/inrupta* in both editions reads as follows: "Allegoricos hoc dicitur. Significat autem eos, qui ita amoris uinculo inter se constricti sunt, ut numquam discerni possint." [This is said allegorically. Moreover, it means those who have been bound mutually by the chain of love so that they never can be separated.]

40. There may be some slight ambiguity in *suprema . . . die* as well. While a standard reference to death, the phrase could also mean here the "last day of the relationship." This would produce a somewhat humorous tautology: happy are those whom love does not loosen until its—that is, love's or the relationship's—last day!

41. I am grateful to Charles Babcock for his willingness to listen to some of my unorthodox thoughts on this poem.

42. Nielsen, "Catullus 45 and Horace *Odes* 3.9: The Glass House"; Pavlock, "Horace's Invitation Poems to Maecenas: Gifts to a Patron"; and Putnam, "Horace *Odes* 3.9: The Dialectics of Desire" reprinted in *Essays on Latin Lyric, Elegy, and Epic*, 107–25, provide useful discussions of this poem.

43. Putnam (*Essays on Latin Lyric, Elegy, and Epic*, 112, note 11) suggests that the door lying open for Lydia indicates a usurping of female power by the male, for normally in Latin love poetry it is the woman's door which is or is not open to the man; Minadeo (*Golden Plectrum*, 47) proposes that the man's control of the door suggests his feminization. The association of the male lover's desire with the door is best seen, not as feminization or usurping of female power, but rather as a tentative openness to the possibility of erotic reciprocity, which responds (albeit somewhat passively) to Lydia's challenge of mutuality.

44. Putnam, *Essays on Latin Lyric, Elegy, and Epic*, 115–17.

45. Ibid., 117.

46. Putnam (*Essays on Latin Lyric, Elegy, and Epic*, 112, note 12) comments on the male lover's use of the present tense rather than an "expected future."

47. Lee, *Word, Sound, and Image in the Odes of Horace*, 107.

48. Putnam, *Essays on Latin Lyric, Elegy, and Epic*, 116.

49. See Adams, *The Latin Sexual Vocabulary*, 159.

BIBLIOGRAPHY

The following list includes all works cited in the text and notes.

Adams, J. N. *The Latin Sexual Vocabulary.* Baltimore, 1982.

Allen, Archibald W. "Sunt qui Propertium malint." In *Critical Essays on Roman Literature: Elegy and Lyric,* edited by J. P. Sullivan, 107–48. Cambridge, Mass., 1962.

Ancona, Ronnie. "A Further Literary-Generic Dimension of Horace's *Integer Vitae* (*Odes* 1.22)." Paper presented at the annual meeting of the Classical Association of the Atlantic States, Princeton, N.J., 1990.

———. "Horace *Odes* 1.25: Temporality, Gender, and Desire." In *Collection Latomus: Studies in Latin Literature and Roman History* 6, edited by C. Deroux, 245–59. Brussels, 1992.

———. "The Subterfuge of Reason: Horace, *Odes* 1.23 and the Construction of Male Desire." *Helios* 16 (1989): 49–57.

Arkins, Brian. "A Reading of Horace, *Carm.* 1.25." *Classica et Mediaevalia* 34 (1983): 161–75.

Armstrong, David. *Horace.* New Haven and London, 1989.

Babcock, Charles L. "The Role of Faunus in Horace, *Carmina* 1.4." *Transactions of the American Philological Association* 92 (1961): 13–19.

———. "*Si Certus Intrarit Dolor*: A Reconsideration of Horace's Fifteenth Epode." *American Journal of Philology* 87 (1966): 400–19.

Barthes, Roland. *A Lover's Discourse.* Translated by Richard Howard. New York, 1978.

Benjamin, Jessica. *The Bonds of Love: Psychoanalysis, Feminism, and the Problem of Domination.* New York, 1988.

———. "The Bonds of Love: Rational Violence and Erotic Domination." In *The Future of Difference,* edited by Hester Eisenstein and Alice Jardine, 41–

70. New Brunswick, N.J., 1985. (This article appears with minor changes under the same title in *Feminist Studies* 6.1 [Spring 1980]: 144–74.)

———. "Master and Slave: The Fantasy of Erotic Domination." In *Powers of Desire: The Politics of Sexuality*, edited by Ann Snitow, Christine Stansell, and Sharon Thompson, 280–99. New York, 1983.

Bennett, Charles E. *Horace: Odes and Epodes*. Loeb Classical Library. London and New York, 1914, reprinted 1919.

———. *Horace: Odes and Epodes*, 1901. Reprint, New Rochelle, N.Y., 1981.

Boyle, A. J. "The Edict of Venus: An Interpretive Essay on Horace's Amatory Odes." *Ramus* 2 (1973): 163–88.

Borzsák, Stephanus, ed. *Q. Horati Flacci Opera*. Leipzig, 1984.

Bradley, Keith R. *Discovering the Roman Family: Studies in Roman Social History*. New York and Oxford, 1991.

Bradshaw, A. "Horace and the Therapeutic Myth: Odes 3,7; 3,11, and 3,27." *Hermes* 106 (1978): 156–76.

———. "Horace, Odes 4.1." *Classical Quarterly* 64 (1970): 142–53.

Cairns, Francis. *Generic Composition in Greek and Roman Poetry*. Edinburgh, 1972.

Cameron, H. D. "Horace's Soracte Ode: (*Carm.* 1.9)." *Arethusa* 22 (1989): 147–59.

Campbell, Archibald Y. *Horace: A New Interpretation*. London, 1924.

Catlow, L. W. "Horace, *Odes* I,25, and IV,13: A Reinterpretation." *Latomus* 35 (1976): 813–21.

Chodorow, Nancy. "Gender, Relation, and Difference in Psychoanalytic Perspective." In *The Future of Difference*, edited by Hester Eisenstein and Alice Jardine, 3–19. New Brunswick, N.J., 1985.

———. *The Reproduction of Mothering: Psychoanalysis and the Sociology of Gender*. Berkeley, 1978.

Cixous, Hélène, and Catherine Clément. *The Newly Born Woman*. Translated by Betsy Wing. Minneapolis, 1975.

Clay, Jenny Strauss. "Ode. 1.9: Horace's September Song." *Classical World* 83 (1989): 102–05.

Clément, Catherine. *Opera, or the Undoing of Women*. Translated by Betsy Wing. Minneapolis, 1988.

Collinge, N. E. *The Structure of Horace's Odes*. London, 1961.

Commager, Steele. *The Odes of Horace: A Critical Study*. New Haven and London, 1962.

Connor, Peter. "Soracte Encore." *Ramus* 1 (1972): 102–12.

Connor, W. R. "The New Classical Humanities and the Old." In *Classics: A Discipline and Profession in Crisis?* edited by Phyllis Culham and Lowell Edmunds, 25–38. Lanham, Md., 1989.

Copley, Frank. *Exclusus Amator: A Study in Latin Love Poetry*. Baltimore, 1956.

Culler, Jonathan. "Beyond Interpretation." In *The Pursuit of Signs: Semiotics, Literature, Deconstruction*, 3–17. Ithaca, 1981.

———. "Changes in the Study of Lyric." In *Lyric Poetry: Beyond New Criticism,* edited by Chaviva Hošek and Patricia Parker, 38–54. Ithaca and London 1985.

Culham, Phyllis, and Lowell Edmunds, ed. *Classics: A Discipline and Profession in Crisis?* Lanham, Md., 1989.

Cunningham, M. P. "Enarratio of Horace *Odes* 1.9." *Classical Philology* 52 (1957): 98–102.

Davis, Gregson. "*Carmina/Iambi*: The Literary-Generic Dimension of Horace's *Integer Vitae* (C. I, 22)." *Quaderni Urbinati di Cultura Classica*, n.s., 27, no. 3 (1987): 67–78.

———. *Polyhymnia: The Rhetoric of Horatian Lyric Discourse*. Berkeley, 1991.

Dewald, Carolyn. "Women and Culture in Herodotus' *Histories*." *Women's Studies* 8 (1981): 93–127.

Dixon, Suzanne. *The Roman Family*. Baltimore and London, 1992.

———. *The Roman Mother*. Norman, Okla., 1988.

Edmunds, Lowell. *From a Sabine Jar: Reading Horace Odes 1.9*. Chapel Hill, N.C., 1992.

Edwards, Catharine. *The Politics of Immorality in Ancient Rome*. Cambridge, 1993.

Eisenstein, Hester, and Alice Jardine. *The Future of Difference*. New Brunswick, N.J., 1985.

Eliot, T. S. "Tradition and the Individual Talent." 1919. Reprinted in *Selected Essays*, new edition, New York, 1950.

Ensor, E. "Notes on the Odes of Horace." *Hermathena* 28 (1902): 105–10.

Ernout, A., and A. Meillet. *Dictionnaire Étymologique de la Langue Latine*. 3d edition. Paris, 1951.

Esler, Carol Clemeau. "Horace, Barine, and the Immortality of Words (*Odes* 2.8)." *Classical Journal* 84 (1989): 105–12.

Estevez, Victor. "Chloe and the Fawn: The Structure of *Odes* 1.23." *Helios* 7.1 (1979–80): 35–44.

Fantham, Elaine. "The Mating of Lalage: Horace, *Odes* 2.5." *Liverpool Classical Monthly* 4 (1979): 47–52.

Fetterley, Judith. *The Resisting Reader: A Feminist Approach to American Fiction*. Bloomington and London, 1978.

Fraenkel, Eduard. *Horace*. Oxford, 1957.

Fredricksmeyer, Ernst A. "Horace's Ode to Pyrrha (*Carm.* 1.5)." *Classical Philology* 60 (1965): 180–85.

Girard, René. *Deceit, Desire, and the Novel*, translated by Yvonne Freccero (Baltimore and London, 1966).

Glare, P. G. W., ed. *The Oxford Latin Dictionary*. Oxford, 1982.

Gould, B. A., ed. *Quinti Horatii Flacci Opera: Accedunt Clavis Metrica et Notae Anglicae Juventuti Accommodatae*. Boston, 1838.

Grassmann, Victor. *Die Erotischen Epoden des Horaz: Literarischer Hintergrund und sprachliche Tradition*. Zetemata 39. Munich, 1966.

Green, Peter, trans. *Juvenal: The Sixteen Satires*. Harmondsworth, England, 1974.

Griffin, Jasper. "Augustan Poetry and the Life of Luxury." *Journal of Roman Studies* 66 (1976): 87–105.

———. *Latin Poets and Roman Life.* Chapel Hill, N.C., 1986.

Habinek, Thomas. "The Marriageability of Maximus: Horace *Ode* 4.1.13–20." *American Journal of Philology* 107 (1986): 407–16.

Hallett, Judith P. *Fathers and Daughters in Roman Society: Women and the Elite Family.* Princeton, 1984.

———. "*Ianua iucunda*: The Characterization of the Door in Catullus 67." *Collection Latomus: Studies in Latin Literature and Roman History* 2, edited by C. Deroux, 106–22. Brussels, 1980.

Hammond, N. G. L., and H. H. Scullard. *The Oxford Classical Dictionary.* 2d edition. Oxford, 1970.

Harrison, S. J. "Horace, *Odes* 3.7: An Erotic *Odyssey?*" *Classical Quarterly* 38 (1988): 186–92.

Havelock, Eric A. *The Lyric Genius of Catullus.* New York, 1939.

Henderson, W. "The Paraklausithyron Motif in Horace's Odes." *Acta Classica* 16 (1973): 51–67.

Holder, Alfred, ed. *Pomponi Porfyrionis Commentum in Horatium Flaccum.* 1894. Reprint, New York, 1979.

Hošek, Chaviva, and Patricia Parker, ed. *Lyric Poetry: Beyond New Criticism.* Ithaca and London, 1985.

Johnson, W. Ralph. *The Idea of Lyric: Lyric Modes in Ancient and Modern Poetry.* Berkeley, 1982.

Jones, F. "Horace, Four Girls and the Other Man." *Liverpool Classical Monthly* 8.3 (1983): 34–37.

Kiessling, A. *Q. Horatius Flaccus: Oden und Epoden.* 11th ed., revised by R. Heinze, afterword and bibliography by E. Burck. Zurich and Berlin, 1964.

Konstan, David. "The Stories in Herodotus' *Histories* Book I." *Helios* 10 (1983): 1–22.

———. "What Is New in the New Approaches to Classical Literature." In *Classics: A Discipline and Profession in Crisis?* edited by Phyllis Culham and Lowell Edmunds, 45–49. Lanham, Md., 1989.

Kresic, Stephanus, ed. *Contemporary Literary Hermeneutics and Interpretation of Classical Texts.* Ottawa, 1981.

La Penna, Antonio. "Tre Poesie Espressionistiche di Orazio." *Belfagor* 18 (1963): 181–93.

Lateiner, Donald. "Mimetic Syntax: Metaphor from Word Order, Especially in Ovid." *American Journal of Philology* 111 (1990): 204–37.

Lee, M. Owen. "Horace *Carm.* 1.23: Simile and Metaphor." *Classical Philology* 60 (1965): 185–86.

———. "Horace, *Odes* 1.25: The Wind and the River." *The Augustan Age* 4 (1985): 39–44.

———. *Word, Sound, and Image in the Odes of Horace.* Ann Arbor, 1969.

Lefèvre, E. "*Rursus bella moves?* Die literarische Form von Horaz, c. 4,I." *Rheinisches Museum* 111 (1968): 166–89.

Liddell, H. G., and R. Scott. *A Greek-English Lexicon.* 9th ed., revised by H. S. Jones. Oxford, 1968.

Lyne, R. O. A. M. *The Latin Love Poets: From Catullus to Horace.* Oxford, 1980.

McDermott, Emily. "Greek and Roman Elements in Horace's Lyric Program." *Aufstieg und Niedergang der Römischen Welt* II 31 3 (Berlin, 1981): 1640–72.

Maltby, Robert. *A Lexicon of Ancient Latin Etymologies.* Leeds, England, 1991.

Meyer, Gulielmus, ed. *Pomponii Porphyrionis Commentarii in Q. Horatium Flaccum.* Leipzig, 1874.

Miller, Nancy K., ed. *The Poetics of Gender.* New York, 1986.

Minadeo, R. *The Golden Plectrum: Sexual Symbolism in Horace's Odes.* Amsterdam, 1982.

———. "Sexual Symbolism in Horace's Love Odes." *Latomus* 34 (1975): 392–424.

Montefiore, Jan. *Feminism and Poetry: Language, Experience, Identity in Women's Writing.* London and New York, 1987.

Murgatroyd, P. "Tibullus and the *Puer Delicatus.*" *Acta Classica* 20 (1977): 105–19.

Murray, Michael. "Horace's Soracte Ode (C. I,9): The Hermeneutic Response." In *Contemporary Literary Hermeneutics and Interpretation of Classical Texts,* edited by Stephanus Kresic, 281–85. Ottawa, 1981.

Mutschler, Fritz-Heiner. "Eine Interpretation der Horazode 'Quid fles Asterie.'" *Symbolae Osloenses* 53 (1978): 111–31.

Nielsen, Rosemary. "Catullus 45 and Horace *Odes* 3.9: The Glass House." *Ramus* 6 (1977): 132–38.

———. "Horace *Odes* 1.23: Innocence." *Arion* 9 (1970): 373–78.

Nielsen, R. M., and R. H. Solomon. "Soracte and Sacred Space: Centuries of *carpe diem.*" *Latomus* 47 (1988): 821–29.

Nisbet, R. G. M. "Romanae Fidicen Lyrae: The Odes of Horace." In *Critical Essays on Roman Literature: Elegy and Lyric,* edited by J. P. Sullivan, 181–218. Cambridge, Mass., 1962.

Nisbet, R. G. M., and Margaret Hubbard. *A Commentary on Horace: Odes Book 1.* Oxford, 1970.

———. *A Commentary on Horace: Odes Book 2.* Oxford, 1978.

Nussbaum, Martha. "Beyond Obsession and Disgust: Lucretius' Genealogy of Love." *Apeiron* 22 (1989): 1–59.

———. "Therapeutic Arguments and Structures of Desire." *differences* 2, Sexuality in Greek and Roman Society (1990): 46–66.

Owens, William M. "The Go-Between: An Interpretation of Horace, Ode 3.7." Paper delivered at the AIA-APA Annual Meetings 1982, abstract in *American Philological Association Abstracts: Annual Meeting 1982.*

———. "*Nuntius Vafer et Fallax*: An Alternate Reading of Horace, C 3.7." *Classical World* 85 (1992): 161–71.

Page, T. E. *Q. Horati Flacci: Opera.* London, 1896.

Palmer, Richard E. "Horace's Soracte Ode (C.I,9): Philosophical Hermeneutics and the Interpretation." In *Contemporary Literary Hermeneutics and Interpretation of Classical Texts*, edited by Stephanus Kresic, 293–98. Ottawa, 1981.

Pasquali, Giorgio. *Orazio Lirico*. Firenze, 1920.

Pavlock, Barbara. "Horace's Invitation Poems to Maecenas: Gifts to a Patron." *Ramus* 11 (1982): 79–98.

Pichon, René. *Index Verborum Amatoriorum*. Hildesheim, Germany, 1966.

Porter, David H. "Horace, *Carmina*, IV,12." *Latomus* 31 (1972): 71–87.

———. *Horace's Poetic Journey: A Reading of Odes 1–3*. Princeton, 1987.

———. "The Recurrent Motifs of Horace, *Carmina* IV." *Harvard Studies in Classical Philology* 79 (1975): 189–228.

Pöschl, Victor. "Horaz C. 1,25." In *Dialogos für Harald Patzer*, edited by J. Cobet, R. Leimbach, and A. Neschke-Hentschke, 187–92. Wiesbaden, 1975.

———. *Horazische Lyrik*. Heidelberg, 1970.

Pucci, Piero. "Lingering on the Threshold." *Glyph* 3 (1978): 52–73.

Putnam, Michael C. J. *Artifices of Eternity: Horace's Fourth Book of Odes*. Ithaca and London, 1986.

———. *Essays on Latin Lyric, Elegy, and Epic*. Princeton, 1982.

———. "Horace *Carm*. 2.9: Augustus and the Ambiguities of Encomium." In *Between Republic and Empire: Interpretations of Augustus and His Principate*, edited by Kurt A. Raaflaub and Mark Toher, 212–38. Berkeley, 1990.

———. "Horace *Odes* 3.9: The Dialectics of Desire." In *Ancient and Modern: Essays in Honor of Gerald F. Else*, edited by John H. D'Arms and John W. Eadie. Ann Arbor, 1977. (Reprinted in Putnam, *Essays on Latin Lyric, Elegy, and Epic*, 107–25.)

Quinn, Kenneth. *Horace: The Odes*. London, 1980.

———. *Latin Explorations*. London, 1963.

Raaflaub, Kurt A., and Mark Toher. *Between Republic and Empire: Interpretations of Augustus and His Principate*. Berkeley, 1990.

Rawson, Beryl, ed. *The Family in Ancient Rome: New Perspectives*. Ithaca, 1986.

Reckford, Kenneth. *Horace*. New York, 1969.

———. "Some Studies in Horace's Odes on Love." *Classical Journal* 55 (1959): 25–33.

Richards, I. A. *Practical Criticism: A Study of Literary Judgment*. New York, 1929.

Richlin, Amy. *The Garden of Priapus: Sexual Aggression in Roman Humor*. New Haven and London, 1983.

Rose, H. J. *A Handbook of Greek Mythology*. New York, 1959.

———. "Some Passages of Latin Poets." *Harvard Studies in Classical Philology* 47 (1936): 1–15.

Rudd, Niall. "Patterns in Horatian Lyric." *American Journal of Philology* 81 (1960): 373–92.

Santirocco, Matthew S. *Unity and Design in Horace's Odes*. Chapel Hill, N.C., and London, 1986.

Saylor, Charles. "*Querelae*: Propertius' Distinctive, Technical Name for his Elegy." *Agon* 1 (1967): 142–49.

Shackleton Bailey, D. R. *Q. Horati Flacci Opera*. Stuttgart, 1985.

Sedgwick, Eve Kosofsky. *Between Men: English Literature and Male Homosocial Desire*. New York, 1985.

Segal, Charles. "Horace's Soracte Ode (C. I,9): Of Interpretation, Philologic and Hermeneutic." In *Contemporary Literary Hermeneutics and Interpretation of Classical Texts*, edited by Stephanus Kresic, 287–92. Ottawa, 1981.

Springer, Carl P. E. "Horace's Soracte Ode: Location, Dislocation, and the Reader." *Classical World* 82 (1988): 1–9.

Stinton, T. C. W. "Horatian Echoes." *Phoenix* 31 (1977): 159–73.

Striar, Brian. "Soracte Reconsidered: The Burden of Youth and the Relief of Age in Horace *Odes* I.9." In *Collection Latomus: Studies in Latin Literature and Roman History* 5, edited by C. Deroux, 203–15. Brussels, 1989.

Suleiman, Susan Rubin. "Pornography, Transgression, and the Avant-Garde: Bataille's *Story of the Eye*." In *The Poetics of Gender*, edited by Nancy K. Miller, 117–36. New York, 1986.

Sullivan, J. P., ed. *Critical Essays on Roman Literature: Elegy and Lyric*. Cambridge, Mass., 1962.

Sylvester, W. "A Note on Horace 'Odes' 1,4." *Classical Journal* 48 (1952–53): 262.

Syndikus, H. P. *Die Lyrik des Horaz: Eine Interpretation der Oden Band 1*. Darmstadt, Germany, 1972.

Vessey, D. W. T. "From Mountain to Lovers' Tryst: Horace's Soracte Ode." *Journal of Roman Studies* 75 (1985): 26–38.

Wender, Dorothea. *Roman Poetry from the Republic to the Silver Age*. Carbondale and Edwardsville, Ill., 1980.

West, Martin L., ed. *Iambi et elegi Graeci ante Alexandrum Cantati*. Vol. 1. Oxford, 1971.

Wilkinson, L. P. *Horace and His Lyric Poetry*. Cambridge, 1946.

Williams, Gordon. *The Third Book of Horace's Odes*. Oxford, 1969.

Winnicott, D. W. "The Capacity to Be Alone" (1958). Reprinted in *The Maturational Process and the Facilitating Environment*, 29–36. New York, 1965.

Woodman, A. J. "Horace's Odes *Diffugere niues* and *Soluitur acris hiems*." *Latomus* 31 (1972): 752–78.

Wordsworth, William. "Preface to the Second Edition of *Lyrical Ballads*." In *Selected Poems and Prefaces*, edited by Jack Stillinger, 445–64. Boston, 1965.

Wyke, Maria. "Mistress and Metaphor in Augustan Elegy." *Helios* 16 (1989): 25–47.

———. "Written Women: Propertius' *Scripta Puella*." *Journal of Roman Studies* 77 (1987): 47–61.

GENERAL INDEX

Achilles, 110–11
Acro. *See* Pseudo-Acro
Adams, J. N., 151 n.4, 154 n.30, 160
  n.46, 162 n.5, 164 n.32, 166 n.14,
  169 n.49
Adhuc, 38–43, 154–55 n.44
Age, 24–26, 28–30, 33, 39, 41, 46,
  48, 51, 52, 61–66, 72–73, 75–102
  passim, 103, 111, 135, 142, 149
  n.28, 152 n.21, n.22, 154 n.29,
  n.41, 156 n.1, 157 n.18, 159 n.41,
  159 n.44, 162 n.2, 163 n.17, 164
  n.27, 164 n.30, n.35, 165 n.40,
  167 n.27
Alcaeus, 147 n.20
Allen, A., 6–7, 147 n.9
Anacreon, 160 n.60
Ancona, R., 150 n.1, 161 n.63, 167–
  68 n.32
Antilochus, 110–12, 167 n.21
Archilochus, 39, 155 n.49
Aristius Fuscus. *See* Fuscus, Aris-
  tius
Arkins, B., 147 n.18
Armstrong, D., 149 n.28
Asterie, 38–43, 155 n.53, 155–56
  n.53
Augustus, 13–14, 104, 106, 112, 114,
  163 n.19, 166 n.3

Autonomy, 7, 9, 14, 18–21, 52, 91–
  93, 95–96, 99–100, 114–18, 134–
  35, 136–37, 141–42. *See also* Dom-
  ination

Babcock, C., 156 n.5, 157 n.10, n.15,
  159 n.31, 163 n.22
Barine, 77–85, 87, 95, 109, 161–62
  n.1, 162 n.7
Barthes, R., 168 n.34
Bataille, G., 152 n.24
Bellerophon, 40, 42
Beloved: feminized, 3, 17–18, 141,
  145–46 n.2; use of term, 3
Benjamin, J., 19–21, 141, 149 n.27,
  150 n.30, n.31, 161 n.63
Bennett, C., 146 n.1, 160 n.54
Bentley, R., 160 n.60
Borzsák, S., 145 n.4
Bowdlerization, 146 n.1
Boyle, A. J., 10–12, 14, 26, 147 n.14,
  n.15, n.17, n.18, n.19, n.20, 150
  n.2, 151 n.11, 151 n.15, 151–52
  n.16, 152–53 n.25, 153 n.25, n.26,
  n.29, 155 n.48
Bradley, K., 149 n.28
Bradshaw, A., 155 n.53, 163 n.15,
  n.19
Bramble, J., 157 n.18

Cairns, F., 154 n.41, 155 n.53
Calais, 134, 137–39
Cameron, H. D., 159 n.39, n.40, 160 n.50, n.51
Campbell, A., 163 n.11
Candaules, 40
Carpe diem, 57
Catlow, L. W., 26, 150 n.2, 151 n.9, 152 n.18, n.21, 153 n.25
Catullus, 4, 5–9, 18, 56–57, 83–85, 115, 120, 147 n.4, 165 n.1, 168 n.33
Chia, 97–100
Chloe, 71–74, 89, 131–39, 154–55 n.44, 161 n.62, 161 n.67
Chloris, 35, 89
Chodorow, N., 19–21, 141, 149 n.26, 150 n.29
Cinara, 88, 163 n.17
Cixous, H., 145 n.1
Clay, J., 159 n.39
Clément, C., 149 n.23
Collinge, N. E., 10, 26, 30, 150 n.2, 151 n.12, n.15, 152 n.24
Commager, S., 33, 44, 72, 115, 152–53 n.25, 154 n.34, 156 n.2, n.5, 157 n.13, n.14, 158 n.28, 158–59 n.31, 159 n.32, n.39, n.44, 160 n.60, 161 n.64, 163 n.15, 164 n.28, 165 n.2, 167 n.30, n.31, 169 n.38
Competition, 122, 132–33, 136, 168 n.34
Connor, P., 159 n.39
Connor, W. R., 145 n.1
Control, 2–3, 13–14, 22–23, 32, 35, 36, 77, 78, 83, 84–85, 87, 104, 109, 124, 132, 139, 167–68 n.32, 169 n.43. *See also* Autonomy; Domination
Copley, F., 26, 151 n.6, n.10, 155 n.53
Crescit, 81, 162 n.6
Criticism: feminist, 2, 15–21, 140, 149 n.23, 149–50 n.28, 152 n.24; traditional, of Horace as a love poet, 1–2, 4–14, 140
Criticism, New. *See* New Criticism
Culler, J., 147 n.16, 148 n.20, 150 n.28

Cunningham, M. P., 159 n.44
Cupid, 62, 80, 98–100, 162 n.4, 164 n.31
Cupido. See Cupid

Davis, G., 115, 148 n.21, 167–68 n.32
Death, 30, 46–52, 53–60, 62–63, 79–80, 101, 107, 110–11, 118, 134, 139, 158–59 n.31, 159 n.44, 160 n.47, 163 n.17
Demeter, 72
Desirability, 25, 27, 29, 30, 32, 48, 76, 78, 79, 87, 95, 96, 97, 99, 100–101, 111, 136, 142
Detachment, 8, 9–10, 51, 90, 147 n.18, 148 n.21. *See also* Autonomy
Dewald, C., 155 n.50
Diana, 58–60
Differentiation, pre-oedipal process of, 19–20
Distance, 35, 137–38. *See also* Autonomy; Detachment; Domination; Irony
Dixon, S., 149 n.28
Domination, 1, 19–20, 44, 58–59, 61, 64, 66–69, 70–74, 103, 104, 106, 110, 111–13, 114, 120–21, 122–23, 125, 128, 129, 140–43, 161 n.63, n.67, n.69, 166 n.3
Dream, erotic, 92–93, 154 n.43, 164 n.26
Dworkin, A., 152 n.24

Edmunds, L., 159 n.39
Edwards, C., 166 n.4
Elegy, 18, 106, 115, 148 n.21, 151 n.6, 165 n.1, n.2, 166 n.4
Eliot, T. S., 6–7, 147 n.6, n.7
Enipeus, 41–43, 155 n.52, 155–56 n.53
Ensor, E., 83, 163 n.13, n.14
Eros. *See* Cupid
Eroticism: use of term, 3. *See also* Mutuality
Esler, C., 161–62 n.1, 162 n.7
Estevez, V., 160 n.60

Faithfulness. *See* Fidelity
Family, Roman, 149 n.28

Fantham, E., 154 n.29
Faunus, 49, 157 n.15, n.19
Fetterley, J., 15–16, 20, 21, 141
Fidelity, 38–43, 44, 82, 84, 156 n.53,
    n.54
Fraenkel, E., 146 n.1, 156 n.3, n.5,
    160 n.49, n.59, 163 n.15, 164
    n.28
Frangere, 73, 161 n.67, n.70
Fredricksmeyer, E., 161 n.63, 161–
    62 n.1
Freud, S., 157 n.19
Fuscus, Aristius, 167–68 n.32

Gender, 2–3, 5, 7–8, 14–21, 81, 140–
    41, 143, 145 n.1, 145–46 n.2, 168
    n.34, 169 n.43; ambiguous, 35.
    See also Autonomy; Control; Crit-
    icism, feminist; Identity; Mutu-
    ality; Psychoanalysis; "Resisting
    reader"; Universalizing
Girard, R., 168 n.34
Glaucon, 41
Gould, B. A., 146 n.1
Grassman, V., 145 n.1
Green, P., 167 n.27
Griffin, J., 147 n.10, n.11
Gyges, 35, 38–43, 154–55 n.44, 155
    n.49, n.50

Habinek, T., 163 n.15, n.19
Hallett, J. P., 149 n.28, 151 n.6
Harrison, S. J., 155 n.49
Havelock, E., 147 n.4
Heinze, R., 155 n.49
Henderson, W., 161 n.69, 165 n.37
Herodotus, 39–41, 155 n.49, n.50
Hippolytus, 58–60
Holder, A., 169 n.39
Homoeroticism, 8, 51, 59, 92–93,
    110–11, 167 n.21, 168 n.34
Homosexuality. *See* Homoeroticism
Human perspective. *See* Univer-
    salizing
Hymen, 83–84

Identity, 12–21, 53, 57, 89, 90, 93,
    101–102, 104, 120, 130–31, 132,
    138, 139, 143; and male develop-
    ment, esp. 15, 18–21. *See also* Au-

tonomy; Domination; Temporal-
    ity: of beloved, public nature of
Indirection, 41, 47–48, 53–54, 115,
    156 n.6, 167–68 n.32
Iners, 55–56, 59, 158 n.26, n.28,
    n.30, 166 n.13
Inrupta. See Irrupta
Insincerity. *See* Allen, A; Richards,
    I. A.
Integer, 38–43, 115–21, 154–55
    n.44
Integritas. See Integer
Interrupta. See Irrupta
Irigaray, L., 17
Irony, 9, 10, 14, 27–28, 30, 34, 38–
    39, 41, 50, 78, 79–80, 83–84, 103,
    105, 107, 125, 127–28, 135, 151
    n.5, 155 n.53. *See also* Allen, A;
    Autonomy; Richards, I. A.
Irrupta, 104, 125–28, 169 n.39
Iugum. See Iungo
Iunctas. See Iungo
Iungo, 24–25, 26, 32, 151 n.4, 154
    n.30

Johnson, W. R., 145 n.3
Jones, F., 154 n.37

Kiessling, A., 155 n.49
Kiessling, A., and Heinze, R., 32,
    150 n.2, 151 n.15, 153 n.27, 165
    n.36
Konstan, D., 145 n.2, 155 n.50, n.51

La Bohème, 149 n.23
Lalage, 35, 114–21, 153 n.29, 167–68
    n.32
La Penna, A., 150 n.1
Lateiner, D., 158 n.23
Lee, M. O., 152 n.23, 156 n.5, 159
    n.39, 160 n.48, 160 n.60, 163
    n.11, n.12, 169 n.47
Lefèvre, E., 163 n.15
Lesbian. *See* Sappho
Leuconoe, 57
Ligurinus, 91–93, 165 n.40
Love. *See* Eroticism
Lucretius, 165 n.1
Lyce, 62, 95–102, 162 n.2, 163 n.17,
    n.19, 164 n.29, n.30

Proetus, 41–42
Propertius, 5–6, 151 n.6
Proserpina. *See* Persephone
Pseudo-Acro, 153 n.29, 155 n.44
Psychoanalysis, 15, 19–21; object-
    relations theory of, 19
Pucci, P., 151 n.6
Puccini, G., 149 n.23
Putnam, M., 12–14, 59, 136, 148
    n.21, 158 n.23, n.26, n.29, n.30,
    159 n.32, n.37, 163 n.15, 164
    n.28, n.31, 166 n.3, n.6, n.17, 167
    n.29, 169 n.42, n.43, n.44, n.45,
    n.46, n.48
Pyrrha, 161–62 n.1, 162 n.7, 167
    n.22

Quinn, K., 154 n.29, 154–55 n.44,
    156 n.4, n.5, 159 n.35, 160 n.53,
    164 n.28, 165 n.36 (chap. 4), n.1
    (chap. 5)

Rationality, 70–74
Rawson, B., 149 n.28
Reader, 6–8, 147 n.16; female, 16.
    See also "Resisting reader"
Reciprocal eroticism. *See* Mutuality
Reckford, K., 34, 148 n.21, 154 n.38,
    n.40
Recollection. *See* Memory
"Resisting reader," 15–16, 141
Richards, I. A., 6–7, 147 n.8
Richlin, A., 162 n.2
Rivalry. *See* Competition
Romantic assumptions about po-
    etry. *See* Poetry, Romantic as-
    sumptions about
Romanticism, 1, 4–5, 8–10, 12, 14,
    92, 103–5, 106, 113, 114, 115, 120,
    125, 127–28, 129–30, 143, 148
    n.21, 165 n.1
Rose, H. J., 161 n.67, 166 n.19
Rudd, N., 159 n.39

Santirocco, M., 149 n.25
Sappho, 34, 115, 120, 167 n.32, 168
    n.33
Saylor, C., 166 n.4
Sedgwick, E. K., 149 n.23, 168 n.34
Segal, C., 159 n.39

Self. *See* Autonomy; Identity
Self-referentiality, 148 n.20, 167–68
    n.32
Servius, 159 n.44
Sestius, 8, 46–52, 57–58, 59, 61,
    145–46 n.2, 157 n.19, 165 n.40
Sexuality. *See* Desirability; Eroticism;
    Gender; Homoeroticism
Shackleton Bailey, D. R., 145 n.4
Shakespeare, W., 17
Shared eroticism. *See* Mutuality
Sincerity. *See* Allen, A.; Richards,
    I. A.
Sonnet, 149 n.24
Sophocles, 98–99, 165 n.37
Springer, C., 159 n.39
Statius, 111
Stinton, T. C. W., 157 n.18
Strato, 111
Striar, B., 159 n.39, n.40, n.42, n.43
Sublimation, 13–14
Suleiman, S. R., 152 n.24
Sylvester, W., 156 n.5, n.7, 157 n.11,
    n.12
Syndikus, H. P., 150 n.1, 151 n.15

Temporal adverb, 22–43 passim, 44,
    75, 141, 150 n.1
Temporality: of beloved, public na-
    ture of, 75–76, 77–85 passim, 95–
    102 passim; of lover, private na-
    ture of, 75–76, 87–93 passim; per-
    sonification of time, 54–56; use of
    term, 3
Time, personification of. *See* Tem-
    porality: personification of time
Theseus, 58–60
Thaliarchus, 63–69
Tempestiva, 73–74
Troilus, 110–12, 167 n.20, n.21
Telephus, 122–28, 168 n.36
Tyro, 155 n.52

Universalizing, 4, 9–12, 14–16, 30,
    59, 75, 140–43, 147 n.18, n.20,
    152–53 n.25

Valgius, 106–13, 163 n.18, 164 n.25,
    165 n.2, 166 n.3, n.6, n.17, 167
    n.21, n.28

Venus, 48, 58, 62, 80, 84, 88–92, 135, 152 n.22, 154 n.32, 163 n.22
Vergil, 29, 162 n.6
Vessey, D. W. T., 160 n.56
Vulcan, 48

Wender, D., 145 n.3
Wilkinson, L. P., 146 n.1, 159 n.39, n.44

Williams, G., 38, 39, 155 n.47
Winnicott, D. W., 19
Woodman, A. J., 156 n.5, 157 n.18, 158 n.22
Wordsworth, W., 6, 147 n.6
Wyke, M., 149 n.24

INDEX OF PASSAGES CITED

RONNIE ANCONA

is Assistant Professor

of Classics and Director,

Master of Arts in the

Teaching of Latin, at

Hunter College.

Library of Congress Cataloging-in-Publication Data

Ancona, Ronnie. 1951–
Time and the erotic in Horace's Odes / Ronnie Ancona.
p.   cm.
Includes bibliographical references (p.) and index.
ISBN 0-8223-1476-2
1. Horace. Carmina.   2. Erotic poetry, Latin—History and criticism.
3. Love poetry, Latin—History and criticism.   4. Psychoanalysis and
literature.   5. Feminism and literature—Rome.   6. Odes—History
and criticism.   7. Women and literature—Rome.   8. Time in literature.
I. Title.
PA6411.A69   1994
874'.01—dc20   93-46913   CIP